BEGINNING
OPENGL®
GAME PROGRAMMING

THOMSON
———— ✳ ————™
OURSE TECHNOLOGY
ofessional ■ Technical ■ Reference

BEGINNING
OPENGL®
GAME PROGRAMMING

DAVE ASTLE
KEVIN HAWKINS

ISBN 13: 978-1-59200-369-3
ISBN 10: 1-59200-369-9
Library of Congress Catalog Card Number: 2004090734
Printed in the United States of America

06 07 08 PH 10 9 8 7 6 5 4

Senior Vice President, Course PTR Group:
Andy Shafran

Publisher:
Stacy L. Hiquet

Senior Marketing Manager:
Sarah O'Donnell

Marketing Manager:
Heather Hurley

Manager of Editorial Services:
Heather Talbot

Senior Acquisitions Editor:
Emi Smith

Associate Marketing Manager:
Kristin Eisenzopf

Project Editor:
Sandy Doell

Technical Reviewer:
Ben Woodhouse

Retail Market Coordinator:
Sarah Dubois

Interior Layout Tech:
Marian Hartsough

Cover Designer:
Steve Deschene

CD-ROM Producer:
Brandon Penticuff

Indexer:
Katherine Stimson

Proofreader:
Gene Redding

THOMSON

COURSE TECHNOLOGY

Professional ■ Technical ■ Reference

Course PTR, a division of Course Technology
25 Thomson Place
Boston, MA 02210
http://www.courseptr.com

For my family and friends
—Kevin

For my crash of rhinos
—Dave

ACKNOWLEDGMENTS

First and foremost, I want to thank my wife Melissa and my kids, Rebi, Evan, Ellie, Tyler, and Nate, for all of your support throughout this project, and for dragging me away from the computer just often enough for me to retain most of my sanity. I love you all.

I'd also like to thank Kevin, my partner and collaborator, without whom I never would have done this. I can't imagine finding a better teammate.

Big thanks to everyone at Premier Press/Course Technology. You're a great group of people to work with, and I genuinely appreciate the confidence you place in me.

Ben Woodhouse deserves special mention for his efforts as technical editor. He provided valuable feedback that helped make this book much better than it would have been otherwise. Thanks also to The Mighty Pete for allowing us to use his skybox images in many of the example programs, and to Jeff Royle from ATI Technologies for providing us with graphics hardware for testing purposes.

Finally, I want to thank everyone who has taught me in some way, including Chuck Hansen, Robert Kessler and my other professors at the University of Utah, my coworkers at Avalanche Software and Qualcomm, the denizens of the GameDev.net forums, and everyone else who has taken the time to share their knowledge and experience via a Web site or book.

—Dave Astle

I'd like to thank Dave, for his work as a good teammate, motivator, and friend. Chances are you would not be holding this book in your hands if he had not used a little friendly coercion on me. I'm amazed at what we were able to accomplish with this project, and a good deal of its success is due to our ability to work together as a team. I also want to thank my family for their constant support for me in everything I do. Oftentimes they don't get as much credit as they should be getting.

My friends and coworkers also deserve a share of the thanks. Whether they know it or not, I've learned from all of them in some form or another and value their friendships: Tucker, Tom, Christie, Mike, Rael, Kristin, Vivian, JP, Andy, Greg R., Greg S., Bill, Kyle, Randall, Jordan, Hack, Justin, Nate, Luke M., Mike M., Johnny Y., Nick M., and so many others that we don't have the space for here. Also, thank you to the Premier Press group for the opportunity to do this project and for maintaining a high degree of support and confidence in both Dave and me, and in GameDev.net.

And finally, I want to thank everyone who has provided me with the ability and talent, directly or indirectly, that has allowed me to create this book, including the professors at Embry-Riddle, my baseball coaches and teammates, Chris Hargrove, Seth Robinson, Jeff Molofee, Rich Benson, and a host of software engineering colleagues.

—Kevin Hawkins

ABOUT THE AUTHORS

DAVE ASTLE has been programming games professionally for several years, working on titles for the Xbox, PlayStation 2, GameCube, PC, and various wireless devices. Currently, he is a lead engineer in the Gaming and Graphics group at Qualcomm, Inc. He is the cofounder and executive producer of GameDev.net, the leading online community for game developers. He has authored or contributed to several game development books and has spoken at industry conferences, including the Game Developers' Conference. He received his bachelor's degree in Computer Science from the University of Utah, where he specialized in graphics, artificial intelligence, networking, software engineering, and compiler theory and design.

KEVIN HAWKINS is a lead software engineer at Raydon Corporation where he designs and develops training simulations for a variety of customers, including the U.S. military. In addition, Kevin is the cofounder and CEO of GameDev.net, the leading online community for game developers. He holds a master's degree in Software Engineering and a bachelor's degree in Computer Science from Embry-Riddle University, where he also played intercollegiate baseball and was drafted by the Cleveland Indians in the 2002 amateur baseball draft.

CONTENTS AT A GLANCE

Contents

INTRODUCTION

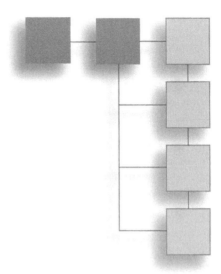

In the spring of 2001, we finished writing *OpenGL Game Programming*. Although the book didn't cover everything we had initially planned, we hoped that it would benefit people learning to program games with OpenGL. The ensuing years have seen that hope realized, as we've come into contact with dozens of people in person and many times that number via e-mail and the Web who had used our book as a starting point into 3D game development.

Given the tremendous effort involved with writing a book, upon the book's completion, we both felt that it would be our first and last book. However, since then, as we gained experience, we began to feel the need to rewrite the book. We noticed areas where it was weak, where it needed to be updated to coincide with the latest OpenGL spec, and where material could be added to provide more complete coverage. We also wanted to explore more advanced subject material. We were torn between rewriting the original book and creating a new advanced book. After some debate, the decision was made to start by taking the core material from the first book and revising it to be up to date and more complete, while removing material that we felt wasn't as relevant for game development. You hold the results of that effort in your hands. With a solid foundation established through this book, we hope to explore more advanced topics in a second volume at some future date.

In this book, you'll begin to learn how to develop games using high-performance graphics and game libraries. You'll learn how to unleash the power of OpenGL 1.5 to create realistic, real-time graphics.

Who Should Read This Book

This book is intended for programmers who are just getting started in 3D game development. We assume that you're comfortable programming in C++ and hope that you have at least a basic understanding of 3D mathematics and graphics. By the end of the book, you should understand all of the basics of OpenGL and be able to apply them to games.

If you're already experienced with OpenGL, you may still find some useful tidbits here, but you're probably better off waiting for the next volume.

What We Will and Won't Cover

The days when you could cover everything you need to know about game development in a single volume (or even two!) are long gone—if they ever existed at all. To keep the size and cost of this book down to the range that is appropriate for a beginner, we had to carefully pick and choose which topics to cover, which required making a few assumptions.

The first assumption is that you know how to program in C++. If not, there are many good books covering it, some of which are listed in Appendix B, "Further Reading." Pick up a few, read them, spend some time programming, and then come back.

The second assumption is that you know how to program on your platform of choice. OpenGL is available on many different platforms, so we can't safely guess which one you're using, nor can we devote space to covering many different platforms. Even if we did pick a popular platform such as Windows, the coverage would be incomplete, and every page we spent on it would be one page less on OpenGL and game programming. So, if you don't already know how to at least get a basic application up and running on your platform of choice, spend some time hitting the books or reading tutorials. That said, in *OpenGL Game Programming*, we included a chapter covering the basics of Win32 programming. Because we believe that the majority of our readers use Windows, we've included that chapter in PDF format on the CD, for your convenience.

Even though we won't be covering platform-specific programming in general, we *will* cover Windows-specific issues related to OpenGL because the way you set up and initialize OpenGL varies from system to system.

The third assumption we make is that you have some understanding of 3D math. Many beginning game programming books (including our original one) provide 3D math primers, but it is such a large topic that these primers are unavoidably incomplete. Rather than give you a half-baked introduction to the topic, we recommend picking up one of the books suggested in Appendix B. In truth, because OpenGL hides much of the mathematics that goes on behind the scenes, you can probably cheat for now and get away with not knowing things like how to compute a dot product or multiply matrices. But if you want to become a graphics guru, you'll want to learn as much as you can about 3D math, and doing so before diving into a book like this one will make your journey easier.

Since we wrote a math primer for the previous book, we went ahead and included it on the CD as well, so if you just want to learn the basics or perhaps brush up a bit, you may find it useful.

Finally, at least in this volume, we've opted not to cover any topics in game development not directly related to graphics or OpenGL. Subjects such as game design, artificial intelligence, networking, audio, and physics are all very important to games, but they all require more than a chapter or two to cover completely—many of them deserve a book of their own.

Now that you know what we won't be covering, let's talk about what we will be covering. As the title suggests, this book is targeted at people who want to make games using OpenGL, but who have never used it before. So you'll learn a lot of OpenGL. You won't learn everything there is to know about it yet—the more advanced aspects will be covered in later volumes, and there are parts of it that aren't particularly useful for games—but you will learn all of the basics, including important topics like texture mapping and vertex arrays. By the end of the book, you'll be able to make non-trivial games.

Our philosophy is to focus on one thing and do it well, rather than trying to cover many things and do them poorly.

What's New

If you've read, or at least looked at, *OpenGL Game Programming*, you may be wondering what's different about this book.

The most obvious change is that this book is much smaller. This book covers most of the material covered through Chapter 13 in *OpenGL Game Programming*. Although we're covering most of the same material as the first edition, this is not merely an update. We've entirely rewritten many sections of the book and thoroughly reviewed and updated everything that hasn't been rewritten. We've added some new sections: some to cover new functionality that has been added to OpenGL, and some to lay the foundation for the next volume. We've also removed a few sections that we felt were of questionable value (don't worry, though; they're on the CD in electronic format, so you're not really missing anything).

About the Target Platform

One of the most important (and difficult!) decisions we faced in writing this book was which target platform to use. Because OpenGL is a cross-platform API, the field was wide open, and we were left with several choices:

1. Write for as many of the major platforms as possible.
2. Use a cross-platform API to abstract the platform-specific details.
3. Write for the most popular platform, and let people on other platforms figure out the differences on their own.

The first option simply isn't practical for space and time reasons. The second option is better, but we felt that there are some platform-specific issues that can't be avoided and are important to understand. Ultimately, we decided on the third option, and it's clear that Windows is still the most popular platform by a very wide margin for people starting off in game development. If you're not using Windows, don't worry, the amount of Windows-specific information is very limited. Almost all of the information covered in this book is readily applicable to any platform OpenGL is supported on.

Using This Book

Note

If you don't read anything else in this introduction, read this section. It contains important information you'll need to get the most out of this book.

The CD

In order to reduce the cost of this book while allowing us to pack in as much information as possible, we've minimized the amount of code that is listed in the book. Full source code for all of the example programs used in the book is included on the CD, so you'll want to open these files or print them out to use in conjunction with the text.

Extensions

You'll learn about extensions in Chapter 8, "OpenGL Extensions." As you'll see there, extensions are especially important under Windows for accessing new features. Throughout the book, whenever we discuss features that are only available as extensions under Windows, we'll provide a box with information about the extension to make it easier for you to use.

Function Names

Many OpenGL functions come in multiple versions to support different numbers and types of parameters. In C++, this could easily be implemented using overloaded functions, but since OpenGL was designed to be used with C and other languages that might not support overloading, another solution was necessary. This solution was to include information about the type and number of parameters in each function's name. In order to be able to avoid listing all of the different variations of a function, we'll use the following convention:

```
glFunction{1234}{bsifd ubusui}(TYPE param);
glFunction{1234}{bsifd ubusui}v(TYPE *params);
```

This notation indicates that the function name will be followed by one of the numbers contained within the first set of curly braces and then one of the letters contained in the second set of curly braces. The letters stand for byte, short, integer, float, double, unsigned byte, unsigned short, and unsigned integer, respectively. TYPE is used as a placeholder for the specific data type accepted by the function. The second form varies from the first only in that it includes a v, which indicates that the function takes an array of values rather than a single value.

When referring to a function that has multiple forms within the text, we will generally refer to it as glFunction() without any parameter information.

Your Tools

In order to use this book, you're going to need a few things. First off, you'll need a C++ compiler. Because knowing C++ is one of the prerequisites for this book, it's safe to assume you already have a C++ compiler. All the code samples for this book were written using Visual C++ 6.0 and Visual C++ .NET, although you should be able to get everything to work with other compilers.

In addition to the compiler, you'll need the headers and libraries for OpenGL. If you're using Visual C++, you already have the latest headers and libraries for Windows. For other platforms, you can visit the official OpenGL Web site at www.opengl.org and download them from there.

Note

The OpenGL implementation included with Visual C++ was (not surprisingly) created by Microsoft. If you search around the Internet, you may come across an OpenGL implementation for Windows created by Silicon Graphics. Because Silicon Graphics is no longer maintaining its implementation, you should stick with Microsoft's implementation.

The specific files needed for OpenGL under Windows are listed below. The filenames for other platforms may be a little different (.a instead of .lib for Linux, for instance), but the function is the same.

gl.h Primary OpenGL header. By convention, this is placed in a subfolder of your compiler's include directory named gl.

glu.h Header for the OpenGL Utility library. This is placed in the same location as gl.h.

opengl32.lib Library containing bindings to OpenGL functions. This is placed in your compiler's library folder.

glu32.lib Library containing bindings to OpenGL Utility Library functions. This is placed in your compiler's library folder.

opengl32.dll Dynamic-link library containing OpenGL function implementations and hooks into video hardware drivers. This is found in the Windows system directory (system32).

glu32.dll Dynamic-link library containing OpenGL Utility Library function implementations. This is found in the Windows system directory (system32).

Whenever making a new project, you'll have to be sure that the OpenGL library files are linked to it. In Visual C++, there are several ways to do this, but the preferred method is by opening the Project menu, selecting the Settings command, clicking the Link tab, and adding opengl32.lib and glu32.lib to the Object/library modules line. You can also include the following two lines anywhere in your project (note that these commands are Microsoft specific and probably won't work with other compilers):

```
#pragma comment(lib, "opengl32.lib")
#pragma comment(lib, "glu32.lib")
```

When you try to compile your program, if you get errors that look like this:

```
error LNK2001: unresolved external symbol __imp__glClear@4
```

it's a sure sign that you haven't linked the OpenGL libraries correctly. Go back and read the preceding several paragraphs again.

Support Web Site

Finally, we maintain a Web site at **http://glbook.gamedev.net** that we will use to provide support for this book. We'll be updating this site regularly to post errata and updates to the example programs as needed. Be sure to check it if you have any problems.

Enough with the introduction, let's get started!

PART I

OpenGL Basics

CHAPTER 1

THE EXPLORATION
BEGINS . . . AGAIN

Before digging into the meat of game development, you need to have a foundational understanding of the medium in which you'll be working. As should be obvious by now, you'll be using the OpenGL API for graphics, so we'll take a look at OpenGL's origins, design, and evolution. We'll also provide an overview of the game industry, as well as a look at the core elements involved in a game.

In this chapter, you will learn:

- What a game is
- About OpenGL and its history
- About libraries that can be used to expand OpenGL's functionality

Why Make Games?

Interactive entertainment has grown by leaps and bounds in the last decade. Computer games, which used to be a niche market, have now grown in to a multi-billion-dollar industry. Recent years have shown a trend of accelerating growth whose end is not in sight. The interactive entertainment industry is an explosive market that pushes the latest computer technologies to the edge and helps drive research in areas such as graphics and artificial intelligence. It is this relentless drive and growth that attracts many people to this industry, but why do people really make games?

From working in the game industry ourselves and talking to many others who do as well, one thing seems to drive people to learn and succeed at the art of game development: *fun*. Games have come to be known as one of the more creative forms of software development, and the amazing games that have been released in recent years are a testament to that. Games like Halo by Bungie Software have pushed the envelope of game design to the point that the industry will never be the same again. Game developers are drawn into this industry by the idea of creating their own virtual world that thousands, if not millions, of other people will one day experience. The game developer strives to be challenged and to discover new technologies and new worlds. According to Michael Sikora, an independent game developer, "It's like a trip I just can't get off." This is what making games is all about.

The World of 3D Games

Although many companies have contributed to the growth of 3D gaming, a special nod must be given to id Software, which was a major catalyst in the rise of 3D games. More than 10 years ago, John Carmack and company unleashed a little game called *Wolfenstein 3D* upon the world. *Wolf3D* brought the gaming world to its knees with realtime raycasting 3D graphics and an immersive world that left gamers sitting at their computers for hours upon hours. The game was a new beginning for the industry, and it never looked back. In 1993, the world of *Doom* went on a rampage and pushed 3D graphics technology past yet another limit with its 2.5D engine. The gaming world reveled in the technical achievement brought by id in their game *Doom*, but it did not stop there. Several years later, *Quake* changed 3D gaming for good. No longer were enemies "fake 3D," but rather full 3D entities that could move around in a fully polygonal 3D. The possibilities were now limited only by how many polygons the CPU (and eventually, the GPU) could process and display on the screen. *Quake* also brought multiplayer gaming over a network to reality as hordes of Internet users joined in the fun of death matches with 30 other people.

Since the release of *Quake*, the industry has been blessed by new technological advancements nearly every few months. The 3D gaming sector has brought on 3D accelerator hardware that performs the 3D math right in silicon. Now, new hardware is released every six months that seems to double its predecessor in raw power, speed, and flexibility. With all these advancements, there could not be a more exciting time than now for 3D game development.

The Elements of a Game

You may now be asking, "How is a game made?" Before we can answer this question, you must understand that games are, at their lowest level, software. Today's software is developed in teams, where each member of a team works on his or her specialty until everyone's work is integrated to create a single, coherent work of art. Games are developed in much the same way, except programming is not the only area of expertise. Artists are required to generate the images and beautiful scenery that is prevalent in so many of today's games. Level designers bring the virtual world to life and use the art provided to them by the artists to create worlds beyond belief. Programmers piece together each element and make sure everything works as a whole. Sound techs and musicians create the audio necessary to provide the gamer with a rich, multimedia, believable, and virtual experience. Designers come up with the game concept, and producers coordinate everyone's efforts.

With each person working on different areas of expertise, the game must be divided into various elements that will get pieced together in the end. In general, games are divided into these areas:

- Graphics
- Input
- Music and sound
- Game logic and artificial intelligence
- Networking
- User interface and menuing system

Each of these areas can be further divided into more specific systems. For example, game logic would consist of physics and particle systems, while graphics might have a 2D and/or 3D renderer. Figure 1.1 shows an example of a simplistic game architecture.

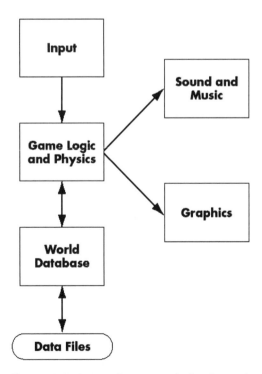

Figure 1.1 A game is composed of various subsystems.

As you can see, each element of a game is divided into its own separate piece and communicates with other elements of the game. The game logic element tends to be the hub of the game, where decisions are made for processing input and sending output. The architecture shown in Figure 1.1 is very simplistic, however; Figure 1.2 shows what a more advanced game's architecture might look like.

As you can see in Figure 1.2, a more complex game requires a more complex architectural design. More detailed components are developed and used to implement specific features or functionality that the game software needs to operate smoothly. One thing to keep in mind is that games feature some of the most complex blends of technology and software designs, and as such, game development requires abstract thinking and implementation on a higher level than traditional software development. When you are developing a game, you are developing a work of art, and it needs to be treated as such. Be ready to try new things on your own and redesign existing technologies to suit your needs. There is no set way to develop games, much as there is no set way to paint a painting. Strive to be innovative and set new standards!

What Is OpenGL?

OpenGL provides the programmer with an interface to graphics hardware. It is a powerful, low-level rendering library, available on all major platforms, with wide hardware support. It is designed for use in any graphics application, from games to modeling to CAD. Many games, such as id Software's *Doom 3*, use OpenGL for their core graphics-rendering engine.

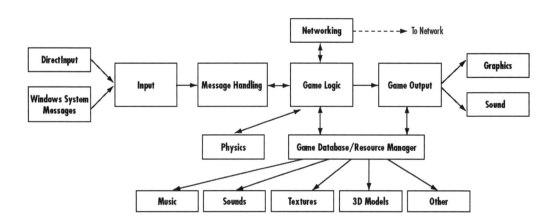

Figure 1.2 A more advanced game architectural design.

OpenGL intentionally provides only low-level rendering routines, allowing the programmer a great deal of control and flexibility. The provided routines can easily be used to build high-level rendering and modeling libraries, and in fact, the OpenGL Utility Library (GLU), which is included in most OpenGL distributions, does exactly that. Note also that OpenGL is just a graphics library; unlike DirectX, it does not include support for sound, input, networking, or anything else not directly related to graphics.

Tip

OpenGL stands for "Open Graphics Library." "Open" is used because OpenGL is an open standard, meaning that many companies are able to contribute to the development. It does not mean that OpenGL is open source.

OpenGL History

OpenGL was originally developed by Silicon Graphics, Inc. (SGI) as a multi-purpose, platform-independent graphics API. Since 1992, the development of OpenGL has been overseen by the OpenGL Architecture Review Board (ARB), which is made up of major graphics vendors and other industry leaders, currently consisting of 3DLabs, ATI, Dell, Evans & Sutherland, Hewlett-Packard, IBM, Intel, Matrox, NVIDIA, SGI, Sun Microsystems, and Silicon Graphics. The role of the ARB is to establish and maintain the OpenGL specification, which dictates which features must be included when one is developing an OpenGL distribution.

At the time of this writing, the most recent version of OpenGL is Version 1.5. OpenGL remained at Version 1.2 for a long time, but three years ago, in response to the rapidly changing state of graphics hardware, the ARB committed to annual updates to the specification.

The designers of OpenGL knew that hardware vendors would want to add features that may not be exposed by core OpenGL interfaces. To address this, they included a method for extending OpenGL. These *extensions* eventually become adopted by other hardware vendors, and when support for an extension is wide enough—or the extension is deemed important enough by the ARB—the extension may be promoted to the core OpenGL specification. Almost all of the most recent additions to OpenGL started out as extensions—many of them directly pertaining to video games. Extensions are covered in detail in Chapter 8, "OpenGL Extensions."

OpenGL Architecture

OpenGL is a collection of several hundred functions providing access to all of the features offered by your graphics hardware. Internally, it acts as a state machine—a collection of states that tell OpenGL what to do and that are changed in a very well-defined manner. Using the API, you can set various aspects of the state machine, including such things as the current color, lighting, blending, and so on. When rendering, everything drawn is affected by the current settings of the state machine. It's important to be aware of what the various states are and the effect they have, because it's not uncommon to have unexpected results due to having one or more states set incorrectly. Although we're not going to cover the entire OpenGL state machine, we'll cover everything that's relevant to the topics covered in this book.

At the core of OpenGL is the rendering pipeline, as shown in Figure 1.3. You don't need to understand everything that happens in the pipeline at this point, but you should at least be aware that what you see on the screen results from a series of stems. Fortunately, OpenGL handles most of these steps for you.

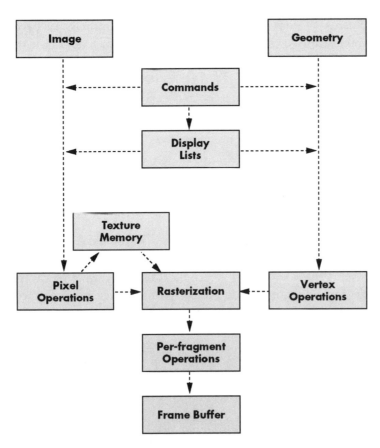

Figure 1.3 The OpenGL rendering pipeline.

Fixed Function Versus Programmability

What you see in Figure 1.3 is the classic *fixed function* pipeline. In the fixed function model, the operations that are performed at each stage are always the same, although you're able to provide input parameters that modify the operations somewhat. For the past several years, the graphics industry has been revolutionized by the development of the *programmable pipeline*. With programmability, a developer is able to take complete control over what happens at certain stages, specifically at the vertex and per-fragment operation stages. This is done through the use of custom programs that actually execute on the graphics hardware. These programs are often referred to as *shaders*.

Shaders can be difficult to understand when you are first learning computer graphics, so in this book we'll be focusing on the fixed function pipeline, which still provides a considerable degree of power and flexibility.

Related Libraries

There are many libraries available that build upon and around OpenGL to add support and functionality beyond the low-level rendering support that it excels at. One of them, GLU, has already been mentioned. We don't have space to cover all of the OpenGL-related libraries, and new ones are cropping up all the time, so we'll limit our coverage here to two of the most important: GLUT and SDL. We'll cover an additional library, GLee, in Chapter 8.

GLUT

GLUT, short for *OpenGL Utility Toolkit*, is a set of support libraries available on every major platform. OpenGL does not directly support any form of windowing, menus, or input. That's where GLUT comes in. It provides basic functionality in all of those areas, while remaining platform independent, so that you can easily move GLUT-based applications from, for example, Windows to UNIX with few, if any, changes.

GLUT is easy to use and learn, and although it does not provide you with all the functionality the operating system offers, it works quite well for demos and simple applications.

Because your ultimate goal is going to be to create a fairly complex game, you're going to need more flexibility than GLUT offers. For this reason, other than a brief example at the end of this chapter, it is not used in the code in the book. However, if you'd like to know more, visit the official GLUT Web page at http://www.opengl.org/resources/libraries/glut.html.

SDL

The Simple Direct Media Layer (SDL) is a cross-platform multimedia library, including support for audio, input, 2D graphics, and many other things. It also provides direct support for 3D graphics through OpenGL, so it's a popular choice for cross-platform game development. More information on SDL can be found at www.libsdl.org.

A Sneak Peek

Let's jump ahead and take a look at some code that you will be using. The code won't make much sense now, but it'll start to in a few chapters. On the CD, look for and open up the project Simple, which you'll find in the directory for this chapter. This example program displays two overlapping colored polygons, as shown in Figure 1.4.

Note that this code uses GLUT for handling all the operating system–specific stuff. This is just to keep things simple rather than confusing the issue with platform-specific setup code. Let's dissect the code. First is the initialization:

```
glEnable(GL_DEPTH_TEST);
```

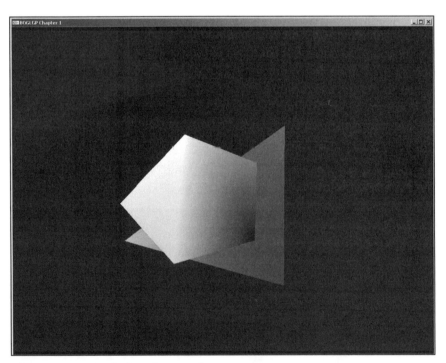

Figure 1.4 A simple OpenGL example.

This line enables zbuffering, which ensures that objects closer to the viewer get drawn over objects that are farther away. This is explained in detail in Chapter 12, "OpenGL Buffers."

Next up is the Reshape() routine, which gets called initially and every time the display window is resized:

```
glViewport(0, 0, (GLsizei) width, (GLsizei) height);
glMatrixMode(GL_PROJECTION);
glLoadIdentity();
gluPerspective(90.0, width/height, 1.0, 100.0);

glMatrixMode(GL_MODELVIEW);
```

This sets up the way in which objects in the world are transformed into pixels on the screen. All of the functions used here will be explained in Chapter 4, "Transformations and Matrices."

The last piece of code to look at is in the Display() routine. This code is called repeatedly to update the screen:

```
glLoadIdentity();
gluLookAt(0.0, 1.0, 6.0,
          0.0, 0.0, 0.0,
          0.0, 1.0, 0.0);

// clear the screen
glClear(GL_COLOR_BUFFER_BIT | GL_DEPTH_BUFFER_BIT);

glBegin(GL_TRIANGLES);
  glColor3f(1.0, 0.0, 0.0);
  glVertex3f(2.0, 2.5, -1.0);
  glColor3f(0.0, 1.0, 0.0);
  glVertex3f(-3.5, -2.5, -1.0);
  glColor3f(0.0, 0.0, 1.0);
  glVertex3f(2.0, -4.0, 0.0);
glEnd();

glBegin(GL_POLYGON);
  glColor3f(1.0, 1.0, 1.0);
  glVertex3f(-1.0, 2.0, 0.0);
  glColor3f(1.0, 1.0, 0.0);
  glVertex3f(-3.0, -0.5, 0.0);
  glColor3f(0.0, 1.0, 1.0);
  glVertex3f(-1.5, -3.0, 0.0);
```

```
    glColor3f(0.0, 0.0, 0.0);
    glVertex3f(1.0, -2.0, 0.0);
    glColor3f(1.0, 0.0, 1.0);
    glVertex3f(1.0, 1.0, 0.0);
glEnd();
```

The first two lines set up the camera, as explained in Chapter 4. glClear()—which you'll learn about in Chapter 12—is then used to clear the screen. The rest of the function draws the two polygons by specifying the vertices that define them, as well as the colors associated with them. These functions will all be explained in Chapter 3, "OpenGL States and Primitives."

Try modifying some of the values in the example program to see what effect they have.

Summary

In this chapter you took a first look at OpenGL, which you'll be using throughout the remainder of this book for graphics demos and games. Now that you have an overview of the API you will be using, you can get into the fun part of actual development!

What You Have Learned

- 3D gaming is a rapidly growing and excited field.
- OpenGL is a graphics library that is used in many games.
- OpenGL has been around for over 10 years. Its development is overseen by the Architectural Review Board.
- Libraries such as GLUT and SDL can be used in conjunction with OpenGL for faster development and added functionality.

Review Questions

1. When was OpenGL first introduced?
2. What is the current version number of OpenGL?
3. Who decides what additions and changes are made to OpenGL?

On Your Own

1. Take the example program and modify it so that the triangle is all red and the polygon is all blue.

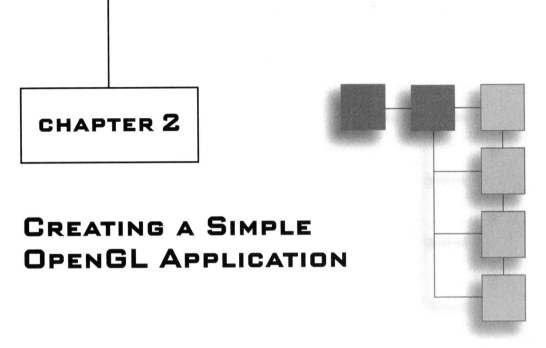

CHAPTER 2

CREATING A SIMPLE OPENGL APPLICATION

As mentioned in the introduction, knowing how to create a basic application on the platform you are using is one of the prerequisites to reading this book. However, even though OpenGL is multiplatform, there are platform-specific things you need to do to be able to use OpenGL. We'll be covering them for Windows here. Over the course of this chapter, you will learn:

- The WGL and related Windows functions that support OpenGL
- Pixel formats
- Using OpenGL with Windows
- Full-screen OpenGL

Introduction to WGL

The set of APIs used to set up OpenGL on Windows is collectively known as WGL, sometimes pronounced "wiggle." Some of the things WGL allows you to do include:

- Creating and selecting a rendering context.
- Using Windows font support in OpenGL applications.
- Loading OpenGL extensions.

We'll cover fonts and extensions in Chapters 11, "Displaying Text," and 8, "OpenGL Extensions," respectively. Rendering contexts are covered here.

Note

WGL provides considerable functionality in addition to what's been listed here. However, the additional features are either rather advanced (and require extensions) or very specialized, so we won't be covering them in this volume.

The Rendering Context

For an operating system to be able to work with OpenGL, it needs a means of connecting OpenGL to a window. If it allows multiple applications to be running at once, it also needs a way to prevent multiple OpenGL applications from interfering with each other. This is done through the use of a *rendering context*. In Windows, the Graphics Device Interface (or GDI) uses a device context to remember settings about drawing modes and commands. The rendering context serves the same purpose for OpenGL. Keep in mind, however, that a rendering context does not replace a device context on Windows. The two interact to ensure that your application behaves properly. In fact, you need to set up the device context first and then create the rendering context with a matching pixel format. We'll get into the details of this shortly.

You can actually create multiple rendering contexts for a single application. This is useful for applications such as 3D modelers, where you have multiple windows or viewports, and each needs to keep track of its settings independently. You could also use it to have one rendering context manage your primary display while another manages user interface components. The only catch is that there can be only one active rendering context per thread at any given time, though you can have multiple threads—each with its own context—rendering to a single window at once.

Let's take a look at the most important WGL functions for managing contexts.

wglCreateContext()

Before you can use a rendering context, you need to create one. You do this through:

```
HGLRC wglCreateContext(HDC hDC);
```

hDC is the handle for the device context that you previously created for your Windows application. You should call this function only after the pixel format for the device context has been set, so that the pixel formats match. (We'll talk about setting the pixel format shortly.) Rather than returning the actual rendering context, a handle is returned, which you can use to pass the rendering context to other functions.

wglDeleteContext()

Whenever you create a rendering context, the system allocates resources for it. When you're done using the context, you need to let the system know about it to prevent those resources from leaking. You do that through:

```
BOOL wglDeleteContext(HGLRC hRC);
```

wglMakeCurrent()

If the currently active thread does not have a current rendering context, all OpenGL function calls will return without doing anything. This makes perfect sense considering that the context contains all of the state information that OpenGL needs to operate. This is done with wglMakeCurrent():

```
BOOL wglMakeCurrent(HDC hdc, HGLRC hRC);
```

You need to make sure both the device context and rendering context you pass to wglMakeCurrent() have the same pixel format for the function to work. If you wish to deselect the rendering context, you can pass NULL for the hRC parameter, or you can simply pass another rendering context.

The wglCreateContext() and wglMakeCurrent() functions should be called during the initialization stage of your application, such as when the WM_CREATE message is passed to the windows procedure. The wglDeleteContext() function should be called when the window is being destroyed, such as with a WM_DESTROY message. It's good practice to deselect the rendering context before deleting it, though wglDeleteContext() will do that for you as long as it's the current context for the active thread.

Here's a code snippet to demonstrate this concept:

```
LRESULT CALLBACK WndProc(HWND hwnd, UINT message, WPARAM wParam, LPARAM lParam)
{
    static HGLRC    hRC;              // rendering context
    static HDC      hDC;              // device context

    switch(message)
    {
    case WM_CREATE:                   // window Is being created
        hDC = GetDC(hwnd);            // get device context for window
        hRC = wglCreateContext(hDC);  // create rendering context
        wglMakeCurrent(hDC, hRC);     // make rendering context current
        break;
```

```
        case WM_DESTROY:                    // window Is being destroyed
            wglMakeCurrent(hDC, NULL);      // deselect rendering context
            wglDeleteContext(hRC);          // delete rendering context
            PostQuitMessage(0);             // send WM_QUIT
            break;
    }  // end switch
}  // end WndProc
```

This little bit of code will create and destroy your OpenGL window. You use static variables for the rendering and device contexts so you don't have to re-create them every time the windows procedure is called. This helps speed the process up by eliminating unnecessary calls. The rest of the code is fairly straightforward as the comments tell exactly what is going on.

Getting the Current Context

Most of the time you will store the handle to your rendering context in a global or member variable, but at times you don't have that information available. This is often the case when you're using multiple rendering contexts in a multithreaded application. To get the handle to the current context, you can use the following:

```
HGLRC wglGetCurrentContext();
```

If there is no current rendering context, this will return NULL.

You can acquire a handle to the current device context in a similar manner:

```
HDC wglGetCurrentDC();
```

Now that you know the basics of dealing with rendering contexts, we need to discuss pixel formats and the PIXELFORMATDESCRIPTOR structure and how you use them to set up your window.

Pixel Formats

OpenGL provides a finite number of *pixel formats* that include such properties as the color mode, depth buffer, bits per pixel, and whether the window is double buffered. The pixel format is associated with your rendering window and device context, describing what types of data they support. Before creating a rendering context, you must select an appropriate pixel format to use.

The first thing you need to do is use the PIXELFORMATDESCRIPTOR structure to define the characteristics and behavior you desire for the window. This structure is defined as

```
typedef struct tagPIXELFORMATDESCRIPTOR {
    WORD  nSize;              // size of the structure
    WORD  nVersion;          // always set to 1
    DWORD dwFlags;           // flags for pixel buffer properties
    BYTE  iPixelType;        // type of pixel data
    BYTE  cColorBits;        // number of bits per pixel
    BYTE  cRedBits;          // number of red bits
    BYTE  cRedShift;         // shift count for red bits
    BYTE  cGreenBits;        // number of green bits
    BYTE  cGreenShift;       // shift count for green bits
    BYTE  cBlueBits;         // number of blue bits
    BYTE  cBlueShift;        // shift count for blue bits
    BYTE  cAlphaBits;        // number of alpha bits
    BYTE  cAlphaShift;       // shift count for alpha bits
    BYTE  cAccumBits;        // number of accumulation buffer bits
    BYTE  cAccumRedBits;     // number of red accumulation bits
    BYTE  cAccumGreenBits;   // number of green accumulation bits
    BYTE  cAccumBlueBits;    // number of blue accumulation bits
    BYTE  cAccumAlphaBits;   // number of alpha accumulation bits
    BYTE  cDepthBits;        // number of depth buffer bits
    BYTE  cStencilBits;      // number of stencil buffer bits
    BYTE  cAuxBuffers;       // number of auxiliary buffer. not supported.
    BYTE  iLayerType;        // no longer used
    BYTE  bReserved;         // number of overlay and underlay planes
    DWORD dwLayerMask;       // no longer used
    DWORD dwVisibleMask;     // transparent underlay plane color
    DWORD dwDamageMask;      // no longer used
} PIXELFORMATDESCRIPTOR;
```

Let's take a look at the more important fields in this structure.

nSize

The first of the more important fields in the structure is nSize. This field should always be set equal to the size of the structure, like this:

```
pfd.nSize = sizeof(PIXELFORMATDESCRIPTOR);
```

This is fairly straightforward and is a common requirement for data structures that get passed as pointers. Often, a structure needs to know its size and how much memory has been allocated for it when performing various operations. A size field allows easy and accurate access to this information with a quick check of the size field.

dwFlags

The next field, dwFlags, specifies the pixel buffer properties. Table 2.1 shows the more common values that you need for dwFlags.

Table 2.1 Pixel Format Flags

Value	Meaning
PFD_DRAW_TO_WINDOW	The buffer can draw to a window or device surface.
PFD_SUPPORT_OPENGL	The buffer supports OpenGL drawing.
PFD_DOUBLEBUFFER	Double buffering is supported. This flag and PFD_SUPPORT_GDI are mutually exclusive.
PFD_DEPTH_DONTCARE	The requested pixel format can either have or not have a depth buffer. To select a pixel format without a depth buffer, you must specify this flag. The requested pixel format can be with or without a depth buffer. Otherwise, only pixel formats with a depth buffer are considered.
PFD_DOUBLEBUFFER_DONTCARE	The requested pixel format can be either single or double buffered.
PFD_GENERIC_ACCELERATED	The requested pixel format is accelerated by the device driver.
PFD_GENERIC_FORMAT	The requested pixel format is supported only in software. (Check for this flag if your application is running slower than expected.)

iPixelType

The iPixelType field specifies the type of pixel data. You can set this field to one of the following values:

- PFD_TYPE_RGBA. RGBA pixels. Each pixel has four components in this order: red, green, blue, and alpha.
- PFD_TYPE_COLORINDEX. Paletted mode. Each pixel uses a color-index value.

For our purposes, the iPixelType field will always be set to PFD_TYPE_RGBA. This allows you to use the standard RGB color model with an alpha component for effects such as transparency.

cColorBits

The cColorBits field specifies the bits per pixel available in each color buffer. At the present time, this value can be set to 8, 16, 24, or 32. If the requested color bits are not available on the hardware present in the machine, the highest setting closest to the one you choose will be used. For example, if you set cColorBits to 24 and the graphics hardware does not support 24-bit rendering, but it does support 16-bit rendering, the device context that is created will be 16-bit.

Setting the Pixel Format

After you have the fields of the PIXELFORMATDESCRIPTOR structure set to your desired values, the next step is to pass the structure to the ChoosePixelFormat() function:

```
int ChoosePixelFormat(HDC hdc, CONST PIXELFORMATDESCRIPTOR *ppfd);
```

This function attempts to find a predefined pixel format that matches the one specified by your PIXELFORMATDESCRIPTOR. If it can't find an exact match, it will find the closest one it can and change the fields of the pixel format descriptor to match what it actually gave you. The pixel format itself is returned as an integer representing an ID. You can use this value with the SetPixelFormat() function:

```
BOOL SetPixelFormat(HDC hdc, int pixelFormat, const PIXELFORMATDESCRIPTOR *ppfd);
```

This sets the pixel format for the device context and window associated with it. Note that the pixel format can be set only once for a window, so if you decide to change it, you must destroy and re-create your window.

The following listing shows an example of setting up a pixel format:

```
PIXELFORMATDESCRIPTOR pfd;
memset(&pfd, 0, sizeof(PIXELFORMATDESCRIPTOR));
pfd.nSize = sizeof(PIXELFORMATDESCRIPTOR);       // size
pfd.dwFlags = PFD_DRAW_TO_WINDOW | PFD_SUPPORT_OPENGL | PFD_DOUBLEBUFFER;
pfd.nVersion = 1;                                // version
pfd.iPixelType = PFD_TYPE_RGBA;                  // color type
pfd.cColorBits = 32;                             // prefered color depth
pfd.cDepthBits = 24;                             // depth buffer
pfd.iLayerType = PFD_MAIN_PLANE;                 // main layer

// choose best matching pixel format, return index
int pixelFormat = ChoosePixelFormat(hDC, &pfd);
```

```
// set pixel format to device context
SetPixelFormat(hDC, pixelFormat, &pfd);
```

One of the first things you might notice about that snippet is that the pixel format descriptor is first initialized to zero, and only a few of the fields are set. This simply means that there are several fields that you don't even need in order to set the pixel format. At times you may need these other fields, but for now you can just set them equal to zero.

An OpenGL Application

You have the tools, so now let's apply them. In this section of the chapter, you will piece together the previous sections to give you a basic framework for creating an OpenGL-enabled window. What follows is a complete listing of an OpenGL window application that displays a window with a lime–green colored triangle rotating about its center on a black background. Let's take a look.

From winmain.cpp:

```
#define WIN32_LEAN_AND_MEAN
#define WIN32_EXTRA_LEAN

#include <windows.h>
#include <gl/gl.h>
#include <gl/glu.h>

#include "CGfxOpenGL.h"

bool exiting = false;        // is the app exiting?
long windowWidth = 800;      // the window width
long windowHeight = 600;     // the window height
long windowBits = 32;        // the window bits per pixel
bool fullscreen = false;     // fullscreen mode?
HDC hDC;                      // window device context

// global pointer to the CGfxOpenGL rendering class
CGfxOpenGL *g_glRender = NULL;
```

The above code defines our #includes and initialized global variables. Look at the comments for explanations of the global variables. The g_glRender pointer is for the CGfxOpenGL class we use throughout the rest of the book to encapsulate the OpenGL-specific code from the operating system–specific code. We did this so that if you want to run the book's examples on another operating system, such as Linux, all you need to do is copy the CGfxOpenGL class and write the C/C++ code in another operating system required to hook the CGfx-OpenGL class into the application. You should be able to do this with relative ease; that is our goal at least.

```
void SetupPixelFormat(HDC hDC)
{
    int pixelFormat;

    PIXELFORMATDESCRIPTOR pfd =
    {
        sizeof(PIXELFORMATDESCRIPTOR),    // size
            1,                            // version
            PFD_SUPPORT_OPENGL |          // OpenGL window
            PFD_DRAW_TO_WINDOW |          // render to window
            PFD_DOUBLEBUFFER,             // support double-buffering
            PFD_TYPE_RGBA,                // color type
            32,                           // prefered color depth
            0, 0, 0, 0, 0, 0,             // color bits (ignored)
            0,                            // no alpha buffer
            0,                            // alpha bits (ignored)
            0,                            // no accumulation buffer
            0, 0, 0, 0,                   // accum bits (ignored)
            16,                           // depth buffer
            0,                            // no stencil buffer
            0,                            // no auxiliary buffers
            PFD_MAIN_PLANE,               // main layer
            0,                            // reserved
            0, 0, 0,                      // no layer, visible, damage masks
    };

    pixelFormat = ChoosePixelFormat(hDC, &pfd);
    SetPixelFormat(hDC, pixelFormat, &pfd);
}
```

The SetupPixelFormat() function uses the PIXELFORMATDESCRIPTOR to set up the pixel format for the defined device context, parameter hDC. The contents of this function are described earlier in this chapter in the "Pixel Formats" section.

```
LRESULT CALLBACK MainWindowProc(HWND hWnd, UINT uMsg, WPARAM wParam, LPARAM lParam)
{
    static HDC hDC;
    static HGLRC hRC;
    int height, width;

    // dispatch messages
    switch (uMsg)
    {
    case WM_CREATE:                  // window creation
        hDC = GetDC(hWnd);
        SetupPixelFormat(hDC);
        hRC = wglCreateContext(hDC);
        wglMakeCurrent(hDC, hRC);
        break;

    case WM_DESTROY:                 // window destroy
    case WM_QUIT:
    case WM_CLOSE:                   // windows is closing

        // deselect rendering context and delete it
        wglMakeCurrent(hDC, NULL);
        wglDeleteContext(hRC);

        // send WM_QUIT to message queue
        PostQuitMessage(0);
        break;

    case WM_SIZE:
        height = HIWORD(lParam);         // retrieve width and height
        width = LOWORD(lParam);

        g_glRender->SetupProjection(width, height);

        break;

    case WM_KEYDOWN:
        int fwKeys;
        LPARAM keyData;
```

```
        fwKeys = (int)wParam;          // virtual-key code
        keyData = lParam;              // key data

        switch(fwKeys)
        {
        case VK_ESCAPE:
            PostQuitMessage(0);
            break;
        default:
            break;
        }

        break;

    default:
        break;
    }
    return DefWindowProc(hWnd, uMsg, wParam, lParam);
}
```

The MainWindowProc() is called by Windows whenever it receives a Windows message. We are not going to go into the details of the Windows messaging system, as any good Windows programming book will do for you, but generally we need to concern ourselves only with the MainWindowProc() during initialization, shutdown, window resizing operations, and Windows-based input functionality. We listen for the following messages:

- WM_CREATE: This message is sent when the window is created. We set up the pixel format here, retrieve the window's device context, and create the OpenGL rendering context.

- WM_DESTROY, WM_QUIT, WM_CLOSE: These messages are sent when the window is destroyed or the user closes the window. We destroy the rendering context here and then send the WM_QUIT message to Windows with the PostQuitMessage() function.

- WM_SIZE: This message is sent whenever the window size is being changed. It is also sent during part of the window creation sequence, as the operating system resizes and adjusts the window according to the parameters defined in the CreateWindowEx() function. We set up the OpenGL projection matrix here based on the new width and height of the window, so our 3D viewport always matches the window size.

- WM_KEYDOWN: This message is sent whenever a key on the keyboard is pressed. In this particular message code we are interested only in retrieving the keycode and seeing if it is equal to the ESC virtual key code, VK_ESCAPE. If it is, we quit the application by calling the PostQuitMessage() function.

You can learn more about Windows messages and how to handle them through the Microsoft Developer Network, MSDN, which comes with your copy of Visual Studio. You can also visit the MSDN Web site at http://msdn.microsoft.com.

```
int WINAPI WinMain(HINSTANCE hInstance, HINSTANCE hPrevInstance, LPSTR lpCmdLine, int
nShowCmd)
{
    WNDCLASSEX windowClass;                 // window class
    HWND       hwnd;                        // window handle
    MSG        msg;                         // message
    DWORD      dwExStyle;                   // Window Extended Style
    DWORD      dwStyle;                     // Window Style
    RECT       windowRect;

    g_glRender = new CGfxOpenGL;

    windowRect.left=(long)0;               // Set Left Value To 0
    windowRect.right=(long)windowWidth;    // Set Right Value To Requested Width
    windowRect.top=(long)0;                // Set Top Value To 0
    windowRect.bottom=(long)windowHeight;  // Set Bottom Value To Requested Height

    // fill out the window class structure
    windowClass.cbSize         = sizeof(WNDCLASSEX);
    windowClass.style          = CS_HREDRAW | CS_VREDRAW;
    windowClass.lpfnWndProc    = MainWindowProc;
    windowClass.cbClsExtra     = 0;
    windowClass.cbWndExtra     = 0;
    windowClass.hInstance      = hInstance;
    windowClass.hIcon          = LoadIcon(NULL, IDI_APPLICATION); // default icon
    windowClass.hCursor        = LoadCursor(NULL, IDC_ARROW);    // default arrow
    windowClass.hbrBackground  = NULL;                           // don't need background
    windowClass.lpszMenuName   = NULL;                           // no menu
    windowClass.lpszClassName  = "GLClass";
    windowClass.hIconSm        = LoadIcon(NULL, IDI_WINLOGO);    // windows logo small
icon

    // register the windows class
    if (!RegisterClassEx(&windowClass))
        return 0;

    if (fullscreen)        // fullscreen?
    {
        DEVMODE dmScreenSettings;                                // device mode
```

```
        memset(&dmScreenSettings,0,sizeof(dmScreenSettings));
        dmScreenSettings.dmSize = sizeof(dmScreenSettings);
        dmScreenSettings.dmPelsWidth = windowWidth;              // screen width
        dmScreenSettings.dmPelsHeight = windowHeight;            // screen height
        dmScreenSettings.dmBitsPerPel = windowBits;              // bits per pixel
        dmScreenSettings.dmFields=DM_BITSPERPEL|DM_PELSWIDTH|DM_PELSHEIGHT;

        if (ChangeDisplaySettings(&dmScreenSettings, CDS_FULLSCREEN) !=
DISP_CHANGE_SUCCESSFUL)
        {
            // setting display mode failed, switch to windowed
            MessageBox(NULL, "Display mode failed", NULL, MB_OK);
            fullscreen = FALSE;
        }
    }

    if (fullscreen)                     // Are We Still In Fullscreen Mode?
    {
        dwExStyle=WS_EX_APPWINDOW;       // Window Extended Style
        dwStyle=WS_POPUP;                // Windows Style
        ShowCursor(FALSE);               // Hide Mouse Pointer
    }
    else
    {
        dwExStyle=WS_EX_APPWINDOW | WS_EX_WINDOWEDGE;        // Window Extended Style
        dwStyle=WS_OVERLAPPEDWINDOW;                         // Windows Style
    }

    // Adjust Window To True Requested Size
    AdjustWindowRectEx(&windowRect, dwStyle, FALSE, dwExStyle);

    // class registered, so now create our window
    hwnd = CreateWindowEx(NULL,                             // extended style
        "GLClass",                                          // class name
        "BOGLGP - Chapter 2 - OpenGL Application",          // app name
        dwStyle | WS_CLIPCHILDREN |
        WS_CLIPSIBLINGS,
        0, 0,                                               // x,y coordinate
        windowRect.right - windowRect.left,
        windowRect.bottom - windowRect.top,                 // width, height
        NULL,                                               // handle to parent
        NULL,                                               // handle to menu
```

```
        hInstance,                              // application instance
        NULL);                                  // no extra params

    hDC = GetDC(hwnd);

    // check if window creation failed (hwnd would equal NULL)
    if (!hwnd)
        return 0;

    ShowWindow(hwnd, SW_SHOW);                  // display the window
    UpdateWindow(hwnd);                         // update the window

    g_glRender->Init();

    while (!exiting)
    {
        g_glRender->Prepare(0.0f);
        g_glRender->Render();
        SwapBuffers(hDC);

        while (PeekMessage (&msg, NULL, 0, 0, PM_NOREMOVE))
        {
            if (!GetMessage (&msg, NULL, 0, 0))
            {
                exiting = true;
                break;
            }

            TranslateMessage (&msg);
            DispatchMessage (&msg);
        }
    }

    delete g_glRender;

    if (fullscreen)
    {
        ChangeDisplaySettings(NULL,0);          // If So Switch Back To The Desktop
        ShowCursor(TRUE);                       // Show Mouse Pointer
    }

    return (int)msg.wParam;
}
```

And there is the main Windows entry point function, WinMain(). The major points in this function are the creation and registration of the window class, the call to the CreateWindowEx() function to create the window, and the main while() loop for the program's execution. You may also notice our use of the CGfxOpenGL class, whose definition is shown below.

From CGfxOpenGL.h:

```cpp
class CGfxOpenGL
{
private:
    int m_windowWidth;
    int m_windowHeight;

    float m_angle;

public:
    CGfxOpenGL();
    virtual ~CGfxOpenGL();

    bool Init();
    bool Shutdown();

    void SetupProjection(int width, int height);

    void Prepare(float dt);
    void Render();
};
```

First we should mention that by no means are we saying that the CGfxOpenGL class is how you should design your applications with OpenGL. It is strictly meant to be an easy way for us to present you with flexible, easy-to-understand, and portable OpenGL applications.

Second, this class is very simple to use. It includes methods to initialize your OpenGL code (Init()), shut down your OpenGL code (Shutdown()), set up the projection matrix for the window (SetupProjection()), perform any data-specific updates for a frame (Prepare()), and render your scenes (Render()). We will expand on this class throughout the book, depending on the needs of our applications.

Here's the implementation, located in CGfxOpenGL.cpp:

```cpp
#ifdef _WINDOWS
#include <windows.h>
#endif
```

```
#include <gl/gl.h>
#include <gl/glu.h>
#include <math.h>
#include "CGfxOpenGL.h"

// disable implicit float-double casting
#pragma warning(disable:4305)

CGfxOpenGL::CGfxOpenGL()
{
}

CGfxOpenGL::~CGfxOpenGL()
{
}

bool CGfxOpenGL::Init()
{
    // clear to black background
    glClearColor(0.0, 0.0, 0.0, 0.0);

    m_angle = 0.0f;

    return true;
}

bool CGfxOpenGL::Shutdown()
{
    return true;
}

void CGfxOpenGL::SetupProjection(int width, int height)
{
    if (height == 0)                    // don't want a divide by zero
    {
        height = 1;
    }

    glViewport(0, 0, width, height);    // reset the viewport to new dimensions
    glMatrixMode(GL_PROJECTION);        // set projection matrix current matrix
    glLoadIdentity();                   // reset projection matrix
```

```
        // calculate aspect ratio of window
        gluPerspective(52.0f,(GLfloat)width/(GLfloat)height,1.0f,1000.0f);

        glMatrixMode(GL_MODELVIEW);          // set modelview matrix
        glLoadIdentity();                    // reset modelview matrix

        m_windowWidth = width;
        m_windowHeight = height;
}

void CGfxOpenGL::Prepare(float dt)
{
        m_angle += 0.1f;
}


void CGfxOpenGL::Render()
{
        // clear screen and depth buffer
        glClear(GL_COLOR_BUFFER_BIT | GL_DEPTH_BUFFER_BIT);
        glLoadIdentity();

        // move back 5 units and rotate about all 3 axes
        glTranslatef(0.0, 0.0, -5.0f);
        glRotatef(m_angle, 1.0f, 0.0f, 0.0f);
        glRotatef(m_angle, 0.0f, 1.0f, 0.0f);
        glRotatef(m_angle, 0.0f, 0.0f, 1.0f);

        // lime greenish color
        glColor3f(0.7f, 1.0f, 0.3f);

        // draw the triangle such that the rotation point is in the center
        glBegin(GL_TRIANGLES);
            glVertex3f(1.0f, -1.0f, 0.0f);
            glVertex3f(-1.0f, -1.0f, 0.0f);
            glVertex3f(0.0f, 1.0f, 0.0f);
        glEnd();
}
```

As you can see, we've put all the OpenGL-specific code in this class. The Init() method uses the glClearColor() function to set the background color to black (0,0,0) and initialize the member variable m_angle, which is used in the Render() method by glRotatef() to perform rotations. In this example, the SetupProjection() method sets up the viewport for perspective projection, which is described in detail in Chapter 4, "Transformations and Matrices."

The Render() method is where we put all OpenGL rendering calls. In this method, we first clear the color and depth buffers, both of which are described in Chapter 12, "OpenGL Buffers." Next, we reset the model matrix by loading the identity matrix with glLoadIdentity(), described in Chapter 4. The glTranslatef() and glRotatef() functions, also described in Chapter 4, move the OpenGL camera five units in the negative z axis direction and rotate the world coordinate system along all three axes, respectively.

Next we set the current rendering color to a lime green color with the glColor3f() function, which is covered in Chapter 5, "Colors, Lighting, Blending, and Fog." Lastly, the transformed triangle is rendered with the glBegin(), glVertex3f(), and glEnd() functions. These functions are covered in Chapter 3, "OpenGL States and Primitives."

You can find the code for this example on the CD included with this book under Chapter 2. The example name is OpenGLApplication.

And finally, what would an example in this book be without a screenshot? Figure 2.1 is a screenshot of the rotating lime green triangle.

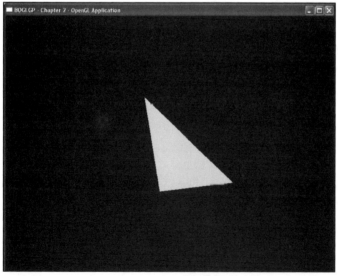

Figure 2.1 Screenshot of the "OpenGLApplication" example.

Full-Screen OpenGL

The code presented in the previous section creates an application that runs in a window, but nearly all 3D games created nowadays are displayed in full-screen mode. It's time to learn how to do that. You'll take the sample program you just created and modify it to give it full-screen capabilities. Let's take a look at the key parts that you need to change.

In order to switch into full-screen mode, you must use the DEVMODE data structure, which contains information about a display device. The structure is actually fairly big, but fortunately, there are only a few members that you need to worry about. These are listed in Table 2.2.

Table 2.2 Important DEVMODE Fields

Field	Description
dmSize	Size of the structure, in bytes. Used for versioning.
dmBitsPerPel	The number of bits per pixel.
dmPelsWidth	Width of the screen.
dmPelsHeight	Height of the screen.
dmFields	Set of bitflags indicating which fields are valid. The flags for the fields in this table are DM_BITSPERPEL, DM_PELSWIDTH, and DM_PELSHEIGHT.

After you have initialized the DEVMODE structure, you need to pass it to ChangeDisplay-Settings():

```
LONG ChangeDisplaySettings(LPDEVMODE pDevMode, DWORD dwFlags);
```

This takes a pointer to a DEVMODE structure as the first parameter and a set of flags describing exactly what you want to do. In this case, you'll be passing CDS_FULLSCREEN to remove the taskbar from the screen and force Windows to leave the rest of the screen alone when resizing and moving windows around in the new display mode. If the function is successful, it returns DISP_CHANGE_SUCCESSFUL. You can change the display mode back to the default state by passing NULL and 0 as the pDevMode and dwFlags parameters.

The following code will be added to the sample application to set up the change to full-screen mode.

```
DEVMODE devMode;
memset(&devMode, 0, sizeof(DEVMODE));    // clear the structure
devMode.dmSize = sizeof(DEVMODE);
```

```
devMode.dmBitsPerPel = g_screenBpp;
devMode.dmPelsWidth = g_screenWidth;
devMode.dmPelsHeight = g_screenHeight;
devMode.dmFields = DM_PELSWIDTH | DM_PELSHEIGHT | DM_BITSPERPEL;

if (ChangeDisplaySettings(&devMode, CDS_FULLSCREEN) != DISP_CHANGE_SUCCESSFUL)
    // change has failed, you'll run in windowed mode
    g_fullScreen = false;
```

Note that the sample application uses a global flag to control whether full-screen mode is enabled.

There are a few things you need to keep in mind when switching to full-screen mode. The first is that you need to make sure that the width and height specified in the DEVMODE structure match the width and height you use to create the window. The simplest way to ensure this is to use the same width and height variables for both operations. Also, you need to be sure to change the display settings *before* creating the window.

The style settings for full-screen mode differ from those of regular windows, so you need to be able to handle both cases. If you are not in full-screen mode, you will use the same style settings as described in the sample program for the regular window. If you are in full-screen mode, you need to use the WS_EX_APPWINDOW flag for the extended style and the WS_POPUP flag for the normal window style. The WS_EX_APPWINDOW flag forces a top-level window down to the taskbar once your own window is visible. The WS_POPUP flag creates a window without a border, which is exactly what you want with a full-screen application. Another thing you'll probably want to do for full-screen is remove the mouse cursor from the screen. This can be accomplished with the ShowCursor() function. The following code demonstrates the style settings and cursor hiding for both full-screen and windowed modes:

```
if (g_fullScreen)
{
    extendedWindowStyle = WS_EX_APPWINDOW;        // hide top level windows
    windowStyle = WS_POPUP;                       // no border on your window
    ShowCursor(FALSE);                            // hide the cursor
}
else
{
    extendedWindowStyle = NULL;                   // same as earlier example
    windowStyle = WS_OVERLAPPEDWINDOW | WS_VISIBLE |
                  WS_SYSMENU | WS_CLIPCHILDREN | WS_CLIPSIBLINGS;
}
```

Take a look at the OpenGLApplication program on the CD in the directory for Chapter 2 to see how you integrate the full-screen mode into your programs. As you can see, you don't need to modify your program too much to add the capability to use full-screen mode. With a little extra Windows programming, you can even ask the user if he or she would like full-screen or windowed mode before the program even starts. Throughout the rest of the book, you will develop games and demos that will have the option of running in either mode.

Summary

In this chapter you learned how to create a simple OpenGL application, particularly within the context of the Microsoft Windows operating system. You learned about the OpenGL rendering context and how it corresponds to the "wiggle" functions wglCreateContext(), wglDeleteContext(), wglMakeCurrent(), and wglGetCurrentContext(). Pixel formats were also covered, and you learned how to set them up for OpenGL in the Windows operating system. Finally, we provided the full source code for a basic OpenGL application and discussed how to set up the window for full-screen mode in OpenGL.

What You Have Learned

- The WGL, or *wiggle*, functions are a set of extensions to the Win32 API that were created specifically for OpenGL. Several of the main functions involve the rendering context, which is used to remember OpenGL settings and commands. You can use several rendering contexts at once.

- The PIXELFORMATDESCRIPTOR is the structure that is used to describe a device context that will be used to render with OpenGL. This structure must be specified and defined before any OpenGL code will work on a window.

- Full-screen OpenGL is used by most 3D games that are being developed. You took a look at how you can implement full-screen mode into your OpenGL applications, and the OpenGLApplication program on the included CD-ROM gives a clear picture of how to integrate the full-screen code.

Review Questions

1. What is the rendering context?
2. How do you retrieve the current rendering context?
3. What is a PIXELFORMATDESCRIPTOR?
4. What does the glClearColor() OpenGL function do?
5. What struct is required to set up an application for full-screen?

On Your Own

1. Take the OpenGLApplication example and a) change the background color to white (1, 1, 1), and b) change the triangle's color to red (1, 0, 0).

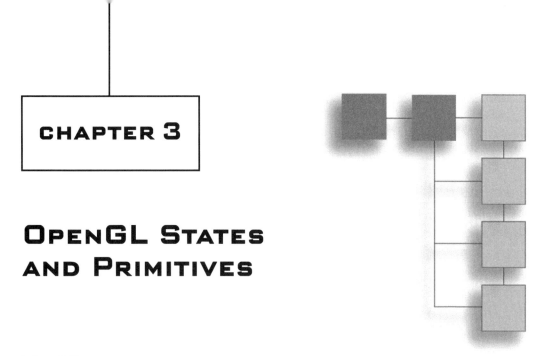

CHAPTER 3

OpenGL States and Primitives

Now it's time to finally get into the meat of OpenGL! To begin to unlock the power of OpenGL, you need to start with the basics, and that means understanding primitives. Before we start, we need to discuss something that is going to come up during our discussion of primitives and pretty much everything else from this point on: the OpenGL state machine.

The OpenGL state machine consists of hundreds of settings that affect various aspects of rendering. Because the state machine will play a role in everything you do, it's important to understand what the default settings are, how you can get information about the current settings, and how to change those settings. Several generic functions are used to control the state machine, so we will look at those here.

As you read this chapter, you will learn the following:

- How to access values in the OpenGL state machine
- The types of primitives available in OpenGL
- How to modify the way primitives are handled and displayed

State Functions

OpenGL provides a number of multipurpose functions that allow you to query the OpenGL state machine, most of which begin with glGet.... The most generic versions of these functions will be covered in this section, and the more specific ones will be covered with the features they're related to throughout the book.

Note

All the functions in this section require that you have a valid rendering context. Otherwise, the values they return are undefined.

Querying Numeric States

There are four general-purpose functions that allow you to retrieve numeric (or Boolean) values stored in OpenGL states. They are

```
void glGetBooleanv(GLenum pname, GLboolean *params);
void glGetDoublev(GLenum pname, GLdouble *params);
void glGetFloatv(GLenum pname, GLfloat *params);
void glGetIntegerv(GLenum pname, GLint *params);
```

In each of these prototypes, the parameter pname specifies the state setting you are query-ing, and params is an array that is large enough to hold all the values associated with the setting in question. The number of possible states is large, so instead of listing all of the states in this chapter, we will discuss the specific meaning of many of the pname values accepted by these functions as they come up. Most of them won't make much sense yet anyway (unless you are already an OpenGL guru, in which case, what are you doing read-ing this?).

Of course, determining the current state machine settings is interesting, but not nearly as interesting as being able to change the settings. Contrary to what you might expect, there is no glSet() or similar generic function for setting state machine values. Instead, there is a variety of more specific functions, which we will discuss as they become more relevant.

Enabling and Disabling States

We know how to find out the states in the OpenGL state machine, so how do we turn the states on and off? Enter the glEnable() and glDisable() functions:

```
void glEnable(GLenum cap);
void glDisable(GLenum cap);
```

The cap parameter represents the OpenGL capability you wish to enable or disable. glEnable() turns it on, and glDisable() turns it off. OpenGL includes over 40 capabilities that you can enable and disable. Some of these include GL_BLEND (for blending operations), GL_TEXTURE_2D (for 2D texturing), and GL_LIGHTING (for lighting operations). As you progress throughout this book, you will learn more capabilities that you can turn on and off with these functions.

glIsEnabled()

Oftentimes, you just want to find out whether a particular OpenGL capability is on or off. Although this can be done with glGetBooleanv(), it's usually easier to use glIsEnabled(), which has the following prototype:

GLboolean glIsEnabled(GLenum cap);

glIsEnabled() can be called with any of the values accepted by glEnable()/glDisable(). It returns GL_TRUE if the capability is enabled and GL_FALSE otherwise. Again, we'll wait to explain the meaning of the various values as they come up.

Querying String Values

You can find out the details of the OpenGL implementation being used at runtime via the following function:

const GLubyte *glGetString(GLenum name);

The null-terminated string that is returned depends on the value passed as name, which can be any of the values in Table 3.1.

Tip

glGetString() provides handy information about the OpenGL implementation, but be careful how you use it. I've seen new programmers use it to make decisions about which rendering options to use. For example, if they know that a feature is supported in hardware on Nvidia GeForce cards, but only in software on earlier cards, they may check the renderer string for geforce and, if it's not there, disable that functionality. This is a bad idea. The best way to determine which features are fast enough to use is to do some profiling the first time your game is run and profile again whenever you detect a change in hardware.

Table 3.1 glGetString() Parameters

Parameter	Definition
GL_VENDOR	The string that is returned indicates the name of the company whose OpenGL implementation you are using. For example, the vendor string for ATI drivers is ATI Technologies Inc. This value will typically always be the same for any given company.
GL_RENDERER	The string contains information that usually reflects the hardware being used. For example, mine returns RADEON 9800 Pro x86/MMX/3DNow!/SSE. Again, this value will not change from version to version.
GL_VERSION	The string contains a version number in the form of either major_number.minor_number or major_number.minor_number.release.number, possibly followed by additional information provided by the vendor. My current drivers return 1.3.4010 Win2000 Release.
GL_EXTENSIONS	The string returned contains a space-delimited list of all of the available OpenGL extensions. This will be covered in greater detail in Chapter 8, "OpenGL Extensions."

Finding Errors

Passing incorrect values to OpenGL functions causes an error flag to be set. When this happens, the function returns without doing anything, so if you're not getting the results you expect, querying the error flag can help you to more easily track down problems in your code. You can do this through the following:

```
GLenum glGetError();
```

This returns one of the values in Table 3.2. The value that is returned indicates the first error that occurred since startup or since the last call to glGetError(). In other words, once an error is generated, the error flag is not modified until a call to glGetError() is made; after the call is made, the error flag will be reset to GL_NO_ERROR.

Table 3.2 OpenGL Error Codes

Value	Meaning
GL_NO_ERROR	Self-explanatory. This is what you want it to be all the time.
GL_INVALID_ENUM	This error is generated when you pass an enumerated OpenGL value that the function doesn't normally accept.
GL_INVALID_VALUE	This error is generated when you use a numeric value that is outside of the accepted range.
GL_INVALID_OPERATION	This error can be harder to track down than the previous two. It happens when the combination of values you passed to a function either doesn't work together or doesn't work with the existing state configuration.
GL_STACK_OVERFLOW	OpenGL contains several stacks that you can directly manipulate, the most common being the matrix stack. This error happens when the function call would have caused the stack to overflow.
GL_STACK_UNDERFLOW	This is like the previous error, except that it happens when the function would have caused an underflow. This usually only happens when you have more pops than pushes, or if one of your pushes would have caused an overflow (because that push would then have been ignored).
GL_OUT_OF_MEMORY	This error is generated when the operation causes the system to run out of memory. Unlike the other error conditions, when this error occurs, the current OpenGL state may be modified. In fact, the entire OpenGL state, other than the error flag itself, becomes undefined. If you encounter this error, your application should try to exit as gracefully as possible.
GL_TABLE_TOO_LARGE	This error is uncommon, since it can only be generated by functions in OpenGL's imaging subset, which isn't used frequently in games. It happens as a result of using a table that is too large for the implementation to handle.

Giving OpenGL a Hint

Some operations in OpenGL may vary slightly from implementation to implementation (or driver to driver), so an attempt was made to allow developers a level of control over the trade-off between image quality and speed. While not all OpenGL implementations follow the command, the `glHint()` function allows you to specify your desired level of trade-off between image quality and speed for several different OpenGL behaviors.

```
void glHint(GLenum target, GLenum hint);
```

The `target` parameter specifies the behavior you want to control. Even though you may not yet fully understand the purpose for the possible OpenGL behaviors, they are listed in Table 3.3. The `hint` parameter can be one of the three options: `GL_FASTEST`, `GL_NICEST`, or `GL_DONT_CARE`. `GL_FASTEST` is used to indicate that the fastest and most efficient implementation should be used, possibly sacrificing quality. `GL_NICEST` is used to indicate that the highest quality implementation should be used, possibly losing performance. `GL_DONT_CARE` indicates that you do not have a preference on the method used to render, so the OpenGL driver will decide what it thinks is best. Keep in mind that hints are implementation-dependent, meaning some implementations might ignore the hints altogether.

Table 3.3 glHint() Behaviors

Parameter	Meaning
`GL_POINT_SMOOTH_HINT`, `GL_LINE_SMOOTH_HINT`, `GL_POLYGON_SMOOTH_HINT`	Specify the sampling quality of points, lines, or polygons during antialiasing.
`GL_FOG_HINT`	If `GL_NICEST` is specified for the `hint` parameter, then fog calculations are performed per pixel. If `GL_FASTEST` is specified for the `hint` parameter, then fog calculations are performed per vertex.
`GL_PERSPECTIVE_CORRECTION_HINT`	Specify the quality of color and texture-coordinate interpolation.

Handling Primitives

So, what are primitives? Merriam-Webster's dictionary defines a primitive as "an unsophisticated person." Well, that doesn't help much, so we'll give it a shot: Simply put, *primitives* are basic geometric entities such as points, lines, and triangles.

You will be using thousands and thousands of these primitives to make your games, so it is important to know how they work. Before we get into specific primitive types, though, we need to talk about a couple of OpenGL functions that you will be using often, at least in simple programs. The first is glBegin(), which has the following prototype:

```
void glBegin (GLenum mode);
```

You use glBegin() to tell OpenGL two things: 1) that you are ready to start drawing, and 2) the primitive type you want to draw. You specify the primitive type with the mode parameter, which can take on any of the values in Table 3.4.

Table 3.4 Valid glBegin() Parameters

Parameter	Definition
GL_POINTS	Individual points.
GL_LINES	Individual line segments composed of pairs of vertices.
GL_LINE_STRIP	Series of connected lines.
GL_LINE_LOOP	Closed loop of connected lines, with the last segment automatically created between the first and last vertices.
GL_TRIANGLES	Single triangles as vertex triplets.
GL_TRIANGLE_STRIP	Series of connected triangles.
GL_TRIANGLE_FAN	Set of triangles containing a common central vertex.
GL_QUADS	Quadrilaterals (polygons with 4 vertices).
GL_QUAD_STRIP	Series of connected quadrilaterals.
GL_POLYGON	Convex polygon with an arbitrary number of vertices. Non-convex polygons can be created using the GLU tesselation functions..

Figure 3.1 illustrates examples of each of the primitive types that you can draw with OpenGL through the glBegin() function. The rest of this chapter provides a detailed look at each of these primitive types.

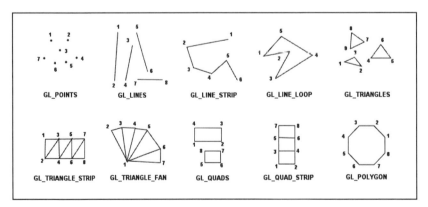

Figure 3.1 OpenGL primitive types.

Each call to glBegin() needs to be accompanied by a call to glEnd(), which has the following form:

```
void glEnd();
```

As you can see, glEnd() takes no parameters. There really isn't much to say about glEnd(), other than that it tells OpenGL that you are finished rendering the type of primitive you specified in glBegin(). Note that glBegin()/glEnd() blocks may not be nested.

Not all OpenGL functions can be used inside a glBegin()/glEnd() block. In fact, only variations of the functions listed in Table 3.5 may be used. Using any other OpenGL calls will generate a GL_INVALID_OPERATION error. While Table 3.4 gives a brief description of each function, we will discuss them in more detail later.

Now we need to talk about one particularly important function—or actually, family of functions—before we move on to primitive types: the glVertex() functions. These functions are used inside a glBegin()/glEnd() block to specify a point in space (a vertex), which is then interpreted appropriately depending on the value passed to glBegin(). The glVertex() function is very important because every object you draw with OpenGL is ultimately described as an ordered set of vertices.

Table 3.5 Valid glBegin()/glEnd Functions

Function	Description
glVertex*()	Sets vertex coordinates
glColor*()	Sets the current color
glSecondaryColor*()	Sets the secondary color
glIndex*()	Sets the current color index
glNormal*()	Sets normal vector coordinates
glTexCoord*()	Sets texture coordinates
glMultiTexCoord*()	Sets texture coordinates for multitexturing
glFogCoord*()	Sets the fog coordinate
glArrayElement()	Specifies attributes for a single vertex based on elements in a vertex array
glEvalCoord*()	Generates coordinates when rendering Bezier curves and surfaces
glEvalPoint*()	Generates coordinates when rendering Bezier curves and surfaces
glMaterial*()	Sets material properties (affect shading when lighting is used)
glEdgeFlag*()	Controls the drawing of edges
glCallList*()	Executes a display list
glCallLists*()	Executes display lists

The glVertex() function has a number of variations that take on the form:

```
void glVertex{234}{dfis}(...);
```

or

```
void glVertex{234}{dfis}v(...);
```

The version of glVertex() you'll be using most often is glVertex3f(), which takes three floating-point values representing the *x*, *y*, and *z* coordinates of the vertex. You should get used to this sort of multidimensional notation of functions because OpenGL uses the notation everywhere!

How about some examples of using the glVertex() function? Here are a few:

```
glVertex2i(5, 20);          // draw a vertex at (5, 20)
glVertex3f(1.5, 0.5, 10.0);  // draw a vertex at (1.5, 0.5, 10.0)

GLfloat v[3] = { 1.5, 0.5, 10.0 };
glVertex3fv(v);              // draw the same vertex as above, except as an array
```

Every time you specify a vertex, other data becomes associated with it, based on what states you currently have enabled. This other data includes the current primary and secondary colors, the current normal, the current texture coordinates, the current material, the current edge flag, and the fog coordinates. All of these things are covered in later chapters, so don't worry about them yet. The important thing to understand is that none of these things matter without a vertex to use them.

That about does it for the basics, so let's move on to some of the most common primitive types you'll be using.

Drawing Points in 3D

It doesn't get any more primitive than a point, so that's what we'll look at first. Drawing a point in 3D is simple and really quite powerful. After all, if you can draw a single pixel on the screen, you can draw anything! So without further ado, here's how to draw a point in OpenGL:

```
glBegin(GL_POINTS);
   glVertex3f(0.0, 0.0, 0.0);
glEnd();
```

In the first line, you tell OpenGL that you're going to be drawing points by passing GL_POINTS to glBegin(). In the next line, you tell it to draw a single point at the origin. Finally, with glEnd() you let OpenGL know you are finished drawing points for now. Note that indenting the code within the glBegin()/glEnd() block is optional, but it is a common practice among OpenGL programmers because it makes the code a bit easier to read.

What if you want to draw a second point, this one at (0.0, 1.0, 0.0)? Well, you could use:

```
glBegin(GL_POINTS);
    glVertex3f(0.0, 0.0, 0.0);
glEnd();
glBegin(GL_POINTS);
    glVertex3f(0.0, 1.0, 0.0);
glEnd();
```

However, that would be horribly inefficient. If you notice, GL_POINTS is plural (in fact, most of the values you can pass to glBegin() are plural), which should suggest that within a single glBegin()/glEnd() block, you can render more than one point, and that's exactly the case. So the preceding code would become:

```
glBegin(GL_POINTS);
    glVertex3f(0.0, 0.0, 0.0);
    glVertex3f(0.0, 1.0, 0.0);
glEnd();
```

Ah . . . shorter, faster, better. You can make as many calls to glVertex() as you want within the glBegin()/glEnd() block, and each will be rendered as a single point.

OpenGL gives you a great deal of control over how primitives are drawn, and points are no exception. There are three things you can modify: the size of the points, whether they are antialiased, and whether distance has an effect on the size and transparency of the point.

Modifying Point Size

To change the point size, you use

```
void glPointSize(GLfloat size);
```

This results in a size-by-size square centered on the vertex coordinates you specified. The default size is 1.0. If point antialiasing is disabled (which it is by default) the point size will be rounded to the nearest integer (with a minimum size of 1) indicating the pixel dimensions of the point. If you like, you can use glGet() with GL_POINT_SIZE to find out the currently selected size. Here's an example:

```
// retrieve current point size
GLfloat oldSize;
glGetFloatv(GL_POINT_SIZE, &oldSize);

// if we have a small point size, make it big (5.0), otherwise make it default
if (oldSize < 1.0)
    glPointSize(5.0);
else
    glPointSize(1.0);
```

Antialiasing Points

Although you can specify primitives with almost infinite precision, there is a finite number of pixels on the screen. This can cause the edges of primitives to look jagged. Antialiasing provides a means of smoothing out the edges to give them a more realistic look. If you want to use antialiasing, you can turn it on by passing GL_POINT_SMOOTH to glEnable() (it can be turned off again by passing the same parameter to glDisable()). If you are unsure whether point antialiasing is currently enabled or disabled, you find out by calling glGet() with GL_POINT_SMOOTH, or with glIsEnabled(GL_POINT_SMOOTH). Here is an example:

```
// if point antialiasing is currently disabled, then enable it
if (!glIsEnabled(GL_POINT_SMOOTH))
  glEnable(GL_POINT_SMOOTH);
```

When antialiasing is enabled, the range of supported point sizes is not necessarily continuous. The only size for which the OpenGL specification requires support with antialiasing is 1.0. If an unsupported size is used, it will be rounded to the nearest supported value. To find out the range of sizes your implementation supports, you can call glGet() with GL_POINT_SIZE_RANGE, and you can use GL_POINT_SIZE_GRANULARITY to find the size difference between adjacent supported sizes. The following code shows how to do both:

```
GLfloat sizes[2];
GLfloat granularity;

// retrieve the point size range
glGetFloatv(GL_POINT_SIZE_RANGE, sizes);
GLfloat minPointSize = sizes[0];
GLfloat maxPointSize = sizes[1];

// retrieve the point size granularity
glGetFloatv(GL_POINT_SIZE_GRANULARITY, &granularity);
```

With antialiasing on, the current point size is used as the diameter of a circle centered at the x and y window coordinates of the point you specified. OpenGL determines how much of each adjacent pixel is covered by the point and adjusts the pixel color accordingly, gradually blending it with the background color toward the point's edges.

Note

It is worth noting that blending needs to be enabled for antialiasing to work. Blending is discussed in Chapter 5, "Colors, Blending, Lighting, and Fog."

Effect of Distance

Normally, points always occupy the same amount of space on the screen, regardless of how far away they are from the viewer. For some applications of points, such as particle systems, you'll want the points to be smaller as they get farther away. You can do this through the use of the glPointParameter() functions:

```
void glPointParameter{if}(enum pname, type param);
void glPointParameter{if}v(enum pname, const type *params);
```

The valid values and uses of pname and param(s) are summarized in Table 3.6.

Extension

Extension name: ARB_point_parameters

Name string: GL_ARB_point_parameters

Promoted to core: OpenGL 1.4

Function names: glPointParameteriARB, glPointParameterivARB, glPointParameterfARB, glPointParameterfvARB

Tokens: GL_POINT_SIZE_MIN_ARB, GL_POINT_SIZE_MAX_ARB, GL_POINT_DISTANCE_ATTENUATION_ARB, GL_POINT_FADE_THRESHOLD_ARB

Table 3.6 Point Parameters

Parameter	Description
GL_POINT_SIZE_MIN	Sets the lower bound on the size OpenGL will scale a point to. Takes a single value.
GL_POINT_SIZE_MAX	Sets the upper bound on the size OpenGL will scale a point to. Takes a single value.
GL_POINT_DISTANCE_ATTENUATION	Takes an array of 3 values which correspond to the a, b, and c coefficients in the attenuation factor: $$1/(a + b * d + c * d^2),$$ where d represents the distance from the point to the eye. The square root of this factor is multiplied by the point size to determine the final size. By default, the values of a, b, and c are (1, 0, and 0), resulting in no distance attenuation.
GL_POINT_FADE_THRESHOLD	This uses a single value that specifies the size below which OpenGL begins to reduce the alpha value of the point, allowing you to gradually fade it as it becomes smaller.

A Pointy Example

The CD that accompanies this book includes an example entitled Points in this chapter that displays a row of points where each point's size increases in the row. Figure 3.2 is a screenshot of this program.

The most important part of the example code is the following lines:

```
float pointSize = 0.5;

// draw a line of points of increasing size
for (float point = -4.0; point < 5.0; point+=0.5)
{
    // set the point size
    glPointSize(pointSize);

    // draw the point
    glBegin(GL_POINTS);
    glVertex3f(point, 0.0, 0.0);
    glEnd();

    // increase the point size for the next point
    pointSize += 1.0;
}
```

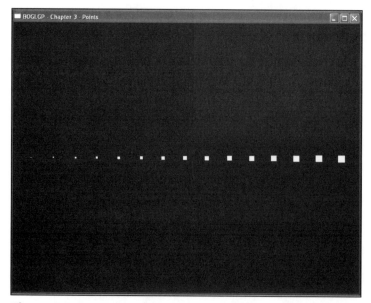

Figure 3.2 Screenshot of the Points example for Chapter 3 on the CD.

These lines of code perform the actual point drawing in a row along the world x-axis, with each point separated by 0.5 units. For each point, we first set the size of the point (starting at a point size of 0.5), and then we draw the point by passing GL_POINTS to glBegin() and using the glVertex3f() function. The point size for the next point is then increased, and the process is repeated.

Now that you have points down, let's move on to something a little more interesting.

Drawing Lines in 3D

Drawing a line in 3D isn't all that different from drawing two points, and because you already know how to do that, let's just dive right in:

```
glBegin(GL_LINES);
    glVertex3f(-2.0, -1.0, 0.0);
    glVertex3f(3.0, 1.0, 0.0);
glEnd();
```

This time, you start off by passing GL_LINES to glBegin() so that OpenGL knows how to interpret the two vertices you are about to specify. After it has both vertices, it knows to draw a line connecting the two of them.

Just as with points, you can draw as many lines as you want to between the calls to glBegin()/glEnd(). Each pair is treated as the endpoints of a new line. If you don't specify an even number of vertices, the last one will just be discarded.

As with points, OpenGL allows you to change several parameters to affect how lines are drawn. In addition to setting the line width and turning on antialiasing, you can specify a stipple pattern.

Modifying Line Width

The default line width is 1.0. To find out the currently selected line width, simply call glGet() with GL_LINE_WIDTH. To change it, you can call glLineWidth() like so:

```
void glLineWidth(GLfloat width);
```

Here's an example of its use:

```
// retrieve the current line width
GLfloat oldWidth;
glGetFloatv(GL_LINE_WIDTH, &oldWidth);

// if our line width is small, make it big
if (oldWidth < 1.0)
    glLineWidth(5.0);
```

Antialiasing Lines

Antialiasing for lines works very much as it does with points. You can turn it on and off by passing GL_LINE_SMOOTH to glEnable() and glDisable(), and the current state can be determined by passing GL_LINE_SMOOTH to glGet() or glIsEnabled(). It is disabled by default.

Again, when using antialiasing, an OpenGL implementation is required only to support the default line width of 1.0. To determine the range and granularity of supported sizes, you can use glGet() with GL_LINE_WIDTH_RANGE and GL_LINE_WIDTH_GRANULARITY, respectively. Here's an example of how to do that:

```
GLfloat sizes[2];
GLfloat granularity;

glGetFloatv(GL_LINE_WIDTH_RANGE, sizes);
GLfloat minLineWidth = sizes[0];
GLfloat maxLineWidth = sizes[1];

glGetFloatv(GL_LINE_WIDTH_GRANULARITY, &granularity);
```

Looks a lot like the points sample above, doesn't it?

Specifying a Stipple Pattern

You can specify a stipple pattern with which to draw the lines. The stipple pattern specifies a mask that will determine which portions of the line get drawn, and it can thus be used for things such as dashed lines. Before using stippling, you need to enable it by passing GL_LINE_STIPPLE to glEnable(). Then, you set the stipple pattern using glLineStipple(), which looks like this:

```
void glLineStipple(GLint factor, GLushort pattern);
```

The factor parameter defaults to 1 and is clamped to fall in the range 1–256. It is used to specify how many times each bit in the pattern is repeated before moving on to the next bit.

The pattern parameter specifies a 16-bit pattern. Any bits that are set in the pattern will result in the corresponding pixels being set; otherwise they are not drawn. Something to be aware of is that the bits in the integer are applied in reverse order, so that the low-order bit affects the left-most pixel; then, as the line progresses to the right, higher order bits are used. This is illustrated in Figure 3.3.

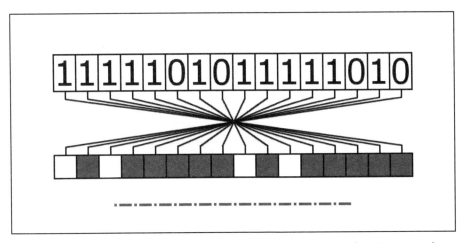

Figure 3.3 A sample stipple pattern demonstrating how the bit order is interpreted.

The following code enables line stippling and then specifies a pattern of alternating dashes and dots:

```
glEnable(GL_LINE_STIPPLE);
GLushort stipplePattern = 0xFAFA;      // 1111 1010 1111 1010

// draws the stipple pattern as 0101 1111 0101 1111
glLineStipple(2, stipplePattern);
```

You can determine the currently selected stipple pattern and repeat factor by calling glGet with GL_LINE_STIPPLE_PATTERN and GL_LINE_STIPPLE_REPEAT. Here's an example:

```
GLushort currentStipplePattern;
GLint currentStippleRepeat;

glGetShortv(GL_LINE_STIPPLE_PATTERN, &currentStipplePattern);
glGetIntv(GL_LINE_STIPPLE_REPEAT, &currentStippleRepeat);
```

Hold the Line Example

On the CD with the previous Points example is an example for lines that demonstrates line widths and line stippling. Figure 3.4 is a screenshot of this line example.

Figure 3.4 Screenshot of the Lines example in Chapter 3 on the CD.

You can see in the screenshot that two columns of lines are displayed. The left column shows lines of increasing width, while the right column shows the same lines of increasing width, but with a stipple pattern applied to them. Here's the code that draws the left column:

```
float lineWidth = 0.5;

// draw a series of lines of increasing width
for (float line = 0.0; line < 7.0; line+=0.5)
{
    // set the line width
    glLineWidth(lineWidth);

    // draw the line
    glBegin(GL_LINES);
        glVertex3f(-5.0, 0.0, line-3.0);
        glVertex3f(-1.0, 0.0, line-3.0);
    glEnd();

    // increase the line width for the next line
    lineWidth += 1.0;
}
```

As you can see, this algorithm is very similar to the Points example in the previous section. For each line, we first set the width of the line, and then we draw the line by passing GL_LINES to glBegin() along with two vertices representing the line endpoints by the glVertex3f() function. The line width is then increased for the next line. Don't worry about the math you see inside the glVertex() function. It's being done so the lines are positioned properly in the viewport.

This next set of code draws the same lines in the right column with a stipple pattern:

```
// reset line width
lineWidth = 0.5;

// enable stippling
glEnable(GL_LINE_STIPPLE);

// 0xAAAA = 1010 1010 1010 1010
short stipplePattern = 0xAAAA;

// set the stipple pattern
glLineStipple(2, stipplePattern);

// draw a series of lines of increasing width with stippling
for (float line = 0.0; line < 7.0; line+=0.5)
{
    // set the line width
    glLineWidth(lineWidth);

    // draw the point
    glBegin(GL_LINES);
        glVertex3f(1.0, 0.0, line-3.0);
        glVertex3f(5.0, 0.0, line-3.0);
    glEnd();

    // increase the point size for the next point
    lineWidth += 1.0;
}
```

Since this code is essentially the same as the previous block that draws the lines in the left column, let us look at the primary difference: the stipple pattern. As you can see, all we have to do is enable the stipple pattern in the OpenGL state machine with the glEnable(GL_STIPPLE_PATTERN) call. Next we tell OpenGL the stipple pattern we want it to use when drawing the next set of lines. We define the stipple pattern as 0xAAAA and set that pattern in OpenGL with the glLineStipple() function. Then when the lines are drawn, the stipple pattern is applied.

Now that you have a handle on lines, let's move on to the heart and soul of almost every 3D game in existence: the all-mighty polygon.

Drawing Polygons in 3D

Although you can (and will) do some interesting things with points and lines, there's no doubt that polygons give you the most power to create immersive 3D worlds, so that's what we'll spend the rest of the chapter on. Before we get into specific polygon types supported by OpenGL (that is, triangles, quadrilaterals, and polygons), we need to discuss a few things that pertain to all polygon types.

You draw all polygons by specifying several points in 3D space. These points specify a region that is then filled with color. At least, that's the default behavior. However, as you'd probably expect by now, the state machine controls the way in which the polygon is drawn, and you're free to change the default behavior. To change the way polygons are drawn, you use

```
void glPolygonMode(GLenum face, GLenum mode);
```

As you will learn in the next subsection, OpenGL handles the front and back faces of polygons separately; as a result, when you call glPolygonMode(), you need to specify the face to which the change should be applied. You do this by setting the face parameter to GL_FRONT for front-facing polygons, GL_BACK for back-facing polygons, or GL_FRONT_AND_BACK for both.

The mode parameter can take on any of the values in Table 3.7.

If, for example, you want to set the front-facing polygons to be drawn filled and the back-facing ones to be rendered as a wire frame (as lines), you could use the following code:

```
glPolygonMode(GL_FRONT, GL_FILL);
glPolygonMode(GL_BACK, GL_LINE);
```

Table 3.7 Polygon Modes

Value	Definition
GL_POINT	Each vertex specified is rendered as a single point, the rendering of which can be controlled by the point states discussed earlier. This basically produces the same effect as calling glBegin() with GL_POINTS.
GL_LINE	This will draw the edges of the polygon as a set of lines. Any of the line states discussed previously will affect how the lines are drawn. This is similar to calling glBegin() with GL_LINE_LOOP.
GL_FILL	This is the default state, which renders the polygon with the interior filled. This is the only state in which polygon stipple and polygon smoothing (see the following) will take effect.

Note that unless you have changed the mode for front-facing polygons elsewhere, the first line is unnecessary, because polygons are drawn filled by default.

To find out the current mode for drawing polygons, you can call glGet() with GL_POLYGON_MODE.

Polygon Mode Example

On the CD you will find a Polygons example that illustrates how polygon modes can be used and the effects they have on OpenGL drawing. Figure 3.5 is a screenshot of this example.

In this example, we have five squares rotating clockwise at the same rate, which means the front faces of the squares face the same direction at the same time (and vice versa for the back faces). Each square is given a different polygon mode and is therefore drawn differently. Starting from the left (square number one), here is each square's configuration:

1) glPolygonMode(GL_FRONT, GL_LINE);

2) glPolygonMode(GL_BACK, GL_POINT);

3) glPolygonMode(GL_FRONT_AND_BACK, GL_FILL);

4) glPolygonMode(GL_BACK, GL_LINE);

5) glPolygonMode(GL_FRONT_AND_BACK, GL_LINE);

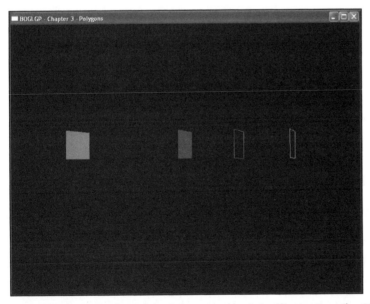

Figure 3.5 Screenshot of the Polygons example in Chapter 3 on the CD.

Polygon Face Culling

Although polygons are infinitely thin, they have two sides, implying that they can be seen from either side. Sometimes, it makes sense to have each side displayed differently, and this is why some of the functions presented here require you to specify whether you're modifying the front face, back face, or both. In any case, the rendering states for each of the sides are stored separately.

When you know that the viewer will be able to see only one side of a polygon, it is possible to have OpenGL eliminate (or more precisely, skip processing) polygons that the viewer can't see. For example, with an object that is completely enclosed and opaque, such as a ball, only the front sides of polygons are ever visible. If you can determine that the back side of a polygon is facing the viewer (which would be true for polygons on the side of the ball opposite of the viewer), you can save time transforming and rendering the polygon because you know it won't be seen. OpenGL can do this for you automatically through the process known as *culling*. To use culling, you first need to enable it by passing GL_CULL_FACE to glEnable(). Then, you need to specify which face you want culled, which is done with glCullFace():

void glCullFace(GLenum mode);

mode can be GL_FRONT to cull front facing polygons, GL_BACK to cull back facing polygons, or GL_FRONT_AND_BACK to cull them both. Choosing the latter causes the polygons to not be drawn at all, which doesn't seem particularly useful. GL_BACK is the default setting.

The next step is telling OpenGL how to determine whether a polygon is front facing or back facing. It does this based on what is called *polygon winding*, which is the order in which you specify vertices. Looking at a polygon head-on, you can choose any vertex with which to begin describing it. To finish describing it, you have to proceed either clockwise or counterclockwise around its vertices. If you're consistent about how you specify your polygons and order your vertices, OpenGL can use the winding to automatically determine whether a polygon face is front or back facing. By default, OpenGL treats polygons with counterclockwise ordering as front-facing and polygons with clockwise ordering as back-facing. The default behavior can be changed using glFrontFace():

void glFrontFace(GLenum mode);

mode should be GL_CCW if you want to use counterclockwise orientation for front-facing polygons and GL_CW if you want to use clockwise orientation.

Note

The winding setting isn't just relevant in culling; it's used by other OpenGL subsystems, including lighting.

Hiding Polygon Edges

It's not uncommon to want to render something in wire-frame mode, and sometimes you may not want to have all the edges of your polygons show up. For example, if you're drawing a square using two triangles, you may not want the viewer to see the diagonal line. This is illustrated in Figure 3.6.

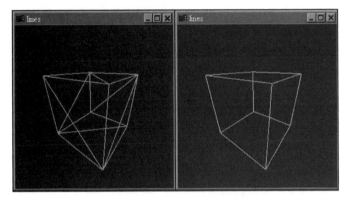

Figure 3.6 Hiding polygon edges you don't want to see.

You can tell OpenGL whether a particular edge of a polygon should be included when rendering it as lines by calling glEdgeFlag(), which can take on one of the two following forms:

- void glEdgeFlag(GLboolean isEdge);
- void glEdgeFlagv(const GLboolean *isEdge);

The only difference between these two forms is that the first takes a single Boolean value as its parameter and the second takes a pointer to an array containing a single Boolean value. (The OpenGL designers must have had a good reason to want to pass a single value in an array, but I can't think of one myself!) Either way, these functions are used to set the edge flag. If the flag is set to GL_TRUE (the default), the edges you specify are drawn; if it is set to GL_FALSE, they are not. Pretty simple.

Antialiasing Polygons

As with points and lines, you can also choose to antialias polygons. You control polygon antialiasing by passing GL_POLYGON_SMOOTH to glEnable() and glDisable(), and the current state can be determined by passing the same parameter to glGet() or glIsEnabled(). As you might expect, it is disabled by default. Here is an example of how to enable polygon antialiasing:

```
// if polygon antialiasing is disabled, then enable it
if (!glIsEnabled(GL_POLYGON_SMOOTH))
    glEnable(GL_POLYGON_SMOOTH);
```

Specifying a Stipple Pattern

The last general polygon attribute you need to look at is polygon stippling, which is similar to line stippling. Rather than filling in a polygon with a solid color, you can set a stipple pattern to fill the polygon. If you've ever set a pattern for your Windows wallpaper, you'll have some idea of the effect.

Polygon stippling is off by default, but you can turn it on by passing GL_POLYGON_STIPPLE to glEnable(). Once it's enabled, you need to specify a stipple pattern, which you do using the following:

```
void glPolygonStipple(const GLubyte *mask);
```

The mask parameter in this call is a pointer to an array containing a 32 × 32 bit pattern. This mask will be used to determine which pixels show up (for bits that are turned on) and which ones don't. Unlike line-stipple patterns, which show up in reverse, polygon-stipple patterns show up exactly as they are specified. Note that the stipple pattern is applied to screen coordinates in 2D. Thus, rotating a polygon doesn't rotate the pattern as well.

Now that we've discussed some general polygon properties, we can look at specific polygonal primitives supported by OpenGL.

Triangles

Triangles are generally the preferred polygon form. There are several reasons for this:

- The vertices of a polygon are always coplanar, because three points define a plane.
- A triangle is always convex.
- A triangle can't cross over itself.

If you try to render a polygon that violates any of these three properties, unpredictable behavior will result. Because any polygon can be broken down into a number of triangles, it makes sense to work with them.

Drawing a triangle in 3D isn't any more difficult than drawing a point or a line. You just need to change the value passed to glBegin() and then specify three vertices:

```
glBegin(GL_TRIANGLES);
    glVertex3f(-2.0, -1.0, 0.0);
    glVertex3f(3.0, 1.0, 0.0);
    glVertex3f(0.0, 3.0, 0.0);
glEnd();
```

Just as with points and lines, you can draw multiple triangles at one time. OpenGL treats every vertex triple as a separate triangle. If the number of vertices defined isn't a multiple of 3, then the extra vertices are discarded.

OpenGL also supports a couple of primitives related to triangles that can improve performance. To understand why you might want to use these, consider Figure 3.7.

Here, you have two connected triangles, which have vertices *A* and *C* in common. If you render these using GL_TRIANGLES, you'll have to specify a total of six vertices (*A*, *B*, and *C* for triangle 1 and *A*, *D*, and *C* for triangle 2). You'll send *A* and *C* down the pipeline twice, performing the same geometrical operations on them each time. Obviously, this is wasteful; compounding this, you can have vertices shared by many triangles in more complex models. If you can reduce the number of times you're sending and transforming redundant vertices, you can improve performance, which is always good.

One way you can do this is by using triangle strips. Simply call glBegin() with GL_TRIANGLE_STRIP, followed by a series of vertices. OpenGL handles this by drawing the first three vertices as a single triangle; after that, it takes every vertex specified and combines it with the previous two vertices to create another triangle. This means that after the first triangle, each additional triangle costs only a single vertex. In general, every set of *n* triangles you can reduce to a triangle strip reduces the number of vertices from 3*n* to *n* + 2. Figure 3.8 illustrates how you can use a triangle strip.

Triangle fans are a similar concept; you can visualize them as a series of triangles around a single central vertex. You draw fans by calling glBegin() with GL_TRIANGLE_FAN. The first vertex specified is the central vertex, and every following adjacent pair of vertices is combined with the center vertex to create a new polygon, as illustrated in Figure 3.9.

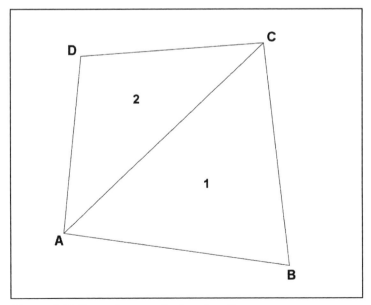

Figure 3.7 Two polygons with shared vertices.

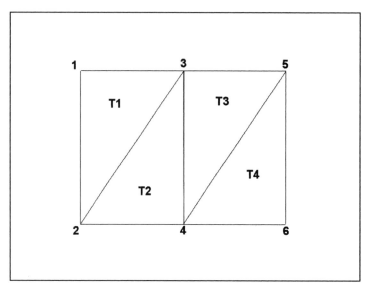

Figure 3.8 A triangle strip creates triangles by combining vertices into triplet sets.

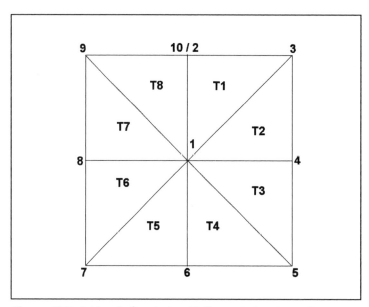

Figure 3.9 A triangle fan starts with the central vertex and spans out as a "fan" of vertices.

Like strips, fans allow you to draw n triangles while specifying only $n + 2$ vertices. However, in practice, the number of triangles that can be packed into a single fan is usually considerably fewer than the number that can be represented as a strip because in most cases, any given vertex won't be shared by a huge number of triangles.

The challenge with either method is in identifying strips and fans, which is relatively easy with simple models but becomes increasingly difficult as the complexity of your models grows. Normally, the process of converting a model represented as triangles into a series of triangle strips (or fans, but usually strips) is done outside of your game engine, either when the model is exported from a modeling program or through a separate tool that optimizes the data for your game. Doing this effectively is beyond the scope of our current discussion.

Quadrilaterals

Quadrilaterals, or quads, are four-sided polygons that can be convenient when you want to draw a square or rectangle. You create them by calling glBegin() with GL_QUADS and then specifying four or more vertices, as Figure 3.10 shows. Like triangles, you can draw as many quads as you want at a time.

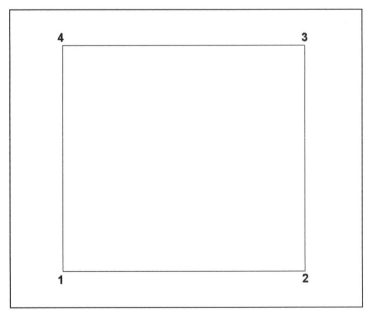

Figure 3.10 A quad is specified with four vertices.

OpenGL provides quad strips as a means of improving the speed of rendering quads. They are specified using GL_QUAD_STRIP. Each pair of vertices specified after the first pair defines a new quad.

Polygons

OpenGL also supports polygons with an arbitrary number of vertices, but in such cases, only one polygon can be drawn within a glBegin()/glEnd() block. The parameter passed is GL_POLYGON (notice that it's not plural), and once glEnd() is reached, the last vertex is automatically connected to the first. If fewer than three vertices are specified, nothing is drawn. Figure 3.11 is an example of polygon drawing.

Using Primitives: Triangles and Quads Example

The final example for this chapter, called TrianglesQuads, shows how you can render a grid using variations of triangles and quads. You can see the screenshot of this example in Figure 3.12.

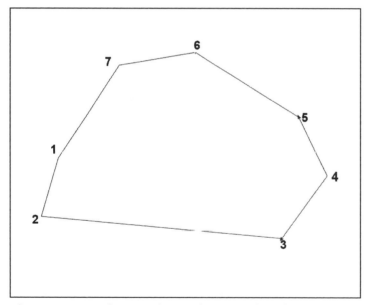

Figure 3.11 A polygon can be an arbitrary number of vertices.

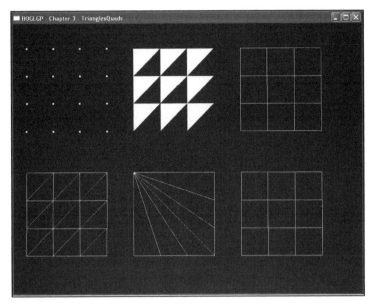

Figure 3.12 Screenshot of the TrianglesQuads example in Chapter 3 on the CD.

As you can see in the screenshot, we render a set of six grids, each with a different primitive type. In the top-left of the figure we have a grid drawn with GL_POINTS so you can see the shape of the grid. The code for drawing this is simply:

```
void DrawPoints()
{
    glPointSize(4.0);
    glBegin(GL_POINTS);
    for (int x = 0; x < 4; x++)
        for (int z = 0; z < 4; z++)
            glVertex3f(x, 0, z);
    glEnd();
}
```

The top-middle grid is drawn with GL_TRIANGLES. We used GL_FILL on this grid so you can see where the actual triangles are drawn (in all other grids the entire grid is filled). The code for this grid is

```
void DrawTriangles()
{
    glBegin(GL_TRIANGLES);
```

```
    for (int x = 0; x < 3; x++)
    {
        for (int z = 0; z < 3; z++)
        {
            glVertex3f(x, 0.0, z);
            glVertex3f((x+1.0), 0.0, z);
            glVertex3f(x, 0.0, (z+1.0));
        }
    }
    glEnd();
}
```

The top–right grid is drawn with GL_QUADS. The code for this grid is

```
void DrawQuads()
{
    glBegin(GL_QUADS);
    for (int x = 0; x < 3; x++)
    {
        for (int z = 0; z < 3; z++)
        {
            glVertex3f(x, 0.0, z);
            glVertex3f((x+1.0), 0.0, z);
            glVertex3f((x+1.0), 0.0, (z+1.0));
            glVertex3f(x, 0.0, (z+1.0));
        }
    }
    glEnd();
}
```

The bottom-left grid is drawn with rows of GL_TRIANGLE_STRIP. The code for this grid is

```
void DrawTriangleStrip()
{
    // 3 rows of triangle strips
    for (int x = 0; x < 3; x++)
    {
        glBegin(GL_TRIANGLE_STRIP);
        for (int z = 0; z < 3; z++)
        {
            glVertex3f(x, 0.0, z);
            glVertex3f((x+1.0), 0.0, z);
            glVertex3f(x, 0.0, (z+1.0));
```

```
            glVertex3f((x+1.0), 0.0, (z+1.0));
        }
        glEnd();
    }
}
```

The bottom-middle grid is drawn with a GL_TRIANGLE_FAN. The code for this grid is

```
void DrawTriangleFan()
{
    glBegin(GL_TRIANGLE_FAN);

    // center vertex of fan
    glVertex3f(0.0, 0.0, 0.0);

    // bottom side
    for (int x = 4; x > 0; x--)
        glVertex3f(x-1, 0.0, 3.0);

    // right side
    for (int z = 4; z > 0; z--)
        glVertex3f(3.0, 0.0, z-1);

    glEnd();
}
```

And finally, the bottom-right grid is drawn with rows of GL_QUAD_STRIP. The code for this grid is

```
void DrawQuadStrip()
{
    for (int x = 0; x < 3; x++)
    {
        glBegin(GL_QUAD_STRIP);
        for (int z = 0; z < 4; z++)
        {
            glVertex3f(x, 0.0, z);
            glVertex3f((x+1.0), 0.0, z);
        }
        glEnd();
    }
}
```

As you can see from the code, each grid's code is slightly different from the others. This is because each primitive accepts data slightly differently, which requires us to modify our algorithms for each primitive type in order for the grids to be drawn properly.

Spend some time looking at and modifying this code to be sure you are comfortable with it. You will be using primitives in every application from here on out, so you had better understand them well!

Attributes

Earlier in this chapter you saw how to set and query individual states from OpenGL. Now let us look at a way to save and restore the values of a set of related state variables with a single command.

An *attribute group* is a set of related state variables that OpenGL classifies into a group. For example, the line group consists of all the line drawing attributes, such as the width, stipple pattern attributes, and line smoothing. The polygon group consists of the same sets of attributes as lines, except for polygons. By using the glPushAttrib() and glPopAttrib() functions, you can save and restore all of the state information for a group in one function call.

```
void glPushAttrib(GLbitfield mask);
void glPopAttrib(void);
```

glPushAttrib() saves all of the attributes for the attribute group specified by mask onto the attribute stack. The mask bits can be logically ORed together to save any combination of attribute bits. glPopAttrib() restores the values of the state variables that were saved with the last glPushAttrib(). Table 3.8 includes a list of a few (certainly not all!) attribute groups that you can pass to glPushAttrib().

Table 3.8 Attribute Groups

Mask	Attribute Group
GL_ALL_ATTRIB_BITS	All OpenGL state variables in all attribute groups
GL_ENABLE_BIT	Enabled state variables
GL_FOG_BIT	Fog state variables
GL_LIGHTING_BIT	Lighting state variables
GL_LINE_BIT	Line state variables
GL_POINT_BIT	Point state variables
GL_POLYGON_BIT	Polygon state variables
GL_TEXTURE_BIT	Texturing state variables

Summary

In this chapter, you learned a little more about the OpenGL state machine. You know how to use glGet() and glIsEnabled() to query the values of parameters within the state machine. You've also seen some specialized functions for altering the state machine, and you should now have an idea of how it works. You'll be looking at other aspects of the state machine as you move on.

You also learned about the primitive types supported by OpenGL and how to modify properties pertaining to them. You should now have no trouble putting points, lines, triangles, and other primitives on the screen. Now that you have state machine basics and primitives under your belt, you can safely move on to more interesting things.

What You Have Learned

- You can query current settings from the OpenGL state machine by using the glGet() and glIsEnabled() functions.

- Primitives are drawn by first specifying the primitive type with the glBegin() function, then sending the vertices and following up with the glEnd() function.

- The glVertex() function specifies a vertex in a glBegin()/glEnd() block and is available in several variations that allow you to define the number of coordinates, the coordinates' data type, and whether the coordinates are being passed individually or as an array.

- You can draw points by passing GL_POINTS as the parameter to glBegin(), modify point size by using the glPointSize() function, turn point antialiasing on by passing GL_POINT_SMOOTH to glEnable(), and control the effect of distance on points with glPointParameter().

- Lines are drawn by passing GL_LINES as the parameter to glBegin(). You can modify line width with the glLineWidth() function, and line antialiasing is turned on by sending GL_LINE_SMOOTH to glEnable(). Line stippling is accomplished through the use of the glLineStipple() function.

- You can change the way OpenGL draws polygons by using the glPolygonMode() function. Passing GL_POINT forces OpenGL to draw only the vertices of polygons; GL_LINE forces OpenGL to draw the edges between polygon vertices as lines; GL_FILL is the default behavior, which renders polygons with the interior filled and allows polygon smoothing and stippling.

- Passing GL_CULL_FACE to glEnable() tells OpenGL to enable its face culling mechanism. Using the glCullFace() function then allows you to specify which polygon side OpenGL should cull.

- By default, OpenGL treats vertices that are ordered counterclockwise in a polygon as the front face of the polygon, while the clockwise vertices are the back face. The glFrontFace() function allows you to modify this setting.

- Triangles are the most important polygon in 3D graphics as any polygon can be broken down into a set of triangles. You draw a triangle in OpenGL by passing GL_TRIANGLES to glBegin().

- You can draw a set of triangles more efficiently by passing GL_TRIANGLE_STRIP or GL_TRIANGLE_FAN to glBegin(). GL_TRIANGLE_STRIP draws a triangle strip, which creates a strip of triangles by combining vertices into sets of triplets. GL_TRIANGLE_FAN starts with the first vertex as the center vertex and draws the rest as a fan of vertices around the center.

- Quadrilaterals may also be drawn by passing GL_QUADS or GL_QUAD_STRIP to glBegin().

- *n*-sided convex polygons may be drawn by passing GL_POLYGON to glBegin().

- You can save and restore OpenGL state variables using the glPushAttrib() and glPopAttrib() functions.

Review Questions

1. How would you determine if OpenGL is drawing antialiased lines?
2. How is culling enabled?
3. In what order does OpenGL draw vertices for a GL_TRIANGLE_STRIP?
4. In what order does OpenGL draw vertices for a GL_TRIANGLE_FAN?
5. What do the following variations of glVertex() mean?

    a. glVertex3f()

    b. glVertex2iv()

    c. glVertex4d()

    d. glVertex3fv()

    e. glVertex2s()

On Your Own

1. You have been tasked to write a function that draws a 2D circle approximation with the option of drawing only the edge of the circle or drawing the circle filled at the world origin (0, 0, 0). Your function must accept the radius of the circle and a value for the number of edges in the circle approximation. Write a function to draw the circle approximation given the following prototype:

```
void DrawCircleApproximation(float radius, int numberOfSides, bool edgeOnly);
```

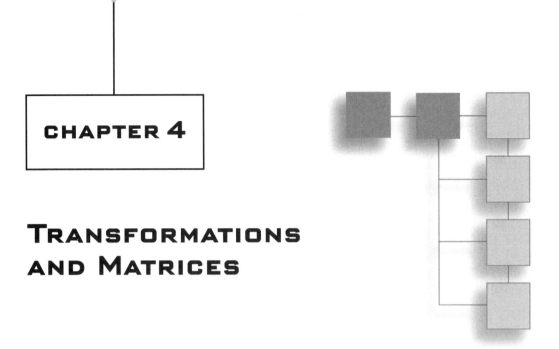

CHAPTER 4

TRANSFORMATIONS AND MATRICES

Now it's time to take a short break from learning how to *create* objects in the world and focus on learning how to *move* the objects around in the world. This is a vital ingredient to generating realistic 3D gaming worlds; without it, the 3D scenes you create would be static, boring, and totally noninteractive. OpenGL makes it easy for the programmer to move objects around through the use of various *coordinate transformations*, discussed in this chapter. You will also take a look at how to use your own matrices with OpenGL, which provides you with the power to manipulate objects in many different ways.

In this chapter you'll learn about:

- The basics of coordinate transformations
- The camera and viewing transformations
- OpenGL matrices and matrix stacks
- Projections
- Using your own matrices with OpenGL

Understanding Coordinate Transformations

Set this book down and stop reading for a moment. Look around you. Now, imagine that you have a camera in your hands, and you are taking photographs of your surroundings. For instance, you might be in an office and have your walls, this book, your desk, and maybe your computer near you. Each of these objects has a shape and geometry described in a *local coordinate system*, which is unique for every object, is centered on the object, and doesn't depend on any other objects. They also have some sort of position and orientation in the world space. You have a position and orientation in world space as well. The relationship between the positions of these objects around you and your position and orientation determines whether the objects are behind you or in front of you. As you are taking photographs of these objects, the lens of the camera also has some effect on the final outcome of the pictures you are taking. A zoom lens makes objects appear closer to or farther from your position. You aim and click, and the picture is "rendered" onto the camera film (or onto your memory card if you have a digital camera). Your camera and its film also have settings, such as size and resolution, which help define how the final picture is rendered. The final image you see in a picture is a product of how each object's position, your position, your camera's lens, and your camera's settings interact to map your surrounding objects' three-dimensional features to the two-dimensional picture.

Transformations work the same way. They allow you to move, rotate, and manipulate objects in a 3D world, while also allowing you to project 3D coordinates onto a 2D screen. Although transformations seem to modify an object directly, in reality, they are merely transforming the object's local coordinate system into another coordinate system. When rendering 3D scenes, vertices pass through four types of transformations before they are finally rendered on the screen:

- **Modeling transformation.** The modeling transformation moves objects around the scene and moves objects from local coordinates into world coordinates.
- **Viewing transformation.** The viewing transformation specifies the location of the camera and moves objects from world coordinates into eye or camera coordinates.
- **Projection transformation.** The projection transformation defines the viewing volume and clipping planes and maps objects from eye coordinates to clip coordinates.
- **Viewport transformation.** The viewport transformation maps the clip coordinates into the two-dimensional viewport, or window, on your screen.

While these four transformations are standard in 3D graphics, OpenGL includes and combines the modeling and viewing transformation into a single *modelview transformation*. We will discuss the modelview transformation in "The Modelview Matrix" section of this chapter.

Table 4.1 shows a summary of all these transformations.

When you are writing your 3D programs, remember that these transformations execute in a specific order. The modelview transformations execute before the projection transformations; however, the viewport can be specified at any time, and OpenGL will automatically apply it appropriately. Figure 4.1 shows the general order in which these vertex transformations are executed.

Table 4.1 OpenGL Transformations

Transformation	Description
Viewing	In 3D graphics, specifies the location of the camera (not a true OpenGL transformation)
Modeling	In 3D graphics, handles moving objects around the scene (not a true OpenGL transformation)
Projection	Defines the viewing volume and clipping planes
Viewport	Maps the projection of the scene into the rendering window
Modelview	Combination of the viewing and modeling transformations

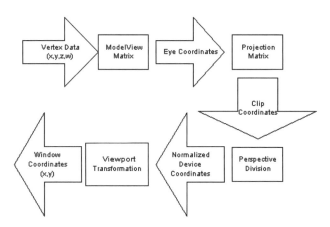

Figure 4.1 The vertex transformation pipeline.

Eye Coordinates

One of the most critical concepts to transformations and viewing in OpenGL is the concept of the *camera*, or eye coordinates. In 3D graphics, the current viewing transformation matrix, which converts world coordinates to eye coordinates, defines the camera's position and orientation. In contrast, OpenGL converts world coordinates to eye coordinates with the *modelview* matrix. When an object is in eye coordinates, the geometric relationship between the object and the camera is known, which means our objects are positioned relative to the camera position and are ready to be rendered properly. Essentially, you can use the viewing transformation to move a camera about the 3D world, while the modeling transformation moves objects around the world. In OpenGL, the default camera (or viewing matrix transformation) is always oriented to look down the negative z axis, as shown in Figure 4.2.

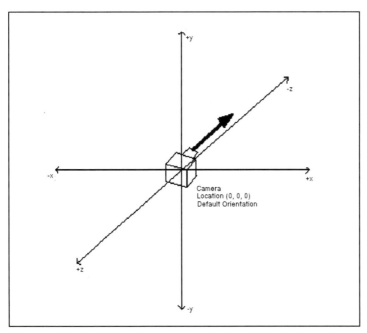

Figure 4.2 The default viewing matrix in OpenGL looks down the negative z axis.

To give you an idea of this orientation, imagine that you are at the origin and you rotate to the left 90 degrees (about the y axis); you would then be facing along the negative x axis. Similarly, if you were to place yourself in the default camera orientation and rotate 180 degrees, you would be facing in the positive z direction.

Viewing Transformations

The viewing transformation is used to position and aim the camera. As already stated, the camera's default orientation is to point down the negative z axis while positioned at the origin (0,0,0). You can move and change the camera's orientation through translation and rotation commands, which, in effect, manipulate the viewing transformation.

Remember that the viewing transformation must be specified before any other modeling transformations. This is because transformations in OpenGL are applied in reverse order. By specifying the viewing transformation first, you are ensuring that it gets applied after the modeling transformations.

How do you create the viewing transformation? First you need to clear the current matrix. You accomplish this through the glLoadIdentity() function, specified as

```
void glLoadIdentity();
```

This sets the current matrix equal to the *identity matrix* and is analogous to clearing the screen before beginning rendering.

Tip

The identity matrix is the matrix in which the diagonal element values in the matrix are equal to 1, and all the other (nondiagonal) element values in the matrix are equal to 0, so that given the 4×4 matrix M: $M(0,0) = M(1,1) = M(2,2) = M(3,3) = 1$. Multiplying the identity matrix I by a matrix M results in a matrix equal to M, such that $I \times M = M$.

After initializing the current matrix, you can create the viewing matrix in several different ways. One method is to leave the viewing matrix equal to the identity matrix. This results in the default location and orientation of the camera, which would be at the origin and looking down the negative z axis. Other methods include the following:

- Using the `gluLookAt()` function to specify a line of sight that extends from the camera. This is a function that encapsulates a set of translation and rotation commands and will be discussed later in this chapter in the "Using `gluLookAt()`" section.
- Using the translation and rotation modeling commands `glTranslate()` and `glRotate()`. These commands are discussed in more detail in the "Using `glRotate()` and `glTranslate()`" section in this chapter; for now, suffice it to say that this method moves the objects in the world relative to a stationary camera.
- Creating your own routines that use the translation and rotation functions for your own coordinate system (for example, polar coordinates for a camera orbiting around an object). This concept will be discussed in this chapter in the "Creating Your Own Custom Routines" section.

Modeling Transformations

The modeling transformations allow you to position and orient a model by moving, rotating, and scaling it. You can perform these operations one at a time or as a combination of events. Figure 4.3 illustrates the three built-in operations that you can use on objects:

- **Translation.** This operation is the act of moving an object along a specified vector.
- **Rotation.** This is where an object is rotated about a vector.
- **Scaling.** This is when you increase or decrease the size of an object. With scaling, you can specify different values for different axes. This gives you the ability to stretch and shrink objects non-uniformly.

The order in which you specify modeling transformations is very important to the final rendition of your scene. For example, as shown in Figure 4.4, rotating and then translating

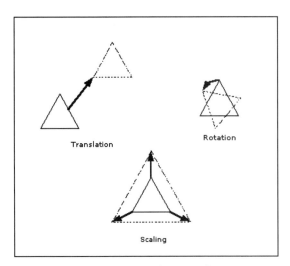

Figure 4.3 The three modeling transformations.

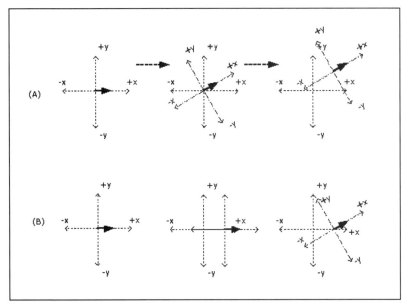

Figure 4.4 (A) Performing rotation before translation; (B) Performing translation before rotation.

an object has a completely different effect than translating and then rotating the object. Let's say you have an arrow located at the origin that lies flat on the x-y plane, and the first transformation you apply is a rotation of 30 degrees around the z axis. You then apply a translation transformation of +5 units along the x axis. The final position of the triangle would be (5, 4.33) with the arrow pointing at a 30-degree angle from the positive x axis. Now, let's swap the order and say you translate the arrow by +5 units along the x axis first. Then you rotate the arrow 30 degrees about the z axis. After the translation, the arrow would be located at (5, 0). When you apply the rotation transformation, the arrow would still be located at (5, 0), but it would be pointing at a 30-degree angle from the x axis.

Projection Transformations

The projection transformation defines the viewing volume and clipping planes. It is performed after the modeling and viewing transformations. You can think of the projection transformation as determining which objects belong in the viewing volume and how they should look. It is very much like choosing a camera lens that is used to look into the world. The field of view you choose when creating the projection transformation determines what type of lens you have. For instance, a wider field of view would be like having a wide-angle lens, where you could see a huge area of the scene without much detail. With a smaller field of view, which would be similar to a telephoto lens, you would be able to look at objects as though they were closer to you than they actually are.

OpenGL offers two types of projections:

- **Perspective projection.** This type of projection shows 3D worlds exactly as you see things in real life. With perspective projection, objects that are farther away appear smaller than objects that are closer to the camera.
- **Orthographic projection.** This type of projection shows objects on the screen in their true size, regardless of their distance from the camera. This projection is useful for CAD software, where objects are drawn with specific views to show the dimensions of an object (i.e. front, left, top views), and can also be used for isometric games.

Viewport Transformations

The last transformation is the *viewport transformation*. This transformation maps the clip coordinates created by the perspective transformation onto your window's rendering surface. You can think of the viewport transformation as determining whether the final image should be enlarged or shrunk, depending on the size of the rendering surface.

OpenGL and Matrices

Now that you've learned about the various transformations involved in OpenGL, let's take a look at how you actually use them. Transformations in OpenGL rely on the *matrix* for all mathematical computations. As you will soon see, OpenGL has what is called the *matrix stack*, which is useful for constructing complicated models composed of many simple objects. You will be taking a look at each of the transformations and look more into the matrix stack in this section.

Tip

In case you need a refresher course, the mathematical concept of the matrix is discussed in the "3D Theory and Concepts" chapter included on the CD.

The Modelview Matrix

The *modelview matrix* defines the coordinate system that is used to place and orient objects. This 4 × 4 matrix can either transform vertices or it can be transformed itself by other matrices. Vertices are transformed by multiplying a vertex vector by the modelview matrix, resulting in a new vertex vector that has been transformed. The modelview matrix itself can be transformed by multiplying it by another 4 × 4 matrix.

Before calling any transformation commands, you must specify whether you want to modify the modelview matrix or the projection matrix. Modifying either matrix is accomplished through the OpenGL function glMatrixMode(), which is defined as

```
void glMatrixMode(GLenum mode);
```

In order to modify the modelview matrix, you use the argument GL_MODELVIEW. This sets the modelview matrix to the current matrix, which means that it will be modified with subsequent transformation commands. Doing this looks like

```
void glMatrixMode(GL_MODELVIEW);
```

Other arguments for glMatrixMode include GL_PROJECTION, GL_COLOR, or GL_TEXTURE. GL_PROJECTION is used to specify the projection matrix; GL_COLOR is used to indicate the color matrix, which we won't be covering; and GL_TEXTURE is used to indicate the texture matrix, which we will discuss in Chapter 7, "Texture Mapping."

Usually at the beginning of your rendering loop, you will want to reset the modelview matrix to the default position (0, 0, 0) and orientation (looking down the negative z axis). To do this, you call the glLoadIdentity() function, which loads the identity matrix as the current modelview matrix, thereby positioning the camera at the world origin and default orientation. Here's a snippet of how you might reset the modelview matrix:

```
glMatrixMode(GL_MODELVIEW);
glLoadIdentity();               // reset the modelview matrix

// ... do other transformations
```

Translation

Translation allows you to move an object from one position in the world to another position in the world. The OpenGL function glTranslate() performs this functionality and is defined as follows:

```
void glTranslate{fd}(TYPE x, TYPE y, TYPE z);
```

The parameters x, y, and z specify the amount to translate along the x, y, and z axes. For example, if you execute the command

```
glTranslatef(3.0f, 1.0f, 8.0f);
```

any subsequently specified objects will be moved three units along the positive x axis, one unit along the positive y axis, and eight units along the positive z axis, to a final position of (3, 1, 8).

Suppose you want to move a cube from the origin to the position (5, 5, 5). You first load the modelview matrix and reset it to the identity matrix, so you are starting at the origin (0, 0, 0). You then perform the translation transformation on the current matrix to position (5, 5, 5) before calling your DrawCube() function. In code, this looks like

```
glMatrixMode(GL_MODELVIEW);      // set current matrix to modelview
glLoadIdentity();                // reset modelview to identity matrix
glTranslatef(5.0f, 5.0f, 5.0f);  // move to (5,5,5)
DrawCube();                      // draw the cube
```

Figure 4.5 illustrates how this code executes.

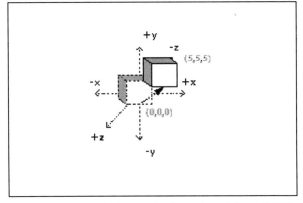

Figure 4.5 Translating a cube from the origin to (5,5,5).

How about a translation example? On the CD under Chapter 4 you will find an example called Translation that illustrates a very simple oscillating translation along the z axis. The example renders a flat square plane at the origin, but because the world coordinate system is being translated, the square plane appears to be moving into and away from the view. Here is the code from the Prepare() function, which performs the oscillation logic:

```
void CGfxOpenGL::Prepare()
{
    // if we're moving in the -z direction, decrement the z position
    if (direction)
        zPos -= 0.01;
    else    // we're moving in the +z direction, increment the z position
        zPos += 0.01;

    // if we have reached the origin or -20 units along the
    // z axis, then change direction
    if (zPos >= 0.0)
        direction = true;
    else if (zPos <= -20.0)
        direction = false;
}
```

This code either increases or decreases the value used to translate the world along the z axis, depending on the "direction" we are currently heading. When the translation value reaches an extreme (0.0 or -20.0), then we change the "direction" of the translation. This code in the Prepare() function is called prior to the Render() function, which looks like this:

```
void CGfxOpenGL::Render()
{
    // clear color and depth buffers
    glClear(GL_COLOR_BUFFER_BIT | GL_DEPTH_BUFFER_BIT);

    // load the identity matrix (clear to default position and orientation)
    glLoadIdentity();

    // translate the world coordinate system along the z axis
    glTranslatef(0.0, 0.0, zPos);

    // draw the plane at the world origin
    DrawPlane();
}
```

The Render() function is very simple. After clearing the color and depth buffers, we load the identity matrix to initialize to the default world position and orientation, translate along the z axis using the value determined in the Prepare() function, and then draw the plane. The DrawPlane() function draws a 4 unit by 4 unit square plane that lies along the x-z plane with its center at the world origin. The resulting execution shows a plane that moves back and forth along the z axis. A screenshot is shown in Figure 4.6.

Rotation

Rotation in OpenGL is accomplished through the glRotate() function, which is defined as

```
void glRotate{fd}(TYPE angle, GLfloat x, TYPE y, TYPE z);
```

With this function, you are performing a rotation around the vector specified by the x, y, and z parameters. The angle of rotation is specified by angle and is measured in degrees in the counterclockwise direction.

For example, if you wanted to rotate around the y axis 135 degrees in the counterclockwise direction, you would use the following:

```
glRotatef(135.0f, 0.0f, 1.0f, 0.0f);
```

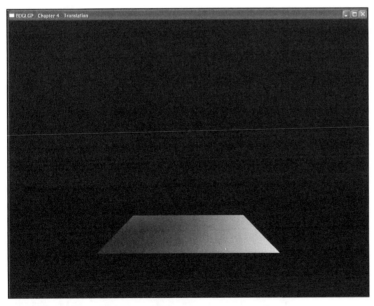

Figure 4.6 A screenshot of the Translation example.

The value of 1.0f for the *y* argument specifies a vector pointing in the direction of the positive y axis. Figure 4.7 illustrates how the glRotate() function works.

If you wanted to rotate clockwise, you would set the angle of rotation as a negative number. To rotate around the y axis 135 degrees in the clockwise direction, you use the following code:

```
glRotatef(-135.0f, 0.0f, 1.0f, 0.0f);
```

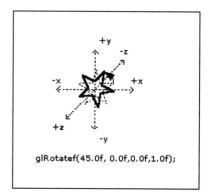

glRotatef(45.0f, 0.0f,0.0f,1.0f);

What if you wanted to rotate around an arbitrary axis? You can accomplish this by specifying the arbitrary axis vector in the x, y, and z parameters. By drawing a line from the relative origin to the point represented by (x,y,z), you can see the arbitrary axis around which you will rotate. For instance, if you rotate 90 degrees about the axis specified by the vector (1, 1, 0), you rotate about the axis that goes from the relative origin to the point (1, 1, 0). In code, this looks like the following:

Figure 4.7 The glRotate() function takes the angle of rotation and a vector for the axis of rotation as parameters.

```
glRotatef(90.0f, 1.0f, 1.0f, 0.0f);
```

Figure 4.8 illustrates how it works.

Rotating about a single axis is fine, but most applications rotate their objects about multiple axes. The order in which you specify rotations is very important when doing this because each rotation you apply changes the local coordinate system of the rotations. For instance, if you rotate an object 60 degrees about

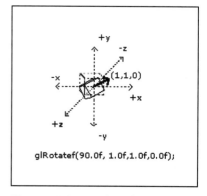

glRotatef(90.0f, 1.0f,1.0f,0.0f);

Figure 4.8 Rotation about an arbitrary axis.

the x axis and then rotate that same object 45 degrees about the y axis in subsequent calls to glRotate(), then the resultant orientation of that object is a result of the two rotations occurring one after the other within the context of the object's local coordinate system. The first rotation will be applied as expected, and the object will be rotated 60 degrees about the x axis. However, the second rotation about the y axis will not be in the context of the world coordinate system. Instead, the y axis rotation occurs in the context of the object's local coordinate system. Because the object has already been rotated 60 degrees about the x axis, the object's new y axis has also been rotated 60 degrees counterclockwise. Your second rotation about the y axis will actually be in this new configuration. Let's look at an example; maybe it will make more sense.

Included on the CD in Chapter 4 you will find an example entitled Rotation. A screenshot of this example is shown in Figure 4.9. If you build and run the example, you will see the

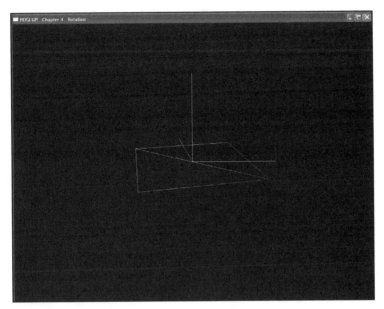

Figure 4.9 A screenshot of the Rotation example.

same plane we created in the Translation example, except this time it is rotating about the origin instead of translating along the z axis. Also being drawn in this example are two sets of lines representing the coordinate system x and y axes. The white lines represent the world coordinate system x and y axes, while the yellow lines represent the x and y axes in the object's local coordinate system. The important part of this example is the following lines in the Render() method:

```
// rotate about x axis then y axis at prescribed angles and draw plane
glRotatef(xAxisAngle, 1.0, 0.0, 0.0);
glRotatef(yAxisAngle, 0.0, 1.0, 0.0);
DrawPlane();
```

You will notice when the example executes that the plane is always rotating about the same world x axis properly, which also seems to be altering the location of the y axis. This is because the rotation about the x axis is specified first, while we are still in the original orientation of the world coordinate system. Once we rotate along the x axis, though, the orientation of the world coordinate system changes to reflect that rotation, and as you can see from the example, the orientation of the y axis changes (the yellow line perpendicular to the plane). Then when we rotate about the y axis, the rotation occurs in the new orientation that has been created as a result of the x axis rotation. Hopefully, through this example you can see how much the order of rotation about different axes matters. Take some time to modify the Rotation example to see how different rotation orders can affect the final rotational outcome of an object.

Scaling

Scaling, in its most simple definition, increases or decreases the size of an object or coordinate system. In other words, when using scaling operations, vertex coordinates for an object are either multiplied by or divided by a scaling factor for each axis. This means that if you would normally place a vertex at the location (1, 1, 1) without scaling, then applying a scaling factor of 2.0 along each axis would place the vertex at the location (2, 2, 2). Scaling is performed in OpenGL through the glScale() function, which is defined as

```
void glScale{fd}(GLfloat x, GLfloat y, GLfloat z);
```

The values passed to the x, y, and z parameters specify the scale factor along each axis. For example, this line applies a scaling factor of 2.0 along each axis:

```
glScalef(2.0f, 2.0f, 2.0f);
```

If you were to draw a 1 × 1 × 1 unit cube after executing the above line, then the cube would really be drawn as a 2 × 2 × 2 cube. Now, let's say you took that cube, and you wanted to double its width (the x axis) without changing its height (the y axis) and depth (the z axis). You would use the following:

```
glScalef(2.0f, 1.0f, 1.0f);
```

What if you wanted to shrink an object? Well, because the scaling factors are each multiplied by the vertices, you simply choose a value less than one, like this:

```
glScalef(0.5f, 0.5f, 0.5f);
```

This line will shrink an object by half its original size. A value of 0.2 would shrink it by one-fifth, 0.1 by one-tenth, and so on. You can even use negative values to mirror, or flip, objects. If you set a scaling factor to 1.0, then the axis the scaling factor belongs to will not be scaled. As you might have guessed from this, scaling is equivalent to multiplying by the scaling factor. Values between 0.0 and 1.0 will shrink the object, and values greater than 1.0 will enlarge the object. Figure 4.10 illustrates the glScale() function.

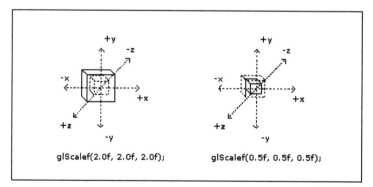

Figure 4.10 The glScale() function.

In the examples so far in this chapter, you've seen an object move around for translation, and you've seen an object rotate for rotation. So naturally, now you are going to see an example for scaling of an object shrinking and expanding. On the CD you will find an example entitled Scaling in the Chapter 4 folder. Taking a look at the Prepare() function in the CGfxOpenGL class, you will see:

```
void CGfxOpenGL::Prepare(float dt)
{
    // increase or decrease scale factor
    if (increaseScale)
        scaleFactor += 0.001;
    else
        scaleFactor -= 0.001;

    if (scaleFactor >= 2.0)
        increaseScale = false;
    else if (scaleFactor <= 0.1)
        increaseScale = true;
}
```

Before we render each frame, the Prepare() function increases or decreases our scaling factor within a range of 0.1 units to 2.0 units. We pass the scaling factor to the glScale() function in the Render() function below:

```
void CGfxOpenGL::Render()
{
    // clear screen and depth buffer
    glClear(GL_COLOR_BUFFER_BIT | GL_DEPTH_BUFFER_BIT);

    // load the identity matrix (clear to default position and orientation)
    glLoadIdentity();

    // move eye back 10 units and orient the plane so we can see it
    glTranslatef(0.0, 0.0, -10.0);
    glRotatef(90.0, 1.0, 0.0, 0.0);

    // scale the plane along all three axes
    glScalef(scaleFactor, scaleFactor, scaleFactor);
    DrawPlane();
}
```

The Render() function sets up the camera 10 units back and rotated onto the z axis so that we can view the plane from above. It then calls the glScale() function, passing the scale factor to all three axis parameters. The result is a plane that increases and decreases in size

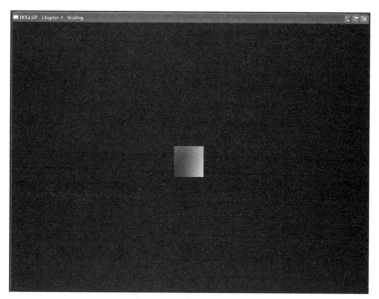

Figure 4.11 A screenshot of the Scaling example. Exciting!

with the value of the scale factor. Although you can't see the plane changing shape, Figure 4.11 is a screenshot of the Scaling example.

Matrix Stacks

The modelview matrix we've been playing with so far is actually only one matrix at the top of a stack of matrices, which is naturally called the OpenGL matrix stack. There are four types of matrix stacks in OpenGL:

- The modelview matrix stack
- The projection matrix stack
- The color matrix stack
- The texture matrix stack

The modelview matrix is the top matrix of the modelview matrix stack, and the projection matrix is the top matrix of the projection matrix stack. Figure 4.12 gives some more information about these matrix stacks. The texture matrix stack is used for the transformation of texture coordinates, and the color matrix can be used to modify colors.

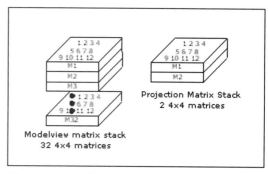

Figure 4.12 The modelview and projection matrix stacks are made up of 32 4 × 4 matrices and two 4 × 4 matrices, respectively, for the Microsoft OpenGL implementation.

In Chapter 3, "OpenGL States and Primitives," you were introduced to two functions, `glPushAttrib()` and `glPopAttrib()`. You learned that you could save the current state of the OpenGL state machine by using `glPushAttrib()`, and you could then retrieve that saved state by using `glPopAttrib()`.

Matrix stacks allow you to do the same thing. The modelview matrix stack allows you to save the current state of the transformation matrix, perform other transformations, and then return to the saved transformation matrix without having to store or calculate the transformation matrix on your own. The projection, texture, and color matrix stacks allow you to do the same thing.

Using the modelview matrix stack essentially allows you to transform from one coordinate system to another while being able to revert back to the original coordinate system. For instance, if we position ourselves at the point (10, 5, 7), and we then push the current modelview matrix onto the current stack, then our current transformation matrix is reset to the local coordinate system centered around the point (10, 5, 7). This means that any transformations we do are now based on the coordinate system at (10, 5, 7). So if we then translate 10 units down the positive x axis with `glTranslate(10.0, 0.0, 0.0)`, we are at the position (10, 0, 0) in the current transformation matrix, but in the world we are positioned at (20, 5, 7). When the matrix stack is popped, we revert back to the original transformation matrix and therefore the original coordinate system, which means we are again positioned at (10, 5, 7).

Two functions allow you to push and pop the matrix stacks: `glPushMatrix()` and `glPopMatrix()`. The `glPushMatrix()` function copies the current matrix and pushes it onto the stack and is defined as:

```
void glPushMatrix();
```

If you push too many matrices onto the stack, then OpenGL gives a `GL_STACK_OVERFLOW` error. The modelview matrix stack is guaranteed to have a stack depth of at least 32, and all of the other matrix stacks have a depth of at least 2. You can find out if your implementation supports larger stacks by calling `glGet()` with `GL_MAX_MODELVIEW_STACK_DEPTH`, `GL_MAX_PROJECTION_STACK_DEPTH`, `GL_MAX_COLOR_STACK_DEPTH`, or `GL_MAX_TEXTURE_STACK_DEPTH`.

The `glPopMatrix()` function pops off the top matrix on the stack and discards its contents. All other matrices in the stack are moved up one position. `glPopMatrix()` is defined as

```
void glPopMatrix();
```

If you try to use this function when there is only one matrix in the stack, OpenGL will give a `GL_STACK_UNDERFLOW` error.

Figure 4.13 shows how the `glPushMatrix()` and `glPopMatrix()` functions operate on the matrix stack.

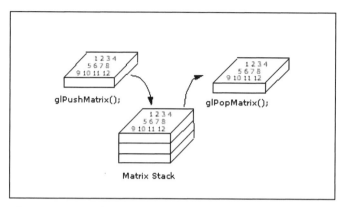

Figure 4.13 Pushing and popping on the matrix stack.

The Robot Example

On the CD you will find the source code for an OpenGL demo called RobotExample that shows an animated walking robot around which the camera rotates. The robot is constructed of cubes that you scale to different shapes and sizes to give the robot arms, legs, feet, a torso, and a head. The glPushMatrix() and glPopMatrix() functions are used to position the robot's body parts in coordinates relative to the center of the robot. Take special note of these functions as you trace through the source code.

Figure 4.14 shows a screenshot of the Robot example.

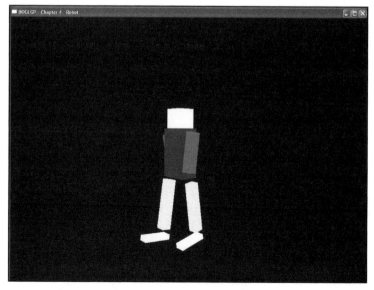

Figure 4.14 A screenshot of the Robot example.

There are two functions that you should focus on as you browse through the source code. The first is the Prepare() method in the Robot class:

```
void Robot::Prepare(float dt)
{
    // if leg is moving forward, increase angle, else decrease angle
    for (int side = 0; side < 2; side++)
    {
        // arms
        if (armStates[side] == FORWARD_STATE)
            armAngles[side] += 20.0f * dt;
        else
            armAngles[side] -= 20.0f * dt;

        // change state if exceeding angles
        if (armAngles[side] >= 15.0f)
            armStates[side] = BACKWARD_STATE;
        else if (armAngles[side] <= -15.0f)
            armStates[side] = FORWARD_STATE;

        // legs
        if (legStates[side] == FORWARD_STATE)
            legAngles[side] += 20.0f * dt;
        else
            legAngles[side] -= 20.0f * dt;

        // change state if exceeding angles
        if (legAngles[side] >= 15.0f)
            legStates[side] = BACKWARD_STATE;
        else if (legAngles[side] <= -15.0f)
            legStates[side] = FORWARD_STATE;
    }
}
```

The Prepare() method modifies the robot arm and leg angles, as well as determining the direction each arm and leg is moving. We use the dt parameter to make the robot's movement frame-rate independent. The armAngles and legAngles arrays store each arm's and leg's angles (array index 0 is the left arm, 1 is the right arm), respectively; the armStates and legStates arrays store the current state of each arm and leg, respectively.

The method you are probably most interested in, though, is the DrawRobot() method in the Robot class:

```
void Robot::DrawRobot(float xPos, float yPos, float zPos)
{
    glPushMatrix();
        glTranslatef(xPos, yPos, zPos);       // draw robot at desired coordinates

        // draw head and torso parts
        DrawHead(1.0f, 2.0f, 0.0f);
        DrawTorso(1.5f, 0.0f, 0.0f);

        // move the left arm away from the torso and rotate it to give "walking" effect
        glPushMatrix();
            glTranslatef(0.0f, -0.5f, 0.0f);
            glRotatef(armAngles[LEFT], 1.0f, 0.0f, 0.0f);
            DrawArm(2.5f, 0.0f, -0.5f);
        glPopMatrix();

        // move the right arm away from the torso and rotate it to give "walking" effect
        glPushMatrix();
            glTranslatef(0.0f, -0.5f, 0.0f);
            glRotatef(armAngles[RIGHT], 1.0f, 0.0f, 0.0f);
            DrawArm(-1.5f, 0.0f, -0.5f);
        glPopMatrix();

        // move the left leg away from the torso and rotate it to give "walking" effect
        glPushMatrix();
            glTranslatef(0.0f, -0.5f, 0.0f);
            glRotatef(legAngles[LEFT], 1.0f, 0.0f, 0.0f);
            DrawLeg(-0.5f, -5.0f, -0.5f);
        glPopMatrix();

        // move the right leg away from the torso and rotate it to give "walking" effect
        glPushMatrix();
            glTranslatef(0.0f, -0.5f, 0.0f);
            glRotatef(legAngles[RIGHT], 1.0f, 0.0f, 0.0f);
            DrawLeg(1.5f, -5.0f, -0.5f);
        glPopMatrix();

    glPopMatrix();        // pop back to original coordinate system
}
```

The DrawRobot() method draws the entire robot at the specified (x, y, z) coordinates. To simplify the code, the method calls several other methods that render the different parts of the robot: DrawHead(), DrawTorso(), DrawArm(), and DrawLeg(). In turn, each of these methods draws its respective part at the specified position, relative to the position of the robot itself because we use the glPushMatrix() and glPopMatrix() functions to position and rotate each robot part.

Projections

We've mentioned projection transformations several times now and even used them in code, so it's high time we discussed how they work. As we've pointed out, there are two general classes of projection transformations available in OpenGL: orthographic (or parallel) and perspective. We'll look at both of these in detail.

By setting a projection transformation, you are, in effect, creating a viewing volume, which serves two purposes. The first is that the viewing volume defines a number of clipping planes, which determine the portion of your 3D world that is visible at any given time. Objects that are outside this volume are not transformed or rendered.

The second purpose of the viewing volume is to determine how objects are drawn. This depends on the shape of the viewing volume, which is the primary difference between orthographic and perspective projections.

Before specifying any kind of projection transformation, though, you need to make sure that the projection matrix is the currently selected matrix stack. As you saw earlier with the modelview matrix, this is done with a call to glMatrixMode():

```
glMatrixMode(GL_PROJECTION);
```

In most cases, you will want to follow this up with a call to glLoadIdentity() to clear out anything that may be stored in the projection matrix, so that previous transformations don't get accumulated. Unlike with the modelview matrix, it is rare to make a lot of changes to the projection matrix.

Once the projection matrix stack is selected, you're ready to specify your projection. We'll look at orthographic projections first and then at the more commonly used perspective transformations.

Orthographic

As we mentioned before, orthographic, or parallel, projections are those that involve no perspective correction. In other words, no adjustment for distance from the camera is made; objects appear the same size onscreen whether they are close or far away. Although this may not look as realistic as perspective projections, it has a number of uses. Traditionally, orthographic projections are included in OpenGL for applications such as CAD, but they can also be used for 2D games or isometric games.

OpenGL provides the `glOrtho()` function to set up orthographic projections:

```
glOrtho(GLdouble left, GLdouble right, GLdouble bottom, GLdouble top, GLdouble near,
GLdouble far);
```

`left` and `right` specify the x-coordinate clipping planes, `bottom` and `top` specify the y-coordinate clipping planes, and `near` and `far` specify the distance to the z-coordinate clipping planes. Together, these coordinates specify a box-shaped viewing volume. More precisely, opposite planes are parallel to each other, and adjacent planes are perpendicular.

Because orthographic projections are commonly used to create 2D scenes, the OpenGL Utility Library provides an additional routine to set up orthographic projections for scenes in which you won't really be using the z coordinate:

```
gluOrtho2D(GLdouble left, GLdouble right, GLdouble bottom, GLdouble top);
```

`left`, `right`, `bottom`, and `top` are as with `glOrtho()` above. Using `gluOrtho2D()` is equivalent to calling `glOrtho()` with `near` set to −1.0 and `far` set to 1.0. When using `gluOrtho2D()`, you'll normally want to use a version of `glVertex()` that takes only two parameters (the x and y coordinates) because the z coordinate isn't usually used. It's common in this case to use integer coordinates and to set the view volume to match the x and y coordinates of the viewport.

Perspective

Although orthographic projections can be interesting, perspective projections create more realistic-looking scenes, so that's what you'll likely be using more often. In perspective projections, as an object gets farther from the viewer, it appears smaller on the screen—an effect commonly referred to as *foreshortening*. The viewing volume for a perspective projection is a *frustum*, which looks like a pyramid with the top cut off, with the narrow end toward the viewer. That the far end of the frustum is larger than the near end is what creates the foreshortening effect. The way this works is that OpenGL transforms the frustum so that it becomes a cube. This transformation affects the objects inside the frustum as well, so objects at the wide end of the frustum get compressed more than objects at the narrow end. The greater the ratio between the wide and narrow ends, the more an object is shrunk. If the ends of the frustum are close in size, there won't be much perspective correction (if they are the same, there will be no correction at all, which is what happens with orthographic projections).

There are a couple of ways you can set up the view frustum, and thus the perspective projection. The first we'll look at is the following:

```
void glFrustum(GLdouble left, GLdouble right, GLdouble bottom, GLdouble top, GLdouble
near, GLdouble far);
```

left, right, top, and bottom together specify the x and y coordinates on the near clipping plane, and near and far specify the distance to the near and far clipping planes. Thus, the top-left corner of the near clipping plane is at (left, top, -near), and the bottom-right corner is at (right, bottom, -near). The corners of the far clipping plane are determined by casting a ray from the viewer through the corners of the near clipping plane and intersecting them with the far clipping plane. So, the closer the viewer is to the near clipping plane, the larger the far clipping plane is, and the more foreshortening is apparent.

Using glFrustum() enables you to specify an asymmetrical frustum, which may be useful in some instances, but it's not typically what you'll want to do. In addition, thinking about what the viewer can see in terms of a frustum is not particularly intuitive. Instead, it's easier to think about the field of view—that is, how wide of an angle he can see. The OpenGL Utility Library provides a function that allows you to directly specify the field of view, and then calculates the frustum for you. This function is

```
void gluPerspective(GLdouble fov, GLdouble aspect, GLdouble near, GLdouble far);
```

fov specifies, in degrees, the angle around the y axis that is visible to the user. aspect is the aspect ratio of the screen, which is the width divided by the height. This determines the field of view around the x axis. near and far have the same meanings they've had in the other projection functions in this section.

One thing we haven't mentioned in our discussion of setting up a frustum is how to determine an appropriate ratio between the width of the far and near end (that is, how wide the field of view is). The appropriate field of view is highly application dependent. If you want to create a fish-eye effect, a very wide field of view may be appropriate. For a realistic perspective, something around 45–90 degrees usually works well. In general, you'll want to experiment to see what looks right for your particular application.

Setting the Viewport

Some of the projection functions we've just discussed are closely related to the size of the viewport (for example, the aspect ratio in gluPerspective). You know that the viewport transformation happens after the projection transformation, so now is as good a time as any to discuss it.

In essence, the viewport specifies the dimensions and orientation of the 2D window into which you'll be rendering. It is set using glViewport():

```
void glViewport(GLint x, GLint y, GLsizei width, GLsizei height);
```

x and y specify the coordinates of the lower-left corner of the viewport, and width and height specify the size of the window in pixels.

When a rendering context is first created and attached to your window, the viewport is automatically set to match the dimensions of the window. That may be good enough for some applications, but in most cases, you'll want to update your viewport any time the window is resized. Although the viewport generally matches your window size, there is nothing requiring it to be the same size. There may be times when you want to limit rendering to a sub-region of your window, and setting a smaller viewport is one way to do this. The Fog demo covered in Chapter 5, "Colors, Lighting, Blending, and Fog," shows an example of using multiple viewports in a single window.

Projection Example

To get a better idea of the differences between the two major projection types, we've included a simple demo that allows you to view the same scene in each mode. The demo starts off with a perspective projection; pressing the spacebar enables you to toggle between orthographic (shown in Figure 4.15) and perspective (shown in Figure 4.16) projections.

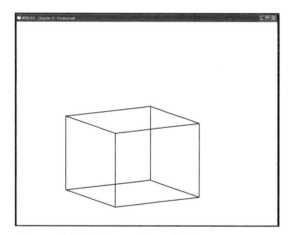

Figure 4.15 Orthographic projection.

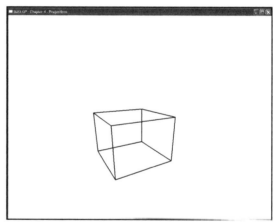

Figure 4.16 Perspective projection.

The relevant portion of this demo is in the ResizeScene() and UpdateProjection() methods of the CGfxOpenGL class, which are listed here for convenience:

```
void CGfxOpenGL::ResizeScene(int width, int height)
{
    // avoid divide by zero
    if (height==0)
    {
        height=1;
    }
```

```
        // reset the viewport to the new dimensions
        glViewport(0, 0, width, height);

        // set up the projection, without toggling the projection mode
        UpdateProjection(false);
}

void CGfxOpenGL::UpdateProjection(bool toggle)
{
        static bool usePerspective = true;

        // toggle the control variable if appropriate
        if (toggle)
            usePerspective = !usePerspective;

        // select the projection matrix and clear it out
        glMatrixMode(GL_PROJECTION);
        glLoadIdentity();

        // choose the appropriate projection based on the currently toggled mode
        if (usePerspective)
        {
            // set the perspective with the appropriate aspect ratio
            glFrustum(-1.0, 1.0, -1.0, 1.0, 1.0, 1000.0);
        }
        else
        {
            // set up an orthographic projection with the same near clip plane
            glOrtho(-1.0, 1.0, -1.0, 1.0, 1.0, 1000.0);
        }

        // select modelview matrix and clear it out
        glMatrixMode(GL_MODELVIEW);
        glLoadIdentity();
}
```

Manipulating the Viewpoint

In this section we are going to introduce you to several options for manipulating the viewpoint, or the "camera." Your first option is to use the gluLookAt() function, which allows you to specify the position of the viewpoint, a directional vector from the viewpoint, and an up vector from the viewpoint to orient and position the viewpoint. The second option is to use a combination of the glTranslate() and glRotate() functions to orient and position the viewpoint. Finally, you can use your own custom routines to define the viewpoint behavior. For instance, you might want the viewpoint to be oriented through the polar coordinate system.

Let's take a look at these options.

Using gluLookAt()

Now let's take a look at the gluLookAt() function, which is defined as

```
void gluLookAt(GLdouble eyex, GLdouble eyey, GLdouble eyez,
               GLdouble centerx, GLdouble centery, GLdouble centerz,
               GLdouble upx, GLdouble upy, GLdouble upz);
```

You can use this function to define the camera's location and orientation instead of the modeling transformations glTranslate() and glRotate(). The first set of three parameters (eyex, eyey, eyez) specifies the location of the camera. The value (0, 0, 0) would naturally specify the origin. The next set of parameters (centerx, centery, centerz) specifies where the camera is pointing, also called the line of sight, which is a vector pointing in the forward direction of the camera. The last set of parameters (upx, upy, upz) is a vector that tells which direction is the up direction. Figure 4.17 shows how all of these parameters work on the camera with the gluLookAt() function.

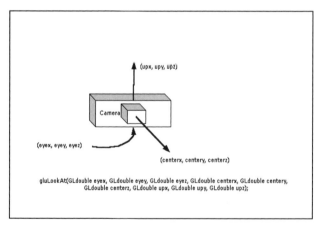

Figure 4.17 The gluLookAt() parameters specify the location and orientation of the camera.

Here is a short code snippet that uses the gluLookAt() function. Don't worry about any code you don't understand yet. You will get to it at some point.

```
void DisplayScene()
{
    glClear(GL_COLOR_BUFFER_BIT);       // clear the color buffer
    glColor3f(1.0f, 0.0f, 0.0f);        // set color to red
    glLoadIdentity();                   // clear the current matrix

    // Now we set the viewing transformation with the gluLookAt() function.
    // This sets the camera at the position (0,0,10) and looking down the
    // negative z axis (0.0, 0.0, -100.0).
    // (eyex, eyey, eyez) = (0.0, 0.0, 10.0)
    // (centerx, centery, centerz) = (0.0, 0.0, -100.0)
    // (upx, upy, upz) = (0.0, 1.0, 0.0)
    gluLookAt(0.0f, 0.0f, 10.0f, 0.0f, 0.0f, -100.0f, 0.0f, 1.0f, 0.0f);

    // draw a triangle at the origin
    glBegin(GL_TRIANGLE);
        glVertexf(10.0f, 0.0f, 0.0f);
        glVertexf(0.0f, 10.0f, 0.0f);
        glVertexf(-10.0f, 0.0f, 0.0f);
    glEnd();
}
```

As you can see, the gluLookAt() function is rather easy to use. By manipulating the parameters, you can move the camera to any position and orientation that you want.

Using glRotate() and glTranslate()

A drawback to gluLookAt() is that you must link the GLU library with your application. What if you don't want to use the GLU library, but you want to get the same functionality? One solution is to simply use the glRotate() and glTranslate() modeling-transformation functions as discussed earlier in this chapter. The code below uses the modeling functions to produce the same effect on the camera as the previous gluLookAt() code.

```
void DisplayScene()
{
    glClear(GL_COLOR_BUFFER_BIT);       // clear the color buffer
    glColor3f(1.0f, 0.0f, 0.0f);        // set color to red
    glLoadIdentity();                    // clear the current matrix
```

```
// Now we set the viewing transformation with the glTranslatef() function.
// We move the modeling transformation to (0.0, 0.0, -10.0), moving the
// world 10 units along the negative z-axis, which effectively moves the
// camera to the position (0.0, 0.0, 10.0).
glTranslatef(0.0f, 0.0f, -10.0f);

// draw a triangle at the origin
glBegin(GL_TRIANGLE);
    glVertexf(10.0f, 0.0f, 0.0f);
    glVertexf(0.0f, 10.0f, 0.0f);
    glVertexf(-10.0f, 0.0f, 0.0f);
glEnd();
}
```

In this case, there isn't a serious difference in code from the gluLookAt() function because all you are doing is moving the camera along the z axis. But if you were orienting the camera at an odd angle, you would need to use the glRotate() function as well (you will see more of glTranslate() and glRotate() soon), which leads to the next way of manipulating the camera: your own custom routines.

Creating Your Own Custom Routines

Suppose you want to create your own flight simulator. In a typical flight simulator, the camera is positioned in the pilot's seat, so it moves and is oriented in the same manner as the plane. Plane orientation is defined by pitch, yaw, and roll, which are rotation angles relative to the center of gravity of the plane (in your case, the pilot/camera position). Using the modeling-transformation functions, you could create the following function to create the viewing transformation:

```
void PlaneView(GLfloat planeX, GLfloat planeY, GLfloat planeZ, // the plane's position
            GLfloat roll, GLfloat pitch, GLfloat yaw)        // orientation
{
    // roll is rotation about the z axis
    glRotatef(roll, 0.0f, 0.0f, 1.0f);

    // yaw, or heading, is rotation about the y axis
    glRotatef(yaw, 0.0f, 1.0f, 0.0f);

    // pitch is rotation about the x axis
    glRotatef(pitch, 1.0f, 0.0f, 0.0f);
    // move the plane to the plane's world coordinates
    glTranslatef(-planeX, -planeY, -planeZ);
}
```

Using this function places the camera in the pilot's seat of your airplane regardless of the orientation or location of the plane. This is just one of the uses of your own customized routines. Other uses include applications of polar coordinates, such as rotation about a fixed point, and use of the modeling-transformation functions to create what is called "*Quake*-like movement," where the mouse and keyboard can be used to control the camera.

The greatest degree of camera control can be obtained by manually constructing and loading your own matrices, which will be covered in the next section.

Using Your Own Matrices

Up until now, we've talked about functions that allow you to modify the matrix stacks without really having to worry about the matrices themselves. This is great because it allows you to do a lot without having to understand matrix math, and the functions OpenGL provides for you are actually quite powerful and flexible. Eventually, though, you may want to create some advanced effects that are possible only by directly affecting the matrices. This will require that you know your way around matrix math, which we're assuming as a prerequisite to reading this book. However, we'll at least show you how to load your own matrix, how to multiply the top of the matrix stack by a custom matrix, and one example of using a custom matrix.

Loading Your Matrix

Before you can load a matrix, you need to specify it. OpenGL matrices are column-major 4×4 matrices of floating point numbers, laid out as in Figure 4.18.

$$\begin{bmatrix} m_0 & m_4 & m_8 & m_{12} \\ m_1 & m_5 & m_9 & m_{13} \\ m_2 & m_6 & m_{10} & m_{14} \\ m_3 & m_7 & m_{11} & m_{15} \end{bmatrix}$$

Figure 4.18 OpenGL's column-major matrix format.

Because the matrices are 4×4, you may be tempted to declare them as two-dimensional arrays, but there is one major problem with this. In C and C++, two-dimensional arrays are row major. For example, to access the bottom-left element of the matrix in Figure 4.18, you might think you'd use matrix[3][0], which is how you'd access the bottom-left corner of a 4×4 C/C++ two-dimensional array. Because OpenGL matrices are column major, however, you'd really be accessing the top-right element of the matrix. To get the bottom-left element, you'd need to use matrix[0][3]. This is the opposite of what you're used to in C/C++, making it counterintuitive and error prone. Rather than using two-dimensional arrays, it's recommended that you use a one-dimensional array of 16 elements. The nth element in the array corresponds to element mn in Figure 4.18.

As an example, if you want to specify the identity matrix (something you'd never need to do in practice due to the glLoadIdentity() function), you could use

```
GLfloat identity[16] = { 1.0, 0.0, 0.0, 0.0, 0.0, 1.0, 0.0, 0.0, 0.0, 0.0, 1.0, 0.0,
0.0, 0.0, 0.0, 1.0 };
```

That's easy enough. So, now that you've specified a matrix, the next step is to load it. This is done by calling glLoadMatrix(), which has two flavors:

```
void glLoadMatrix{fd}(const TYPE matrix[16]);
```

When glLoadMatrix() is called, whatever is at the top of the currently selected matrix stack is replaced with the values in the matrix array, which is a 16-element array as specified previously.

Multiplying Matrices

In addition to loading new matrices onto the matrix stack (and thus losing whatever information was previously in it), you can multiply the contents of the active matrix by a new matrix. Again, you'd specify your custom matrix as above and then call the following:

```
void glMultMatrix{fd}(const TYPE matrix[16]);
```

Again, matrix is an array of 16 elements. glMultMatrix() uses post-multiplication; in other words, if the active matrix before the call to glMultMatrix() is Mold, and the new matrix is Mnew, then the new matrix will be Mold × Mnew. Note that the ordering is important; because matrix multiplication is not commutative, Mold × Mnew in most cases will not have the same result as Mnew × Mold.

Transpose Matrices

Extension

Extension name: ARB_transpose_matrix

Name string: GL_ARB_transpose_matrix

Promoted to core: OpenGL 1.3

Function names: glLoadTransposeMatrixfARB(), glLoadTransposeMatrixdARB(), glMultTransposeMatrixfARB(), glMultTransposeMatrixdARB()

Tokens: GL_MODELVIEW_MATRIX_ARB, GL_PROJECTION_MATRIX_ARB, GL_TEXTURE_MATRIX_ARB, GL_COLOR_MATRIX_ARB

We mentioned earlier that OpenGL uses column-major matrices, which conflicts with the row-major two-dimensional arrays used by C and C++. In OpenGL 1.3, two new functions were introduced that allow you to use row-major matrices instead:

```
glLoadTransposeMatrix{fd}(const TYPE matrix[16]);
glMultTransposeMatrix{fd}(const TYPE matrix[16]);
```

These functions work exactly the same way as `glLoadMatrix()` and `glMultMatrix()`, except that the matrices are the transposition of what OpenGL uses internally. By using them, you can specify your matrices as two-dimensional arrays in C or C++ and address the matrix elements in an intuitive way.

Summary

In this chapter, you learned how to manipulate objects in your scene by using transformations. You've also examined how to change the way in which the scene itself is viewed, through setting up projections. In the process, you've learned about the projection and modelview matrices and how to manipulate them using both built-in functions and matrices you define yourself. You now have the means to place objects in a 3D world, to move and animate them, and to move around the world.

What You Have Learned

- Transformations allow you to move, rotate, and manipulate objects in a 3D world, while also allowing you to project 3D coordinates onto a 2D screen.
- The viewing transformation specifies the location of the camera.
- The modeling transformation moves objects around the 3D world.
- The projection transformation defines the viewing volume and clipping planes.
- The viewport transformation maps the projection of the scene into the viewport, or window, on your screen.
- The OpenGL modelview transformation is a combination of the modeling and viewing transformations.
- The viewpoint is also called the "camera" or "eye coordinates."
- Translation is the act of moving an object along a vector.
- Rotation is the act of rotating an object about a vector-defined axis.
- Scaling is the act of increasing or decreasing the size of an object.
- Perspective projection shows 3D worlds exactly as you see things in real life. Objects that are farther away appear smaller than objects that are closer to the camera.

- Orthographic projection shows objects on the screen in their true size, regardless of their distance from the camera.
- The modelview matrix defines the coordinate system that is used to place and orient objects. You set the modelview matrix to the current matrix by using the `glMatrixMode()` function with `GL_MODELVIEW` as the parameter. Using `GL_PROJECTION` as the parameter sets the current matrix to the projection matrix.
- `glLoadIdentity()` restores the current matrix to the identity matrix.
- Translation is performed in OpenGL with the `glTranslate()` function.
- Rotation is performed in OpenGL with the `glRotate()` function.
- Scaling is performed in OpenGL with the `glScale()` function.
- Saving and restoring the current matrix is accomplished via the `glPushMatrix()` and `glPopMatrix()` functions.
- The `glOrtho()` and `gluOrtho2D()` functions are used to set up orthographic projections.
- The `glFrustum()` and `gluPerspective()` functions are used to set up perspective projections.
- `gluLookAt()` can be used to position and orient the OpenGL viewpoint.
- Use the `glLoadMatrix()` function to load a user-defined matrix as the current OpenGL matrix.
- Use the `glMultMatrix()` function to multiply the current OpenGL matrix by a user-defined matrix.

Review Questions

1. Write the line of code to position an object at the point (29, 3, 15).
2. Write the line of code to rotate an object 15 degrees about the x axis.
3. Write the lines of code to a) triple the size of an object and b) halve the size of an object.
4. What are the four types of matrix stacks?
5. What function restores the current matrix to the identity matrix?
6. What do the `glPushMatrix()` and `glPopMatrix()` functions accomplish?

On Your Own

1. Write a function that positions and rotates a cube, given as parameters the (x, y, z) position of the cube and the rotation angles about each axis. You can assume that the function to draw the cube is `DrawCube()`, and the prototype of your function is

```
void PositionAndRotate(float xPos, float yPos, float zPos, float xAngle, float
yAngle, float zAngle);
```

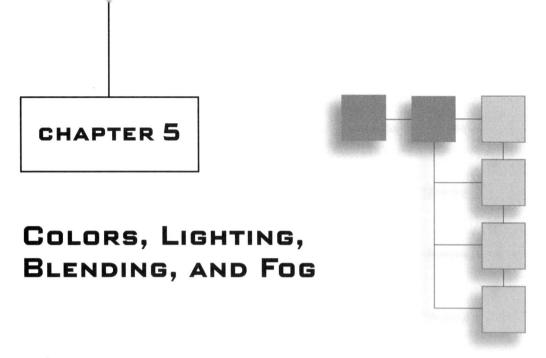

Colors, Lighting, Blending, and Fog

A world without color would be pretty boring, not to mention confusing and depressing. Likewise, moving around in a 3D world drawn in shades of black and white on a computer screen would get to be rather monotonous for most people. It wouldn't be particularly realistic. Fortunately, OpenGL offers plenty of magic to fill your world with color.

This chapter begins by taking a look at how basic colors work in OpenGL. Then we'll move on to more realistic colors using lighting and materials. Then we'll look at how transparency and other effects can be achieved through blending. Finally, we'll take a look at OpenGL's built-in fog support, which can be used to both create realism and improve performance. As you can see, the fun is just beginning!

In this chapter, you'll learn about:

- Colors in OpenGL
- Shading
- OpenGL lighting
- Light sources
- Materials
- Blending and transparency
- Fog

Using Colors in OpenGL

When you pass primitives to OpenGL, it assigns colors to them by one of two methods: using lighting or using the current color. When lighting is used, the color for each vertex is computed based on a number of factors, including the position and color of one or more lights, the current material, the vertex normal, and so on. If lighting is disabled, then the current color is used instead. In *RGBA mode*, which is what you'll almost always be using, OpenGL keeps track of a primary and a secondary color consisting of red, green, blue, and alpha components.

Note

The alternative to RGBA mode is *color-index* mode. In color-index mode, rather than specifying color values directly, you specify indices into a palette of colors maintained by the windowing system. Unless you intend to target very old computers, you can ignore color-index mode entirely. Because it is no longer relevant, we won't be covering it here.

In this chapter you'll first learn about how to use the current color, and later on about lighting.

Setting the Color

In RGBA mode, you specify colors by indicating the intensity of the red, green, and blue components. There is also an optional fourth component, called alpha, which is usually used for transparency. We'll discuss using the alpha value later in this chapter.

The color components are usually expressed using floating point values, with 0.0 being the minimum intensity and 1.0 being the maximum. So black would be represented by setting the red, green, and blue components to 0.0, whereas white would be represented by setting all three components to 1.0.

To specify the primary color in OpenGL, you will use one of the many variations of glColor*():

```
void glColor{34}{bsifd ubusui}(T components);
void glColor{34}{bsifd ubusui}v(T components);
```

The first set of functions takes each color component individually, whereas the second set of functions takes them in an array of the appropriate size. The byte, short, and integer versions of glColor() internally remap the values to a floating point value, so that the maximum possible integer value is mapped to 1.0 and the minimum value is mapped to 0.0.

When using the versions of glColor() that take only three components, the alpha value is automatically set to 1.0.

Let's look at a few samples of how glColor() is used. The following calls all set the current primary color to yellow.

```
// using floats
glColor3f(1.0, 1.0, 0.0);
```

```
// using unsigned bytes
glColor3ui(255, 255, 0);

// using signed bytes in an array
GLbyte yellow[] = {127, 127, 0};
glColor3iv(yellow);
```

The primary color is used to determine vertex colors when lighting is not enabled. Every time you specify a vertex using glVertex(), the current primary color is checked and applied to that vertex. You can change the color as often as you like, although if you change it more than once between vertices, only the last change will have an effect.

Tip

At first glance, using the primary color might not seem terribly useful. Directly specifying a color for each vertex might work well for simple demos, but most things in the real world can't be described accurately using such a simple model. However, it does have practical applications. For example, in most games, many of the lights and most of the geometry are static, i.e. they don't change from frame to frame. Rather than redundantly recomputing lighting every frame, one common solution is to compute it before the program is run—possibly using a more realistic lighting model than that used by most graphics APIs, such as radiosity—and then store—or "bake"—the computed value into the vertex data as the vertex color. Then, when the geometry is displayed, this value is combined with textures and possibly dynamic lighting to produce the final color.

Secondary Color

Extension

Extension name: EXT_secondary_color

Name string: GL_EXT_secondary_color

Promoted to core: OpenGL 1.4

Function names: glSecondaryColor{msifd ubusui}EXT, glSecondaryColor{msifd ubusui}vEXT

Tokens: GL_COLOR_SUM_EXT

In addition to a primary color, OpenGL keeps track of a secondary color, which was added in OpenGL 1.4. The secondary color came about as the result of adding separate specular color, which we'll cover later in this chapter. Because vertices had to carry around a second piece of color information anyway, the OpenGL designers decided to allow developers to make use of it even when they aren't using lighting. The secondary color is interpolated across the primitive and added to the fragment color after the texture environment has been applied—which simply means that the secondary color is added after everything else. The one main difference between the primary and secondary colors is that the secondary color does not include an alpha component.

The secondary color can be set using one of the following:

```
glSecondaryColor3{bsifd ubusui}(TYPE red, TYPE green, TYPE blue);
glSecondaryColor3{bsifd ubusui}v(TYPE color);
```

By default, the secondary color is not used during rasterization when lighting is disabled. To make use of the secondary color, you need to enable it as follows:

```
glEnable(GL_COLOR_SUM);
```

Among other things, you can use this to specify the specular component if you're doing lighting yourself.

Shading

So far, we have talked about using glColor() to set the color at each vertex. But how does OpenGL decide what color to use for pixels in the middle of a triangle? If all three vertices are the same color, then it should be obvious that every pixel in the triangle should use that color as well. But what happens if you use a different color for each vertex of a primitive?

To find out, let's consider a line with two vertices of different colors. We'll keep things simple and say that the first vertex is black and the second vertex is white. So what is the color of the line itself? This answer comes from what is known as the *shading model*.

Shading can either be *flat* or *smooth*. When flat shading is used, the entire primitive is drawn with a single color. With the exception of points, primitives are drawn using more than one vertex. Because each vertex may have a different color, OpenGL has to choose one of them to use for the primitive's color. For lines, triangles, and quads, the color of the last vertex is used. For line strips and line loops, the color of the second vertex in each individual segment is used. For triangle strips and fans and quad strips, the color of the last vertex in each sub-triangle or quad is used. For polygons, the color of the first vertex is used.

Smooth shading, based on the *Gouraud shading* model, is the more realistic of the two and uses interpolation to determine the colors between the vertices of a primitive. This process will be made clearer as we continue with the line example.

If we use flat shading on our sample line, the line will be white because the last vertex specified is white. However, if we use smooth shading, then our line will progress from the color black at the first vertex to gray at the middle of the line to white at the second vertex. This effect is illustrated in Figure 5.1.

Vertex 1   Vertex 2

Figure 5.1 Smooth shading of a line with black at the first
vertex and white at the second vertex.

As you can see, interspersed between the first vertex and the middle of the line are progressively lighter shades of gray. The progression continues on the other half of the line as
the colors shift through lighter shades of gray until you reach white.

The idea of smooth shading with polygonal primitives is essentially the same as smooth
shading with a line. For example, drawing the triangle using smooth shading with a different color for each vertex yields a triangle where each vertex color progressively changes
to the other two vertices' colors as it moves across the polygon's surface. Smooth shading
is useful for simulating the effect of a curved surface when lighting is enabled.

Now that you know what these shading modes are all about, how do you use them? The
glShadeModel() function lets you specify the current shading model before you begin drawing. It is defined as:

```
glShadeModel(GLenum mode);
```

You can specify either GL_SMOOTH for smooth shading or GL_FLAT for flat shading as the *mode*
parameter. The default setting is GL_SMOOTH.

So with this information, you can now create some code that will draw a smooth-shaded
triangle.

```
// use smooth shading
glShadeModel(GL_SMOOTH);

// draw our smooth-shaded triangle
glBegin(GL_TRIANGLES);
  glColor3f(1.0f, 0.0f, 0.0f);    // red vertex
  glVertex3f(-10.0f, -10.0f, -5.0f);
  glColor3f(0.0f, 1.0f, 0.0f);    // green vertex
  glVertex3f(20.0f, -10.0f, -5.0f);
  glColor3f(0.0f, 0.0f, 1.0f);    // blue vertex
  glVertex3f(-10.0, 20.0f, -5.0f);
glEnd();
```

The output is shown in Figure 5.2 (refer to the CD for a full-color version). The red, green, and blue colors from each of the vertices progressively change as they move across the triangle's surface. In the middle, the three colors converge to create the color gray, which means that the three colors (RGB) are each at the same intensity.

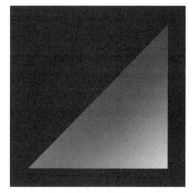

Figure 5.2 A smooth-shaded triangle with red, green, and blue vertices.

A Colorful Example

The sample program from this section, which you'll find in the Colors directory in the Chapter 5 folder, illustrates the use of colors and shading. Figure 5.3 shows the same quad drawn four times. The top row uses flat shading, the bottom uses smooth, the right column uses secondary color, and the left column does not.

Lighting in OpenGL

You have now arrived at one of the most important aspects of 3D graphics: lighting. It is one of the few elements that can make or break the realism of your 3D game. So far, you've looked at how to build objects, move objects, put color on objects, and shade them. Now let's look at how to make these objects come to life with materials, lights, and lamps.

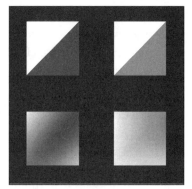

Figure 5.3 A quad drawn with four different shading and color settings.

OpenGL Lighting and the Real World

Let's take a quick step back and look at a simple explanation of how light works in the real world. Light sources, such as the sun or a light bulb, produce photons of many different wavelengths, covering the full spectrum of colors. Many of these photons strike objects, which absorb some of them and reflect others, depending on what the object is made of. The reflected photons may be reflected fairly uniformly if the object has a smooth surface, or they may be scattered if the surface is rough. The reflected photons may then strike other objects, and the process continues. We are able to see the world around us because some of these photons eventually enter our eyes.

Modeling the complex interaction of light photons and even a fairly small number of objects is computationally expensive. Although it is certainly possible to create a computer-based model of real-world lighting that very accurately models nature, the methods for doing so are too expensive to be used in games and other real-time applications. For this reason, OpenGL and other graphics libraries use simplified lighting models that trade accuracy for speed. Although the results do not match the real world exactly, they are close enough to be believable. If you would rather have more accurate lighting than that which OpenGL provides, you can do your own calculations either by passing pre-lit vertices to OpenGL or by using your own custom calculations through the use of a vertex program.

OpenGL calculates lighting by approximating the light into red, green, and blue components. This means that the color a light emits is determined by the amount of red, green, and blue light it emits. Light is further broken down into four different terms, which together attempt to simulate the major effects of real-world lighting:

- **Ambient light** simulates light bouncing between surfaces so many times that the source of the light is no longer apparent. This component is not affected by the position of either the light or the viewer.
- **Diffuse light** comes from a certain direction, but once it strikes a surface, it is reflected equally in all directions. The diffuse lighting component is affected by the position or direction of the light, but not the position of the viewer.
- **Specular light** is directional and reflected off a surface in a particular direction. Specularity is often referred to as shininess. The specular term is affected by the position of both the light and the eye.
- **Emissive light** is a cheap way to simulate objects that emit light. OpenGL does not actually use the emissive term to illuminate surrounding objects; it simply causes the emissive object to be more intensely lit.

The final results of lighting depend on several major factors, each of which is discussed in detail in this section. The factors are

1. One or more light sources. Each light source will have the ambient, diffuse, specular, and emissive terms listed above, each specified as RGBA values. In addition, they will either have a position or direction or have terms that affect attenuation and may have a limited area of effect (for example, a spotlight).

2. The orientation of surfaces in the scene. This is determined through the use of normals, which are associated with each vertex.

3. The material each object is made of. Material properties define what percentages of the RGBA values of each lighting term should be reflected. They also define how shiny the surface is.

4. The lighting model, which includes a global ambient term (independent of any light source), whether or not the position of the viewer has an effect on lighting calculations, and other parameters.

When the light strikes a surface, OpenGL uses the material of the surface to determine the percentage of red, green, and blue light that should be reflected by the surface. Even though they are approximations, the equations used by OpenGL can be computed rather quickly and produce reasonably good results.

Light Sources

It's time to turn on the lights and get on with the show! The first thing you need to do to take advantage of OpenGL's lighting is to enable it, which is done as follows:

```
glEnable(GL_LIGHTING);
```

This call causes the lighting equation to be applied to every vertex, but it does not actually turn on any lights. You need to explicitly turn on any lights you'll be using by calling glEnable():

```
glEnable(GL_LIGHTx);
```

x takes on a numeric value ranging from 0 to a maximum value that can vary across different OpenGL implementations. You're guaranteed to always have at least eight lights, though, so GL_LIGHT0 through GL_LIGHT7 are always valid. If you want to find out whether or not more than eight lights are available, you can pass GL_MAX_LIGHTS to glGet():

```
GLint maxLights;
glGetIntegerv(GL_MAX_LIGHTS, &maxLights);
```

Tip

Eight lights may not seem like a lot; you certainly have more than eight in your home. There are good reasons for keeping the maximum number of lights relatively small, though. First of all, lighting is fairly expensive. Even enabling three or four lights can have a noticeable impact on your frame rate. Second, OpenGL's lights are really needed only for *dynamic lighting*. Dynamic lighting is used when either the light source is moving or one or more of the objects being lit are moving. Only a small percentage of game objects fit into this category; everything else can use *static lighting*. Because static lighting doesn't change, it can be calculated in advance, usually by a 3D modeling program or other external tool, and encoded within the model vertex data. Finally, if you really need more than eight lights (or the implementation-defined maximum, if more than eight), it's unlikely that any one object needs to be lit by more than eight lights, so you can update each light as needed on a per-model basis.

Assigning Light Properties

Each light has several properties associated with it that define its position or direction in the world, the colors of its ambient, diffuse, specular, and emissive terms, and whether the light radiates in all directions or is limited to a spotlight-like cone. These properties are controlled through glLight():

```
glLight{fi}(GLenum light, GLenum pname, type param);
glLight{fi}v(GLenum light, GLenum pname, const type *params);
```

light identifies which light's properties you are modifying and uses GL_LIGHTx, as in the previous section. The next several sections cover each of the possible values of pname and the params associated with them, which are summarized in Table 5.1.

Table 5.1 glLight*() Parameters

Parameter	Meaning
GL_AMBIENT	Ambient intensity of light
GL_DIFFUSE	Diffuse intensity of light
GL_SPECULAR	Specular intensity of light
GL_POSITION	Position of light as vector (x, y, z, w)
GL_SPOT_DIRECTION	Direction of spotlight as vector (x, y, z)
GL_SPOT_EXPONENT	Spotlight exponent
GL_SPOT_CUTOFF	Spotlight cutoff angle
GL_CONSTANT_ATTENUATION	Constant attenuation value
GL_LINEAR_ATTENUATION	Linear attenuation value
GL_QUADRATIC_ATTENUATION	Quadratic attenuation value

Position and Direction

Each light can have either a position or a direction. Lights with a position are often called *positional* or *point lights*. *Directional lights* represent lights that are infinitely far away. There are no true directional lights in nature, since nothing is infinitely far away, but some light sources are far enough away that they can be treated as directional lights. The sun is an excellent example of this. The main advantage to using directional lights is that they simplify the lighting calculation. With positional lights, you have to calculate the direction vector between the light source and the surface. With directional lights, the direction is the same for every surface. Even so, the extra cost associated with positional lights is necessary and worth it for lights that truly are positional, which includes almost every light source you can actually see in your game. Use whichever form is appropriate for the light in question.

You set a light's position using GL_POSITION, passing a four-element vector of the form (x, y, z, w). *x*, *y*, and *z* represent either the position or direction. The *w* term is used to indicate whether this is a directional or positional light. If it is 0.0, it is directional. Otherwise, it is positional. The following code shows you how to set up a directional light pointing down the negative y axis.

```
GLfloat lightDir[] = { 0.0, 1.0, 0.0, 0.0 };
glLightfv(GL_LIGHT0, GL_POSITION, lightDir);
```

To set up a positional light located at (2, 4, –3), you'd use the following:

```
GLfloat lightPos[] = { 2.0, 4.0, -3.0, 1.0 };
glLightfv(GL_LIGHT0, GL_POSITION, lightDir);
```

The default position for all lights is (0, 0, 1, 0), which is directional, pointing down the negative z axis.

Whenever you make a call to glLight() with GL_POSITION, the position vector you specify is modified by the current modelview matrix, just as vertices are, and stored in eye coordinates. We'll discuss this in greater detail in "Moving and Rotating Lights" later on in this chapter.

Light Color

Light sources are composed of three of the lighting terms we discussed earlier: ambient, diffuse, and specular. To set each of these terms, you call glLight() with a pname of GL_AMBIENT, GL_DIFFUSE, or GL_SPECULAR, respectively, and an array of four values representing the RGBA color of the term. The following code sample shows an example of setting up a blue light with white specular.

```
GLfloat white[] = {1.0, 1.0, 1.0, 1.0};
GLfloat blue[] = {0.0, 0.0, 1.0, 1.0};

glLightfv(GL_LIGHT0, GL_AMBIENT, blue);
glLightfv(GL_LIGHT0, GL_DIFFUSE, blue);
glLightfv(GL_LIGHT0, GL_SPECULAR, white);
```

The default color for all terms for all lights is black (0.0, 0.0, 0.0, 1.0), with two exceptions: Light zero has a default diffuse and specular term of white (1.0, 1.0, 1.0, 1.0).

Attenuation

In the real world, the farther an object is away from a light, the less effect that light has on the object. For example, if you look at a street lamp at night (especially in the fog), you'll be able to see the intensity of the light dropping off away from the lamp. This phenomenon is known as *attenuation*. This effect is modeled in graphics by using an attenuation factor, which can reduce the effect of a light's contribution to the color of an object based on the distance to the object. The attenuation factor is calculated as follows:

$$\frac{1}{k_c + k_l d + k_q d^2}$$

d is the distance from the light to the vertex. k_c, k_l, and k_q are the constant, linear, and quadratic attenuation factors, respectively. These default to (1, 0, 0), which results in no attenuation. You can change them by passing GL_CONSTANT_ATTENUATION, GL_LINEAR_ATTENUATION, or

GL_QUADRATIC_ATTENUATION to glLight(). The following sample code sets the attenuation factors to (4, 1, 0.25).

```
glLightf(GL_LIGHT0, GL_CONSTANT_ATTENUATION, 4.0f);
glLightf(GL_LIGHT0, GL_LINEAR_ATTENUATION, 1.0f);
glLightf(GL_LIGHT0, GL_QUADRATIC_ATTENUATION, 0.25);
```

The attenuation factor affects only positional light sources. Attenuation doesn't make sense for directional lights because these light sources are at an infinite distance. It also does not affect the emission or global light values; it affects only diffuse, specular, and light-specific ambient light.

There is one drawback to using attenuation. Because the equation for calculating the attenuation at a certain distance requires a division and maybe some additions and multiplications, attenuation incurs an additional cost.

Spotlights

Normally, positional lights radiate light in all directions. However, you can limit the effect of the light to a specific cone. This is called a *spotlight*. To create a spotlight, you set up a positional light as you normally would and then set a few spotlight-specific parameters: the spotlight cutoff, the spotlight's direction, and the spotlight's focus.

Let's think about what a spotlight looks like for a moment. If you were looking at a spotlight in pure darkness, you would see that the light creates a cone of light in the direction that the spotlight is pointing. With OpenGL, you can define how wide this cone of light should be by specifying the angle between the edge of the cone and its axis with the GL_SPOT_CUTOFF parameter, as illustrated in Figure 5.4.

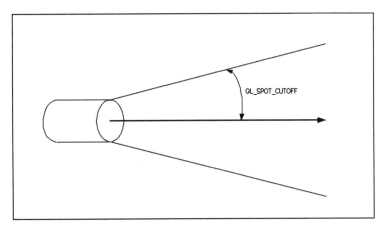

Figure 5.4 The GL_SPOT_CUTOFF parameter defines the angle between the edge of the light cone and the cone's axis.

A GL_SPOT_CUTOFF value of 10 degrees, for example, results in a spotlight with a cone of light that spreads out a total of 20 degrees in the spotlight's direction. OpenGL accepts only values between 0.0 and 90.0 for the GL_SPOT_CUTOFF parameter, except for the special value of 180.0 degrees, which is the default value, and which is used when you want to convert a spotlight back into a regular light.

If you want to specify a cone of light that spreads a total of 30.0 degrees, you use the glLight() function like this:

```
glLightf(GL_LIGHT0, GL_SPOT_CUTOFF, 15.0f);    // 30 degree light cone
```

The next thing you need to do is specify the direction that the spotlight is facing. This is done with GL_SPOT_DIRECTION, which takes a vector of the format (x, y, z). The default direction is (0.0, 0.0, −1.0), which points the spotlight down the negative z axis. You can specify your own direction for the spotlight by using glLight(), like so:

```
float spotlightDirection[] = { 0.0, -1.0, 0.0 };
glLightfv(GL_LIGHT0, GL_SPOT_DIRECTION, spotlightDirection);
```

These two lines will point the spotlight down the negative y axis.

And finally, you can specify the focus of the spotlight, which can be defined as the concentration of the spotlight in the center of the light cone. As you move away from the center of the cone, the light is attenuated until there is no more light at the edge of the cone. You can use GL_SPOT_EXPONENT to control this. A higher spot exponent results in a more focused light source that drops off quickly. The following line sets the GL_SPOT_EXPONENT parameter to a value of 10.0:

```
glLightf(GL_LIGHT0, GL_SPOT_EXPONENT, 10.0f);
```

The spot exponent can range from 0 to 128. A value of 0, which is the default, results in no attenuation, so the spotlight is evenly distributed.

Moving and Rotating Lights

What do you need to do to make a light move around? Think about how you would make any other object in the world move around. One way is to set the position of the object after you translate or rotate it. You can do the same thing with lights. When you call glLight*() to define the position or direction of a light, the information you specify is modified by the current modelview matrix.

For static lights (ones that don't move), you'd merely position the light after you set up the camera (by calling gluLookAt(), for example) but without applying any other transformations to the modelview matrix.

A common item in 3D games is a flashlight. Flashlights, or headlights, are simply another way to position and move a light around the world. This more general problem is having a light position stay fixed relative to the eye, or camera, position. To achieve this effect, you need to specify the light position before setting up the camera transformation. First you set the modelview matrix to the identity matrix, then you define your light position at the origin, and then you set up the camera transformation as you normally would:

```
glMatrixMode(GL_MODELVIEW);
glLoadIdentity();

// position the light at the origin
GLfloat lightPos(0.0, 0.0, 0.0, 1.0);
glLightfv(GL_LIGHT0, GL_POSITION, lightPos);

// set up the camera
gluLookAt(eye.x, eye.y, eye.z, at.x, at.y, at.z, up.x, up.y, up.z);
```

If you do not specify a direction, you get the effect of a lantern or lamp located at the position of the camera. If you want a headlight or flashlight effect, you need to set the light direction to point down the negative z axis. Because your light position is fixed, you only need to specify it once when you initialize your application, which will eliminate the need to redefine the light position every time you render a frame.

Materials

OpenGL approximates material properties based on the way the material reflects red, green, and blue light. For example, if you have a surface that is pure green, it reflects all the incoming green light while absorbing all the incoming red and blue light. If you were to place this surface under a pure red light, it would appear to be black. This is because the surface reflects only green light; when it is placed under red light, the surface absorbs the light and reflects nothing—so you see black. If you were to place the green surface under a white light, you would see a green surface because the green component of the white light is being reflected while the red and blue components are being absorbed. Lastly, if the surface were placed in green light, you would see a green surface, because the green light is being reflected back to you—the visual effect would be the same as placing it under a white light.

Materials have the same three color terms as light: ambient, diffuse, and specular. These properties determine how much light the material reflects. A material with high ambient, low diffuse, and low specular reflectance will reflect only ambient light sources well while absorbing the diffuse and specular light sources. A material with a high specular reflectance will appear shiny while absorbing the ambient and diffuse light sources. The values specified by the ambient and diffuse reflectances typically determine the color of the material and are usually identical in value. In order to make sure that specular highlights end up being the color of the light source's specular intensity, specular reflectance is normally set to be gray or white. A good way to think about this is to think of a bright white light pointing at a shiny blue surface. Although the surface would mostly show up as blue, the specular highlight on the surface would appear as white.

Defining Materials

Now that you have a general understanding of what materials are, let's look at how to use them. Actually, setting a material is fairly similar to creating a light source. The difference is the function that is used:

```
void glMaterial{if}(GLenum face, GLenum pname, TYPE param);
void glMaterial{if}v(GLenum face, GLenum pname, const TYPE *params);
```

The face parameter in these functions specifies how the material will be applied to the object's polygons, implying that materials can affect front and back faces differently. It can be one of three values: GL_FRONT, GL_BACK, or GL_FRONT_AND_BACK. Only the face you specify will be modified by the call to glMaterial(). Most often, you'll use the same values for both faces. The next parameter, pname, tells OpenGL which material properties are being set. This parameter can be any of the values listed in Table 5.2. The last parameter is either a scalar or array value as appropriate for the property being set. The meaning of each of these parameters will be explained in the following sections.

Table 5.2 glMaterial*() Parameters

Parameter	Meaning
GL_AMBIENT	Ambient color of material
GL_DIFFUSE	Diffuse color of material
GL_AMBIENT_AND_DIFFUSE	Ambient and diffuse color of material
GL_SPECULAR	Specular color of material
GL_SHININESS	Specular exponent
GL_EMISSION	Emissive color of material

Material Colors

The ambient, diffuse, and specular components specify how a material interacts with a light source and, thus, determine the color of the material. These values are set by passing GL_AMBIENT, GL_DIFFUSE, or GL_SPECULAR to glMaterial(). Frequently, the same values are used for both the ambient and diffuse term, so OpenGL allows you to use GL_AMBIENT_AND_DIFFUSE to specify them both together, saving you a function call.

If you want to set the ambient material color to red for the front and back of polygons, then you would do this:

```
float red[] = { 1.0f, 0.0f, 0.0f, 1.0f };
glMaterialfv(GL_FRONT_AND_BACK, GL_AMBIENT, red);
```

Similarly, to set both the ambient and diffuse materials to white for the front of polygons, you do this:

```
float white[] = { 1.0f, 1.0f, 1.0f, 1.0f };
glMaterialfv(GL_FRONT, GL_AMBIENT_AND_DIFFUSE, white);
```

Keep in mind that any polygons you draw after calling glMaterial() will be affected by the material settings until there is another call to glMaterial().

Shininess

Try looking at something metallic and something cloth under a direct light. You'll notice that the metallic object appears to be shiny, while the cloth object isn't. This is because light striking the cloth object is mostly scattered by the rough cloth surface, whereas light is directly reflecting off of the metal surface. Figure 5.5 illustrates this. The sphere on the left uses a material such as metal. The illusion of shininess is caused by the bright spot, known as a *specular highlight*. The sphere on the right uses a cloth-like material and thus appears dull.

The shininess of a material is simulated by the size of the specular highlight. This is controlled via a single scalar value, which you can set using GL_SHININESS. This value can range from 0 to 128, with values of 128 representing an extremely shiny material with a

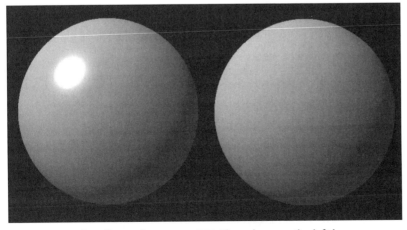

Figure 5.5 The effects of GL_SHININESS. The sphere on the left has a shininess of 128; the sphere on the right has a shininess of 0.

small specular highlight, and 0 representing a material that is not shiny at all with a very large specular highlight.

The following code was used to set up the shininess for the metallic sphere in Figure 5.5.

```
glMaterialf(GL_FRONT_AND_BACK, GL_SHININESS, 128);
```

Emissive Materials

The emissive property of materials allows you to cheaply simulate objects that emit light, such as an area light or anything that glows. It's important to note that the object won't really emit light, so it won't illuminate nearby objects. The emissive term is simply added to the other lighting components to cause the object to appear brighter than it normally would. The emissive term is set using GL_EMMISION, as follows:

```
// use a dark gray color
GLfloat emissiveColor[] = {0.3, 0.3, 0.3, 1.0};

// set the emissive term for both the front and back face
glMaterialfv(GL_FRONT_AND_BACK, GL_EMISSION, emmisiveColor);
```

This causes the object to appear slightly brighter than it otherwise would. By default, the emissive term is (0.0, 0.0, 0.0, 1.0);

Color Tracking

Another way to set material properties is by what is called *color tracking*. Color tracking allows you to set material properties with calls to the glColor() function instead of using glMaterial(), which often allows for more efficient code. You can use color tracking by passing the GL_COLOR_MATERIAL parameter to the glEnable() function. Then you use glColorMaterial() function to specify which material parameters will be affected by calls to glColor(). The prototype for glColorMaterial() is

```
void glColorMaterial(GLenum face, GLenum mode);
```

The face parameter can be GL_FRONT, GL_BACK, or GL_FRONT_AND_BACK. The mode parameter can be GL_AMBIENT, GL_DIFFUSE, GL_SPECULAR, GL_AMBIENT_AND_DIFFUSE, or GL_EMISSION. Most often, you will use the default values of GL_FRONT_AND_BACK and GL_AMBIENT_AND_DIFFUSE.

Here is some sample code to set the diffuse property of the fronts of polygons to track the current color:

```
glEnable(GL_COLOR_MATERIAL);                // enable color tracking
glColorMaterial(GL_FRONT, GL_DIFFUSE);      // front of polygons, diffuse material
glColor3f(1.0f, 0.0f, 0.0f);                // set color to red
glBegin(GL_TRIANGLES);
    // draw triangles
glEnd();
```

As you can see, color tracking is very simple to set up and use.

Normals

Normals are vectors that are perpendicular to a surface. They are important in lighting because they can be used to describe the orientation of that surface. When a light source is specified, it is either at some specific point in space or shines in a particular direction. When you draw an object, the light rays from this light source approach and strike the surfaces of the object at some angle. Using the angle between the incoming light ray and the normal, combined with lighting and material properties, you can calculate the color of the surface. This is illustrated in Figure 5.6.

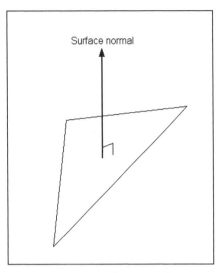

Figure 5.6 The surface normal.

In OpenGL, normals are specified on a per-vertex basis, rather than per-polygon. The advantage of this is that when you have only one normal per polygon, it assumes that all points on the polygon have the same orientation. This would be fine for flat surfaces, but often, a group of small triangles is used to represent curved surfaces. With vertex normals, each normal can have a slightly different orientation, allowing you to simulate curved surfaces. In addition, if you really want a flat surface, you can use the same normal values for each vertex, so this approach is much more flexible.

OpenGL maintains a current normal in its internal state. Any time you specify a vertex when lighting is enabled, the current normal is associated with it. You will typically modify the current normal once per vertex or once per polygon. To change the current normal, you use the following:

```
void glNormal3{bsifd}(TYPE nx, TYPE ny, TYPE nz);
void glNormal3{bsifd}v(const TYPE *v);
```

The values passed to glNormal() represent a three-dimensional vector specifying the normal. The following code specifies a triangle with a normal pointing in the positive y direction.

```
glBegin(GL_TRIANGLES);
   glNormal3f(0.0, 1.0, 0.0);
   glVertex3f(-3.0, 0.0, 2.0);
   glVertex3f(2.0, 0.0, 0.0);
   glVertex3f(-1.0, 0.0, -3.0);
glEnd();
```

As you can see, all three vertices use the same normal. If you wanted to specify a different normal for each vertex, it would look something like the following:

```
glBegin(GL_TRIANGLES);
    glNormal3f(-0.707f, 0.707f, 0.0);
    glVertex3f(-3.0, 0.0, 2.0);
    glNormal3f(0.707f, 0.707f, 0.0);
    glVertex3f(2.0, 0.0, 0.0);
    glNormal3f(0.0, 0.707f, -0.707f);
    glVertex3f(-1.0, 0.0, -3.0);
glEnd();
```

Calculating Normals

Finding the normal for a flat surface is easy. You just need to apply a little vector math—in particular, the cross product. As a reminder, given two 3D vectors A and B, the cross product will produce a vector that is perpendicular to both A and B. The equation for calculating the cross product is

$$A \times B = (A_yB_z-A_zB_y, \; A_zB_x-A_xB_z, \; A_xB_y-A_yB_x)$$

This means that you need two vectors, A and B, to calculate your surface's normal. Where can you find two vectors? For any triangle, you have three points, P1, P2, and P3. You can then define two vectors V1 and V2 that go from P1 to P2 and P1 to P3. respectively. Figure 5.7 illustrates this.

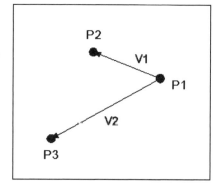

Now all you have to do is take the cross product of V1 and V2, and you get your normal. Remember that when taking the cross product, the order of the vectors matters. V1 × V2 points in the opposite direction as V2 × V1. When computing the surface normal this way, you have to be sure that you are consistent with the vertex winding. So, if you are using counterclockwise winding, with the vertices ordered P1, P2, and P3, the vectors should be constructed as follows:

Figure 5.7 You can define two vectors, V1 and V2, out of three points.

$$V1 = P2-P1$$

$$V2 = P3-P1$$

The normal would then be V1 × V2.

This method is very straightforward, but it works only for a flat shading model where all of the vertices in a polygon have the same normals. If you are using multiple polygons to simulate a complex rounded surface, then each normal will be slightly different to vary the lighting across the surface. One way to achieve this is to compute the surface normal for every triangle touching a vertex and then take the average of them, possibly weighting them based on the area of each triangle. This breaks down when the mesh contains hard edges. For instance, imagine applying this algorithm to a cube. You'd end up with the corners looking rounded, which isn't correct. There are solutions to this, such as using *smoothing groups*, which identify groups of triangles to be used together when averaging normals. Alternatively, you could set a threshold, such that any triangle with a surface normal more than x degrees different from the current normal is not used in the average.

The Unit Normal and Normalization

Many operations involving vectors can be simplified if you know the vectors have a length of 1. These are known as *unit vectors*. If you remember your vector math, given a vector A, you can find the length using the equation

$$|A| = sqrt(A_x^2 + A_y^2 + A_z^2)$$

Unit normals are simply unit vectors that are used as normals. OpenGL assumes that any normals you pass to it are already of unit length. If you use normals that are not of unit length, you'll get strange lighting results. Usually, the normals stored in standard 3D model formats will already be of unit length. If you're calculating the normals on the fly, you'll have to convert them to unit length yourself. This process is known as *normalization*. Doing so is simply a matter of dividing each component of the normal by the length of the normal.

An alternative to manually normalizing your normals is to tell OpenGL to do it for you by enabling GL_NORMALIZE, as follows:

```
glEnable(GL_NORMALIZE);
```

This approach isn't terribly efficient. Most of the time, you'll calculate your normals only once, so it makes more sense to normalize them at the same time, rather than having OpenGL repeatedly normalize them every frame.

The main reason OpenGL includes the ability to normalize normals is that the inverse transposition of the modelview matrix is applied to normals prior to lighting. If the modelview matrix includes scaling, the normals may not be of unit length after this operation. If you are using scaling, you should definitely enable GL_NORMALIZE to ensure that unit normals are being used in lighting.

If you are using only uniform scaling—in other words, if you are scaling equally in all three directions—then you can use a potentially cheaper alternative to GL_NORMALIZE. GL_RESCALE_NORMAL extracts the scale factor from the modelview matrix and uses it to rescale the normal after the matrix is applied. You enable GL_RESCALE_NORMAL as follows:

```
glEnable(GL_RESCALE_NORMAL);
```

Extension

Extension name: `EXT_rescale_normal`

Name string: `GL_EXT_rescale_normal`

Promoted to core: OpenGL 1.2

Tokens: `GL_RESCALE_NORMAL_EXT`

Unlike `GL_NORMALIZE`, which works with normals of any length, `GL_RESCALE_NORMAL` assumes that the original normals were of unit length.

The Lighting Model

In addition to individual lights and materials, there are additional global components of the lighting model that the final color values compute by lighting. These are

- A global ambient term.
- Whether the location of the viewer is local or infinite (affects specular calculation).
- Whether lighting is one sided or two sided.
- Whether the calculated specular color is stored separately from the other color values and passed on to the rasterization stage.

You control these elements of the lighting model with the `glLightModel()` function, which is defined as

```
void glLightModel{if}(GLenum pname, TYPE param);
void glLightModel{if}v(GLenum pname, const TYPE *param);
```

The first parameter of each of these functions, `pname`, specifies which lighting model property you are modifying. The second parameter is the value that you are setting for the lighting model property. It will be either a single value or an array of values, depending on the version of the function used. The `pname` parameter can be set to any of the values listed in Table 5.3.

Table 5.3 glLightModel*() Parameters

Parameter Name	Meaning
`GL_LIGHT_MODEL_AMBIENT`	Ambient intensity of the scene (RGBA); default value is (0.2, 0.2, 0.2, 1.0).
`GL_LIGHT_MODEL_LOCAL_VIEWER`	Viewpoint is local or infinite; default value is `GL_FALSE` (infinite).
`GL_LIGHT_MODEL_TWO_SIDE`	One-sided or two-sided lighting; default value is `GL_FALSE` (one-sided).
`GL_LIGHT_MODEL_COLOR_CONTROL`	Specular color is stored separate from ambient and diffuse color; default value is `GL_SINGLE_COLOR` (not separate).

Global Ambient Light

In addition to the ambient light contributed by individual light sources, there is a *global ambient light* that is present whether or not any light sources are enabled. This is used to model light for which the source can't be determined. This value is controlled with GL_LIGHT_MODEL_AMBIENT. The following code sets the global ambient light to a blue-green color, perhaps for an underwater scene.

```
float globalAmbient [] = { 0.0, 0.2, 0.3, 1.0 };  // dim blue-green light
glLightModelfv(GL_LIGHT_MODEL_AMBIENT, globalAmbient);
```

Local or Infinite Viewer

When calculating the specular term, the direction from the vertex being calculated and the viewpoint affect the intensity of the specular highlight. The GL_LIGHT_MODEL_LOCAL_VIEWER parameter lets you specify whether the viewpoint is local (i.e. based on the viewer's actual position in the world) or an infinite distance away. Having a local viewpoint will increase the realism of your scene but will be more expensive because the direction has to be calculated for each vertex. An infinite viewpoint (set with GL_FALSE) is used by default, but you can change it to a local viewpoint with this line:

```
glLightModeli(GL_LIGHT_MODEL_LOCAL_VIEWER, GL_TRUE);
```

The difference between a local and an infinite viewer is most evident at close range. Using a local viewer is more accurate but more expensive, so enable it only if you really need it.

Two-Sided Versus One-Sided Lighting

The next parameter you can specify is GL_LIGHT_MODEL_TWO_SIDE. This parameter deals with whether you want to calculate the lighting for the back of polygons correctly. For example, if you were to take an enclosed object such as a cube and cut it in half, you would see that the back, or inside, of the polygons is not correctly illuminated. If you want the inside of these polygons to be illuminated correctly, you set the GL_LIGHT_MODEL_TWO_SIDE parameter to GL_TRUE like so:

```
glLightModeli(GL_LIGHT_MODEL_TWO_SIDE, GL_TRUE);
```

When you set this parameter to GL_TRUE, you are telling OpenGL to reverse the surface normals for the back-face of polygons, which results in all of the polygons being illuminated correctly. With this extra calculation, two-sided lighting naturally performs a bit more slowly than one-sided lighting. Again, to switch back to one-sided lighting, set the value to GL_FALSE.

Separate Specular Color

The final light model property you can set is the GL_LIGHT_MODEL_COLOR_CONTROL property. This control was added because when you use lighting with texturing, the specular highlight tends to get washed out when the texture is applied. In other words, due to modulation (which you'll understand after reading Chapter 7, "Texture Mapping"), specular highlights that are very bright are reduced, causing the object to look less shiny than it should. When you enable separate specular color, rather than adding together the ambient, diffuse, specular, and emissive lighting values as it normally does, OpenGL creates two colors for each vertex of the object being lit: the primary color, consisting of the non-specular components, and a secondary color that containing the specular component. When texture mapping occurs, only the primary color is used. Then afterwards, the secondary specular color is added to the result. This leads to more visible specular highlights. You tell OpenGL to separate the specular components from the others with this line of code:

```
glLightModeli(GL_LIGHT_MODEL_COLOR_CONTROL, GL_SEPARATE_SPECULAR_COLOR);
```

If you want to combine the specular component with the other components, you call this function with the value GL_SINGLE_COLOR instead of GL_SEPARATE_SPECULAR_COLOR.

Extension

Extension name: EXT_separate_specular_color

Name string: GL_EXT_separate_specular_color

Promoted to core: OpenGL 1.2

Tokens: GL_LIGHT_MODEL_COLOR_CONTROL_EXT, GL_SINGLE_COLOR_EXT, GL_SEPARATE_SPECULAR_COLOR_EXT

Lighting in Action

The CD that accompanies this book contains a demo for this section in the lights folder. This demo, shown in Figure 5.8, uses three lights to illuminate a cube. The first light is white and is used as a flashlight, positioned on the viewer with a spotlight facing into the scene. The flashlight can be toggled on and off with the spacebar. The second light is a red light positioned statically to the right of the cube. The third light is green and rotates around the cube. The cube itself is composed of a bluish material. Each side of the cube uses normals that are exactly perpendicular to the surface.

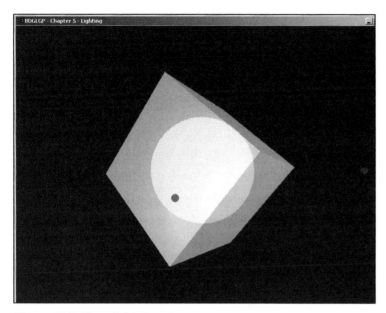

Figure 5.8 Three lights in action.

Blending

OpenGL allows you to blend incoming fragments with pixels already onscreen, which enables you to introduce effects such as transparency into your scenes. With transparency you can simulate water, windows, glass, and other objects in the world that you can see through.

Remember the alpha value we've been ignoring all this time? Well, now that we're talking about blending, you need to learn how to use it. When you enable blending, you are telling OpenGL to combine the color of the incoming primitive with the color that is already in the

---

Fragments

The term *fragment* may be new to you, but it will come up several times throughout this book, so now's a good time to discuss what fragments are.

As OpenGL processes the primitives you pass to it, during the rasterization stage, it breaks them into pixel-sized chunks called fragments. Sometimes the terms pixel and fragment are used interchangeably, but there is a subtle difference. *Pixel* usually refers to values that actually get written to the color buffer. A *fragment* is a piece of a primitive that may eventually become a pixel after it is depth tested, alpha tested, blended, combined with a texture, combined with other fragments, and so on.

frame buffer and store the result back in the frame buffer. Blending operations are typically specified with the RGB values representing the color and the alpha value representing the opacity, although other combinations are possible, as you'll see shortly. From now on, we will refer to the incoming fragment as the *source* and the currently stored pixel as the *destination*.

To enable blending in OpenGL, you call the glEnable() function with the GL_BLEND parameter. You then call glBlendFunc() to define the source and destination blend factors. Blend factors are values in the range 0.0 to 1.0 that are multiplied by the RGBA components of both the source and destination colors. The resulting colors are then combined (usually by adding them) and clamped to the range 0.0 to 1.0. glBlendFunc() looks like this:

```
void glBlendFunc(GLenum sfactor, GLenum dfactor);
```

sfactor is the source blend factor, and dfactor is the destination blend factor. Table 5.4 shows all of the blend factors that you can use. The default blend factors are GL_ONE for the

Table 5.4 Blending Factors

Factor	Description
GL_ZERO	Each component is multiplied by 0, effectively setting the color to black.
GL_ONE	Each component is multiplied by 1.0, leaving the color unchanged.
GL_SRC_COLOR	Each component is multiplied by the corresponding component
GL_ONE_MINUS_SRC_COLOR*	Each component is multiplied by (1.0 – source color).
GL_DST_COLOR**	Each component is multiplied by the corresponding component in the destination color.
GL_ONE_MINUS_DST_COLOR**	Each component is multiplied by (1.0 – destination color).
GL_SRC_ALPHA	Each component is multiplied by the source alpha value.
GL_ONE_MINUS_SRC_ALPHA	Each component is multiplied by (1.0 – source alpha value).
GL_DST_ALPHA	Each component is multiplied by the destination alpha value.
GL_ONE_MINUS_DST_ALPHA	Each component is multiplied by (1.0 – destination alpha value).
GL_CONSTANT_COLOR***	Each component is multiplied by the constant color set via glBlendColor().
GL_ONE_MINUS_CONSTANT_COLOR***	Each component is multiplied by (1– the constant color).
GL_CONSTANT_ALPHA***	Each component is multiplied by the alpha value of the constant color set via glBlendColor().
GL_ONE_MINUS_CONSTANT_ALPHA***	Each component is multiplied by (1– the alpha value of the constant color).
GL_SRC_ALPHA_SATURATE	Multiplies the source color by the minimum of the source and (1 – destination). The alpha value is not modified. Only valid as the source blend factor.

* Only available as a source blend factor in OpenGL 1.4 or later.

** Only available as a destination blend factor in OpenGL 1.4 or later.

*** Only available via the EXT_blend_color extension under Windows.

source and GL_ZERO for the destination, which produces the same results as not using blending at all.

Many different effects can be created with these blending factors, some of which are more useful in imaging than they are in games. To better understand how they work, let's look at a common application that *is* useful in games: transparency. Typically, transparency is implemented using GL_SRC_ALPHA for the source and GL_ONE_MINUS_SRC_ALPHA for the destination. You would set this up as follows:

```
glEnable(GL_BLEND);
glBlendFunc(GL_SRC_ALPHA, GL_ONE_MINUS_SRC_ALPHA);
```

To get an idea of how this works, let's say you first draw a red (1.0, 0.0, 0.0, 1.0) triangle, and then draw a blue (0.0, 0.0, 1.0, 0.5) triangle on top of it. With an alpha value of 0.5, the blue triangle is 50% transparent. So with the blend factors we've chosen, the source color will be multiplied by the source alpha (0.5), and the destination color will be multiplied by one minus the source alpha (1.0−0.5, or 0.5). The source and destination colors are thus calculated as follows:

```
source color = S_R*S_A, S_G*S_A, S_B*S_A, S_A*S_A = 0*0.5, 0*0.5, 1*0.5, 0.5*0.5 = 0, 0, 0.5, 0.25
destination color = D_R*(1-S_A), S_G*(1-S_A), S_B*(1-S_A), S_A*(1-S_A) = 1*0.5, 0*0.5, 0*0.5,
1*0.5 = 0.5, 0, 0, 0.5
```

These two values are then added together to obtain the final result of (0.5, 0, 0.5, 0.75). You can see the results of this in Figure 5.9.

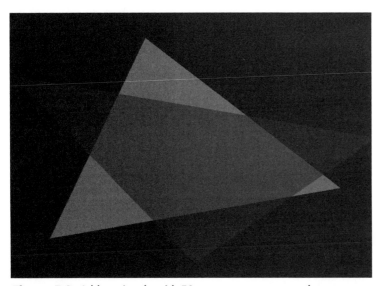

Figure 5.9 A blue triangle with 50 percent transparency drawn over a red triangle.

This simple example ignores one very important thing: You have to pay attention to the depth of objects and the order in which they are drawn when using transparency. When drawing without transparency, you can use the z-buffer normally to make sure that distant objects don't get drawn on top of closer objects, even if the closer objects were drawn first. You don't really have to care about the order objects get drawn in, at least as far as correct rendering is concerned (it can make a performance difference, though, as you'll see in Chapter 10, "Up Your Performance"). When you use transparency, however, the order matters. If you draw a transparent object that appears in front of an opaque object, you should be able to see the opaque object. But if you draw the transparent object first, the opaque object will fail the depth test and never be drawn.

The most common way of handling this problem is to draw all of your opaque objects first. This will fix part of the problem, but a hidden problem remains. What if the distant object is also transparent? If it's drawn after the closer transparent object, it'll still fail the depth test and not be drawn. There are two common ways of resolving this issue.

The first method is to disable depth buffer writes (effectively making the z-buffer read-only) when drawing transparent objects. The objects are still tested against the z-buffer, so opaque objects can still occlude them, but the transparent objects themselves don't update the z-buffer, so they can never occlude anything else. You disable depth buffer writes by passing GL_FALSE to glDepthMask(), as follows:

```
glDepthMask(GL_FALSE);
```

You turn depth buffer writes back on with GL_TRUE.

Unfortunately, this works only with some blending operations, such as simple additive blending (for example, using a source and destination blend factor of GL_SOURCE_ALPHA, GL_ONE, respectively). In most blending operations, the order the fragments are drawn in makes a difference.

The second method of dealing with transparent object order is to sort them based on distance from the viewer and draw the more distant objects first. This can generally be done fairly quickly and cheaply, since the number of transparent objects in your world will usually be fairly small.

Which method you use depends on the effect you are trying to attain. The visual results of the two approaches are not the same, so they are not interchangeable.

Separate Blend Functions

Extension

Extension name: EXT_blend_func_separate

Name string: GL_ EXT_blend_func_separate

Promoted to core: OpenGL 1.4

Function names: glBlendFuncSeparateEXT

Tokens: GL_DST_RGB_EXT, GL_SRC_RGB_EXT, GL_DST_ALPHA_EXT, GL_SRC_ALPHA_EXT

When using glBlendFunc(), the same factor is used for both the RGB and alpha components. This isn't always desirable. For instance, the alpha channel is sometimes used to store information that has nothing to do with blending. In that case, you wouldn't want blending to modify the alpha channel at all. To address this need, OpenGL includes an alternative to glBlendFunc() called glBlendFuncSeparate():

void glBlendFuncSeparate(GLenum sfactorRGB, GLenum dfactorRGB, GLenum sfactorAlpha, GLenum dfactorAlpha);

sfactorRGB_and dfactorRGB are used to set the blend factor for the source and destination RGB blend factors, respectively. sfactorAlpha and dfactorAlpha are used for the source and destination alpha blend factors. Any of the values in Table 5.4 can be used for these parameters. Suppose you wanted to set up blending to use transparency but keep the alpha value intact. You'd use something like the following:

glBlendFuncSeparate(GL_SRC_ALPHA, GL_ONE_MINUS_SRC_ALPHA, GL_ONE, GL_ZERO);

That's all there is to it.

The Blend Equation

Extension

Extension name: EXT_blend_minmax

Name string: GL_EXT_blend_minmax

Promoted to core: Optional in OpenGL 1.2, required in 1.4

Function names: glBlendEquationEXT

Tokens: GL_FUNC_ADD_EXT, GL_MIN_EXT, GL_MAX_EXT, GL_BLEND_EQUATION_EXT

Extension

Extension name: EXT_blend_subtract

Name string: GL_EXT_blend_subtract

Promoted to core: Optional in OpenGL 1.2, required in 1.4

Tokens: GL_FUNC_SUBTRACT_EXT, GL_FUNC_REVERSE_SUBTRACT_EXT

By default, after multiplying the source color by the source blend factor and the destination color by the destination blend factor, the two values are then added together to get the final color. What if you wanted to subtract one from the other? The operation performed on the two values is called the *blend equation*, and OpenGL allows you to change it. You do this through the use of glBlendEquation():

```
void glBlendEquation(GLenum mode);
```

The values accepted by the mode parameter and the meanings associated with them are listed in Table 5.5. C_S and C_D represent the source and destination colors, S and D represent the source and destination blend factors, and C represents the final color.

Table 5.5 Blending Equations

Equation	Description
GL_FUNC_ADD	$C = (C_S * S) + (C_D * D)$. Result is clamped to [0, 1]. This is the default.
GL_FUNC_SUBTRACT	$C = (C_S * S) - (C_D * D)$. Result is clamped to [0, 1].
GL_FUNC_REVERSE_SUBTRACT	$C = (C_D * D) - (C_S * S)$. Result is clamped to [0, 1].
GL_MIN	$C = \min(C_S, C_D)$.
GL_MAX	$C = \max(C_S, C_D)$.

Note

When using the min or max blend equations, you'll notice that the blend factor isn't being used at all. The comparison is done using the original values and is done component-wise. So if the source color is (0.2, 0.6, 0.1, 1.0) and the destination color is (1.0, 0.3, 0.5, 0.7), min results in a final color of (0.2, 0.3, 0.1, 0.7) and max results in a final color of (1.0, 0.6, 0.5, 1.0).

You can determine the current blend equation by calling glGet() with GL_BLEND_EQUATION.

Constant Blend Color

Extension

Extension name: EXT_blend_color

Name string: GL_EXT_blend_color

Promoted to core: Optional in OpenGL 1.2, required in 1.4

Function names: glBlendColorEXT

Tokens: GL_CONSTANT_COLOR_EXT, GL_ONE_MINUS_CONSTANT_COLOR_EXT, GL_CONSTANT_ALPHA_EXT, GL_ONE_MINUS_CONSTANT_ALPHA_EXT, GL_BLEND_COLOR_EXT

Several of the blend factors listed in Table 5.4 make use of a constant blend color, so it's time to explain what that is. The constant blend color simply allows you to set a constant value to use as a weighting factor. You might use this to blend an image that does not contain alpha values, rather than adding an alpha channel yourself with identical values for every pixel.

You set the constant color using glBlendColor():

```
void glBlendColor(GLclampf red, GLclampf green, GLclampf blue, GLclampf alpha);
```

The red, green, blue, and alpha parameters should be self-explanatory by now. The GLclampf type is used to indicate floating point values that OpenGL internally clamps to the range 0.0 to 1.0.

The default constant blending color is (0, 0, 0, 0). You can determine the current constant blend color by passing GL_BLEND_COLOR to glGet().

Disk Blender

To demonstrate some of the many blending combinations, we've included the Disk Blender demo on the CD (found in the folder blender for this chapter). Disk Blender is drawn with a black background with an alpha of 1.0. A green disk with some transparency is drawn first, without blending. Then a semi-transparent red disk is drawn on top of it with blending enabled. By pressing the S, D, and E keys, you can cycle through all of the available source factors, destination factors, and blend equations. A screenshot of the demo is shown in Figure 5.10.

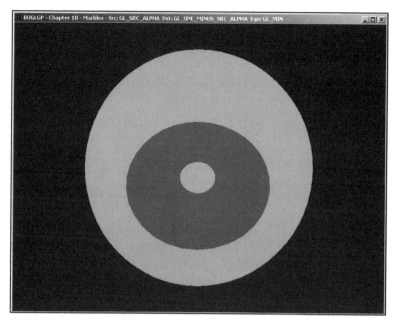

Figure 5.10 Disks drawn with `GL_MIN`.

Fog

Adding fog to your world has more than one purpose. Besides trying to give the player the impression of actual fog, it can be used to obscure objects in the distance and have them gradually become clearer as the player gets closer. This is beneficial both in allowing you to reduce the amount of geometry on the scene at one time (and thus improving performance) and in preventing objects from suddenly popping into view as they enter the view frustum.

There is more than one way to implement fog, but because OpenGL provides native support for it, that's the approach we'll cover here.

OpenGL Fog

OpenGL's built-in fog support works by blending each pixel with the color of the fog, using a *blend factor* dependent on the distance from the viewer, the density of the fog, and the currently selected fog mode. The blend factor is used in the following equation:

$$\text{color}_{out} = \text{blendFactor} \times \text{color}_{in} + (1 - \text{blendFactor})\text{color}_{fog}$$

The details of how the blend factor is determined will be covered momentarily.

To use fog, you first have to enable it, which, not surprisingly, is done with a call to glEnable():

glEnable(GL_FOG);

Fog has several states associated with it, which you can control with calls to glFog():

glFog{fi}(GLenum pname, type param);
glFog{fi}v(GLenum pname, const type *params);

The accepted values of pname and their meanings are listed in Table 5.6.

Table 5.6 Fog Parameters

Parameter	Description
GL_FOG_MODE	This parameter can be GL_LINEAR, GL_EXP, or GL_EXP2, specifying which equation is used to calculate the blend factor. The default is GL_EXP.
GL_FOG_DENSITY	This parameter is a single value representing the density of the fog, used in the equations below. The value must be positive, and the default is 1.0.
GL_FOG_START	This parameter is a single value defining the start, or near distance, used in the fog equations.
GL_FOG_END	This parameter is a single value defining the end, or far distance, used in the fog equations.
GL_FOG_INDEX	This parameter specifies the color index to use for fog when using 8-bit color.
GL_FOG_COLOR	This specifies the color to be used for fog. It is an array—and so requires one of the array versions of glFog()—representing color values. The default fog color is black.
GL_FOG_COORD_SRC	This parameter can be either GL_FOG_COORD or GL_FRAGMENT_DEPTH. This controls what OpenGL uses as the depth term in the blend factor equations.

The mode determines which of three equations is used to determine the blending factor. The three equations are defined as follows:

GL_LINEAR: blendFactor = (end-depth) / (end-start)
GL_EXP: blendFactor = $e^{(-density \times depth)}$
GL_EXP2: blendFactor = $e^{(-density \times depth)^2}$

The density, end, and start terms in these equations correspond to the values of GL_FOG_DENSITY, GL_FOG_START, and GL_FOG_END, respectively. Note that the start and end values matter only if you are using GL_LINEAR mode, and density matters only when you are using GL_EXP or GL_EXP2 mode.

Fog Coordinates

Extension

Extension name: EXT_fog_coord

Name string: GL_EXT_fog_coord

Promoted to core: OpenGL 1.4

Function names: glFogCoord{fd}EXT, glFogCoord{fd}vEXT

Tokens: GL_FOG_COORD_SRC_EXT, GL_FOG_COORD_EXT, GL_FRAGMENT_DEPTH_EXT

The depth term in the above equations by default represents the distance between the viewer and the fragment, which OpenGL calculates automatically. However, you may want to use something other than the depth in the blend factor equations. For example, you might want to have the amount of fog vary based on how far above sea level the polygon is, for a ground fog type of effect. This can be accomplished through the use of *fog coordinates,* which allow you to directly control the depth term used in the blend factor equations. Fog coordinates consist of a single-valued parameter that can be specified per vertex. This value is then interpolated across the polygon's surface. You set the fog coordinates via the following APIs:

```
glFogCoord{fd}(type coord);
glFogCoord{fd}v(type *coord);
```

In addition to specifying the fog coordinates, you also have to tell OpenGL to use them instead of the computed depth value. You do this as follows:

```
glFogi(GL_FOG_COORD_SRC, GL_FOG_COORD);
```

To switch back to using the computed depth value, use the following:

```
glFogi(GL_FOG_COORD_SRC, GL_FRAGMENT_DEPTH);
```

Tip

Prior to OpenGL 1.5, GL_FOG_COORD_SRC and GL_FOG_COORD were named GL_FOG_COORDINATE_SOURCE and GL_FOG_COORDINATE, respectively.

And that's it! As you can see, adding OpenGL's native fog to your game is really quite simple. You may have to tweak the parameters to get it to look the way you want, but with a little experimentation, you should soon be quite comfortable with OpenGL's fog support.

Note

You can turn fog on and off at will, so that you can have it affect only some of the objects in your scene.

Fog in Action

The Fog demo included on the CD shows several different examples of using fog, as you'll see in Figure 5.11. The demo renders a simple heightmap-based terrain, with a large quad drawn in blue at ground level to represent water. The top left panel shows the terrain without any fog, the top right panel uses GL_LINEAR fog, the bottom left panel shows GL_EXP fog with a fairly low density, and the bottom right panel shows GL_EXP2 fog with fog coordinates set so that the fog is thicker where the terrain is lower (near the water), thinning quickly at higher elevations.

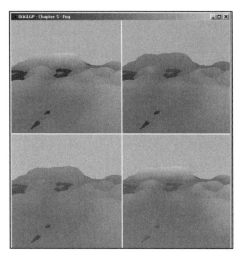

Figure 5.11 Simple terrain with several fog modes.

Summary

This chapter covered a lot of new information! You've learned about how OpenGL handles colors, how shading works, what the elements of the lighting model are and how to control them, how to use blending, and how to take advantage of OpenGL's built-in fog. You now have the knowledge to create fairly complex OpenGL applications, even including simple games.

What You Have Learned

- Colors are represented with red, green, blue, and alpha components. You can specify the current primary and secondary colors using glColor() and glSecondaryColor().

- You can choose whether to use flat or smooth (a.k.a. Gouraud) shading using glShadeModel().

- OpenGL's lighting model is composed of ambient, diffuse, specular, and emissive terms.

- You can control lights using glLight() and define materials for your objects using glMaterial().

- You can move and rotate lights just like any other object in OpenGL. When you call glLight() to define the position or direction of a light, the information you specify is manipulated by the current modelview matrix.

- All objects in your world should have normals associated with them to ensure that lighting works as expected. You specify normals using glNormal().

- OpenGL's lighting model includes several global components that you can control via glLightModel().

- Through blending, you have a great deal of control over how incoming fragments are combined with values already in the color buffer. In addition to being able to define a wide range of blending factors with glBlendFunc() or glBlendFuncSeparate(), you can specify a constant blend factor with glBlendColor() and change the blend equation with glBlendEquation().

- You can use fog to allow objects to fade to a background color as they get farther away, allowing you to use a smaller view frustum and avoid having objects pop into view as they enter the frustum. Fog is controlled through glFog(). You can take greater control over how fog is calculated by using fog coordinates.

Review Questions

1. What is the minimum number of lights that an OpenGL implementation must provide, and how can you find out how many are available?

2. How do you set the fog color?

3. How can you change the specular color of a material using glColor()?

4. (True or False) The space reserved for storing separate specular color is wasted when you're not using lighting.

5. Which of the following blend factors can be used only for the source color?

   a. GL_CONSTANT_COLOR

   b. GL_ALPHA_SATURATE

   c. GL_DST_ALPHA

   d. GL_SRC_COLOR

On Your Own

1. Modify the lights demo as follows:
   - Add an emissive property to the cube's material.
   - Add attenuation to the red light.
   - Make the beam of the flashlight more focused.
   - Add a transparent sphere surrounding the cube, and set the material for it using color tracking.

CHAPTER 6

Bitmaps and Images with OpenGL

Now it's time to break off from the world of 3D graphics and take a look at the world of *raster graphics*, which are graphics in which an image is composed of an array of pixels arranged in rows and columns. In this chapter you'll be looking specifically at how you can use OpenGL to perform various functions on bitmaps and images. We'll also be discussing how to load and save the Targa (.tga) image file format.

In this chapter you will discover:

- How to use OpenGL bitmaps
- OpenGL pixel functions
- How to load and save the Targa image format

The OpenGL Bitmap

The term *bitmap* in the context of OpenGL is defined as a rectangular array of pixels, where one bit of information (a 0 or 1) is stored about each pixel. Bitmaps are composed of a mask encapsulated in a two-dimensional array representing a rectangular area of the window. You can use them for rendering font characters, 2D objects in a game, or as elements in a GUI. For instance, take a 16 × 16 bitmap and divide it into a 16 × 16 grid as shown in Figure 6.1. When you draw this bitmap, every bit in the two-dimensional array that is set to 1 corresponds to a pixel in the current raster color on the screen. If the bit is not set, then nothing is drawn. Given this behavior, the 16×16 bitmap shown in Figure 6.1 will be drawn by OpenGL as the letter X. You will see an example in this chapter that does something similar.

Actually specifying the bitmap data is slightly different than that shown in Figure 6.1. Bitmap data is always stored in 8-bit multiple chunks, although the width of the actual bitmap does not need to be a multiple of 8. OpenGL draws the bitmap by starting at the lower-left corner and working its way up, row by row. Therefore, you need to specify your bitmap's data in this order, so that the bottom of the bitmap is the first set of data and the top of the bitmap is the last set of data.

Figure 6.1 A 16×16 bitmap divided into a grid of zeroes and ones.

An example of bitmap data for Figure 6.1 in code looks like:

```
unsigned char bitmapX[] = {
                    0x80, 0x01,    // 1000 0000 0000 0001
                    0x40, 0x02,    // 0100 0000 0000 0010
                    0x20, 0x04,    // 0010 0000 0000 0100
                    0x10, 0x08,    // 0001 0000 0000 1000
                    0x08, 0x10,    // 0000 1000 0001 0000
                    0x04, 0x20,    // 0000 0100 0010 0000
                    0x02, 0x40,    // 0000 0010 0100 0000
                    0x01, 0x80,    // 0000 0001 1000 0000
                    0x01, 0x80,    // 0000 0001 1000 0000
                    0x02, 0x40,    // 0000 0010 0100 0000
                    0x04, 0x20,    // 0000 0100 0010 0000
                    0x08, 0x10,    // 0000 1000 0001 0000
                    0x10, 0x08,    // 0001 0000 0000 1000
                    0x20, 0x04,    // 0010 0000 0000 0100
                    0x40, 0x02,    // 0100 0000 0000 0010
                    0x80, 0x01,    // 1000 0000 0000 0001
};
```

Positioning the Bitmap

The glRasterPos() function specifies the current raster coordinates for drawing bitmaps in the OpenGL window. The coordinates sent to the function define the bottom-left corner of the bitmap's rectangle. For example, passing the coordinates (30, 10) to the `glRasterPos()` function draws the next bitmap with its bottom-left corner at (30, 10). The function is defined as:

```
void glRasterPos{234}{sifd}(TYPE x, TYPE y, TYPE z, TYPE w);
void glRasterPos{234}{sifd}v(TYPE *coords);
```

To set the current raster coordinates to (30, 10), you would call the function like this:

```
glRasterPos2i(30, 10);
```

When setting the raster coordinates in a 3D viewport and projection matrix, the coordinates sent to `glRasterPos()` are converted to 2D screen coordinates, in much the same way as when you use the `glVertex()` function. If you want to specify the raster coordinates in screen coordinates, then you need to set up a 2D viewport and projection matrix with the width and height of the viewport equal to the width and height of the OpenGL window. You can use the `glOrtho()` or `gluOrtho2D()` function to define a 2D viewport with orthographic projection, as described in Chapter 4, "Transformations and Matrices."

For error checking, you can find out if the raster position you passed to the function is a valid raster position by passing the `GL_CURRENT_RASTER_POSITION_VALID` parameter to the `glGetBooleanv()` function. If the function returns `GL_FALSE`, the position is invalid.

If you would like to obtain the current raster position, you can simply pass `GL_CURRENT_RASTER_POSITION` as the first parameter to `glGetFloatv()`. The second parameter should be a pointer to an array of floats to hold the (x, y, z, w) values that are returned by `glGetFloatv()`.

Drawing the Bitmap

After you set the current raster position, you can draw your bitmap with the `glBitmap()` function, which is defined as:

```
void glBitmap(GLsizei width, GLsizei height, GLfloat xOrigin, GLfloat yOrigin,
              GLfloat xIncrement, GLfloat yIncrement, const GLubyte *bitmap);
```

This function draws a bitmap with the specified width and height in pixels at the coordinates (xOrigin, yOrigin) relative to the current raster position. The values xIncrement and yIncrement specify step increments that are added to the current raster position after the bitmap is drawn. Figure 6.2 shows how a bitmap is affected by these parameters.

Note

One drawback to OpenGL bitmaps is that you can neither rotate nor zoom them, but you can do these operations with pixel maps, or images, as you will soon see.

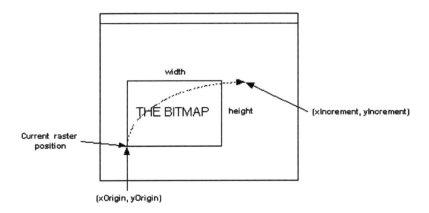

Figure 6.2 The effect of glBitmap() parameters when drawing a bitmap.

An OpenGL Bitmap Example

The following example displays 50 16 × 16 bitmaps in random locations during each frame. The end result is a window with 50 letter *A*s popping up and disappearing randomly. You will find the RandomABitmap example on the CD under Chapter 6.

First, you need to define your character *A* as an array of bit information. This is declared at the top of the CGfxOpenGL.cpp file:

```
unsigned char letterA[] = {
                    0xC0, 0x03,
                    0xC0, 0x03,
                    0xC0, 0x03,
                    0xC0, 0x03,
                    0xC0, 0x03,
                    0xDF, 0xFB,
                    0x7F, 0xFE,
                    0x60, 0x06,
                    0x30, 0x0C,
                    0x30, 0x0C,
                    0x18, 0x18,
                    0x18, 0x18,
                    0x0C, 0x30,
                    0x0C, 0x30,
                    0x07, 0xE0,
                    0x07, 0xE0
};
```

The bits specified for the `letterA` array translate to the bitmap you see in Figure 6.3. Keep in mind that you are storing the bitmap upside down, but the bitmap will be rendered correctly as shown in Figure 6.3.

First, take a look at the `Prepare()` method:

```
void CGfxOpenGL::Prepare(float dt)
{
    // store the random (x, y) position of the bitmaps
    for (int idx = 0; idx < MAX_BITMAPS; idx++)
    {
        m_bitmaps[idx].xPos = rand() % m_windowWidth;
        m_bitmaps[idx].yPos = rand() % m_windowHeight;
    }
}
```

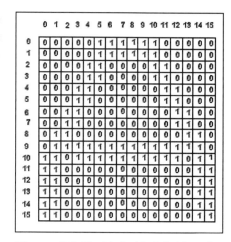

Figure 6.3 The bit-by-bit definition of our letter *A*.

The `Prepare()` method stores the random (x, y) positions of the bitmaps, based on the window size, in an array of `BitmapStructs`, which is a struct defined in `CGfxOpenGL.h` that stores the bitmap x and y positions.

Next is the `Render()` method:

```
void CGfxOpenGL::Render()
{
    // clear screen and depth buffer
    glClear(GL_COLOR_BUFFER_BIT | GL_DEPTH_BUFFER_BIT);

    // load the identity matrix (clear to default position and orientation)
    glLoadIdentity();

    // single byte alignment
    glPixelStorei(GL_UNPACK_ALIGNMENT, 1);

    // color white
    glColor3f(1.0, 1.0, 1.0);

    // render all the bitmaps
    for (int idx = 0; idx < MAX_BITMAPS; idx++)
    {
        glRasterPos2i(m_bitmaps[idx].xPos, m_bitmaps[idx].yPos);
        glBitmap(16, 16, 0.0, 0.0, 0.0, 0.0, letterA);
    }
}
```

The Render() method is fairly straightforward. Of particular interest is the loop at the bottom of the method that sets the current raster position and renders the bitmap. The glRasterPos2i() function positions each bitmap, and the glBitmap() function draws them. Very simple, isn't it?

Note

For the moment, disregard our use of the glPixelStorei() function in the Render() method of the RandomABitmap example. This function is explained in more detail in the "Managing Pixel Storage" section of this chapter.

Also notice that we are setting up the orthographic projection to match the viewport in the SetupPerspective() method. This allows us to use the window raster coordinates, as explained earlier in this chapter.

The end result, or a single frame anyway, is shown in Figure 6.4.

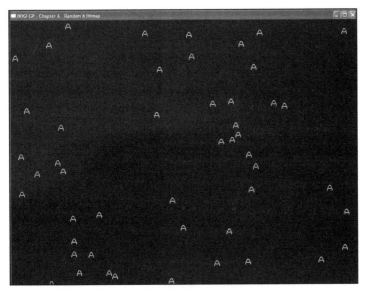

Figure 6.4 A screenshot of the RandomABitmap example.

Using Images

In most cases, when performing raster graphics, developers use *images* instead of the OpenGL bitmap. While similar to bitmaps, images differ in the amount of information they hold for each pixel. For instance, an OpenGL bitmap holds a single bit of information per pixel indicating whether that pixel is on (1) or off (0), but an image might hold anywhere from 8 bits of information per pixel to 32 bits per pixel. Such a bit resolution can tell OpenGL specifically which color a pixel should be by specifying the individual red, green, blue, and alpha components of the color.

With OpenGL you can manipulate images pixel by pixel. Sometimes images are referred to as *pixel maps* or *pixmaps*. Although we will be talking about displaying images on the screen in this chapter, you can also use images as textures on polygons. We discuss texture mapping in Chapter 7, "Texture Mapping."

Drawing Image Data

Assuming you already have your image data loaded into memory, you use the OpenGL function glDrawPixels() to display the image data at a specified raster position in the window. Like glBitmap(), you specify the current raster position by using the glRasterPos() function. The glDrawPixels() function looks like this:

```
void glDrawPixels(GLsizei width, GLsizei height, GLenum format, GLenum type,
                  const GLvoid *pixels);
```

You specify the width and height of the image along with the pixel format and pixel type of the pixel data that is passed to the function. The pixel format can be any of the formats listed in Table 6.1. An example image format would be one with red, green, and blue values for each pixel, in which case you'll want to use the GL_RGB pixel format. This tells OpenGL that the pixel data being passed to glDrawPixels() is coming as a set of red, green, and blue pixel components, where the size of each component is defined by the pixel type.

Table 6.1 Pixel Formats

Pixel Format	Description
GL_ALPHA	Alpha color pixels
GL_BGR*	Pixel components ordered as blue, green, red
GL_BGRA*	Pixel components ordered as blue, green, red, alpha
GL_BLUE	Blue pixels
GL_COLOR_INDEX	Color-index pixels
GL_GREEN	Green pixels
GL_RED	Red pixels
GL_RGB	Pixel components ordered as red, green, blue
GL_RGBA	Pixel components ordered as red, green, blue, alpha
GL_LUMINANCE	Single luminance component in pixel
GL_LUMINANCE_ALPHA	Luminance component followed by alpha component
GL_STENCIL_INDEX	Single stencil index
GL_DEPTH_COMPONENT	Single depth component

* Only available via the EXT_bgra extension under Windows.

The pixel type can be any of the types listed in Table 6.2. This parameter defines the data type of each pixel element.

Table 6.2 Pixel Types

Pixel Type	Description
GL_BITMAP	A single bit (0 or 1)
GL_BYTE	Signed 8-bit integer (1 byte)
GL_UNSIGNED_BYTE	Unsigned 8-bit integer (1 byte)
GL_SHORT	Signed 16-bit integer (2 bytes)
GL_UNSIGNED_SHORT	Unsigned 16-bit integer (2 bytes)
GL_INT	Signed 32-bit integer (4 bytes)
GL_UNSIGNED_INT	Unsigned 32-bit integer (4 bytes)
GL_FLOAT	Single-precision floating point (4 bytes)
GL_UNSIGNED_BYTE_3_3_2	Packed into unsigned 8-bit integer. R3, G3, B2
GL_UNSIGNED_BYTE_2_3_3_REV	Packed into unsigned 8-bit integer. B2, G3, R3
GL_UNSIGNED_SHORT_5_6_5	Packed into unsigned 16-bit integer. R5, G6, B5
GL_UNSIGNED_SHORT_5_6_5_REV	Packed into unsigned 16-bit integer. B5, G6, R5
GL_UNSIGNED_SHORT_4_4_4_4	Packed into unsigned 16-bit integer. R4, G4, B4, A4
GL_UNSIGNED_SHORT_4_4_4_4_REV	Packed into unsigned 16-bit integer. A4, B4, G4, R4
GL_UNSIGNED_SHORT_5_5_5_1	Packed into unsigned 16-bit integer. R5, G5, B5, A1
GL_UNSIGNED_SHORT_1_5_5_5_REV	Packed into unsigned 16-bit integer. A1, B5, G5, R5
GL_UNSIGNED_INT_8_8_8_8	Packed into unsigned 32-bit integer. R8, G8, B8, A8
GL_UNSIGNED_INT_8_8_8_8_REV	Packed into unsigned 32-bit integer. A8, B8, G8, R8
GL_UNSIGNED_INT_10_10_10_2	Packed into unsigned 32-bit integer. R10, G10, B10, A2
GL_UNSIGNED_INT_2_10_10_10_REV	Packed into unsigned 32-bit integer. A2, B10, G10, R10

* Packed formats available only via the EXT_packed_pixels extension under Windows.

Here is some code that uses the glDrawPixels() function to draw an RGB image of a width and height imageWidth and imageHeight, respectively, that you have stored in the variable imageData at the screen position (300, 300):

```
unsigned char *imageData;
int             imageWidth, imageHeight;
...
glRasterPos2i(300, 300);
glDrawPixels(imageWidth, imageHeight, GL_RGB, GL_UNSIGNED_BYTE, imageData);
```

We specify the GL_RGB pixel format because the image is an RGB image, and we specify the GL_UNSIGNED_BYTE pixel type since the imageData is stored as an array of unsigned char.

Reading from the Screen

There may be times when you want to read the pixels already on the screen so that you can save them to disk as an image file or can manipulate them in memory (i.e., for special effects). OpenGL allows you to do this by providing you with the glReadPixels() function, which is defined as:

```
void glReadPixels(GLint x, GLint y, GLsizei width, GLsizei height, GLenum format,
                  GLenum type, GLvoid *pixels);
```

glReadPixels() has essentially the same parameters as glDrawPixels() with the addition of an (x, y) coordinate. The (x, y) coordinate specifies the lower-left corner of the rectangle with dimensions defined by width and height that will be read from the screen and stored in the pixels parameter. The format and type parameters work the same way as glDrawPixels() and can be the same values as those defined in Tables 6.1 and 6.2.

As an example, if you want to read the top half of your OpenGL window into an RGB buffer, you might use the glReadPixels() function like this:

```
void *imageData;
int  screenWidth, screenHeight;
...
glReadPixels(0, screenHeight/2, screenWidth, screenHeight/2, GL_RGB, GL_UNSIGNED_BYTE,
             imageData);
```

Note

Since glReadPixels() is reading from the frame buffer and hence across the AGP bus of the video card, the execution time of the function can be relatively long. Try not to use glReadPixels() often, if at all, during runtime.

Copying Screen Data

Aside from reading and writing to the screen, OpenGL also lets you copy pixels from one portion of the screen to another with the glCopyPixels() function, defined as:

```
glCopyPixels(GLint x, GLiny y, GLsizei width, GLsizei height, GLenum buffer);
```

This function copies the pixel data in the frame buffer with a rectangle whose lower-left corner is at the screen location (x, y) and has dimensions defined by width and height to the current raster position. The buffer parameter can be any of the values defined in Table 6.3.

Table 6.3 glCopyPixels() Buffer Values

Buffer Value	Description
GL_COLOR	Copy from the color buffer
GL_DEPTH	Copy from the depth buffer
GL_STENCIL	Copy from the stencil buffer

One application of glCopyPixels() is for magnifying a portion of the OpenGL window, such as for a magnifying glass or a sniper gun scope. By copying a specific portion of the screen and using the next function we are going to describe, glPixelZoom(), you can zoom in on areas of your 3D world.

Magnification, Reduction, and Flipping

OpenGL lets you enlarge, reduce, and flip images with the glPixelZoom() function, defined as:

```
void glPixelZoom(GLfloat xZoom, GLfloat yZoom);
```

By default, the xZoom and yZoom parameters are 1.0, meaning the pixel zoom is set to normal viewing mode. Values greater than 0.0 and less than 1.0 reduce the image; values greater than 1.0 magnify the image. This behavior is similar to the glScale() function mentioned in Chapter 4. When you specify negative values, the image is reflected about the current raster position. Here are some examples, with their effects in comments:

```
glPixelZoom(-1.0f, -1.0f);      // flip image horizontally and vertically
glPixelZoom(0.5f, 0.5f);        // reduce image to half its original size
glPixelZoom(5.0f, 5.0f);        // magnify the image 5 times in all directions
```

Managing Pixel Storage

Images stored in memory are composed of between one and four chunks of data, stored as array elements. These data chunks can refer to anything from the color index or luminance to the red, green, blue, and alpha components for each pixel. Pixel formats, or the arrangements of pixel data, help to determine the number and order of elements stored for each pixel.

Often you may find that you need to take into account such issues as displaying a subimage that corresponds to a subrectangle of the image data array, or maybe different machines with different byte-ordering conventions, or even simply machines that are more efficient at moving data to and from the frame buffer if the data is aligned on certain byte boundaries (i.e., 2, 4, 8-byte boundaries). When you run into these issues, you will likely want to control the byte alignment. Luckily, OpenGL provides a function to do just that: glPixelStore().

```
void glPixelStore{if}(GLenum pname, TYPE param);
```

Managing pixel storage can get to be rather complicated, so we are going to keep the discussion simple. If you would like more information on pixel storage, be sure to follow up the topic with one of the references provided in Appendix B, "Further Reading."

The pname parameter can take many different values, but the ones we're interested in are GL_PACK_ALIGNMENT and GL_UNPACK_ALIGNMENT. Each of these can have param values of 1, 2, 4, or 8. When you specify the GL_PACK_ALIGNMENT parameter, you are telling OpenGL how your pixels are aligned in each row when passing memory to OpenGL via glDrawPixels() or the glTexImage*() APIs you'll learn about in Chapter 8, "OpenGL Extensions." When you specify the GL_UNPACK_ALIGNMENT parameter, you are telling OpenGL how to align memory for pixels at the start of each pixel row when it passes data to your program through functions such as glReadPixels(). By default, both parameters are equal to 4, indicating a 4-byte alignment.

As an example, the following line of code tells OpenGL that there is no byte alignment when unpacking the image data from memory, since the alignment is set to 1:

```
glPixelStorei(GL_UNPACK_ALIGNMENT, 1);
```

Targa Image Files

Now we're going to talk about the Targa image format. This format is fairly simple to work with, and it brings the added bonus of an alpha channel. With the addition of the alpha channel, you can incorporate transparency and other cool special effects when you load Targa files and use them as bitmaps or textures.

The Targa File Format

In its most simple form, the Targa format is divided into two parts: the header and the data. The header consists of fields that are arranged in this structure:

```
struct tgaheader_t
{
    unsigned char   idLength;
    unsigned char   colorMapType;
    unsigned char   imageTypeCode;
    unsigned char   colorMapSpec[5];
    unsigned short  xOrigin;
    unsigned short  yOrigin;
    unsigned short  width;
    unsigned short  height;
    unsigned char   bpp;
    unsigned char   imageDesc;
};
```

Note

We are providing only a basic overview of the Targa image format. If you would like a more detailed explanation of the Targa format, visit the Web site Wotsit's File Formats at http://www.wotsit.org. Wotsit's is a repository for many file formats ranging from images to 3D models.

While loading, you will want to use the header information as a guide for loading the rest of the image. You should pay particular attention to the idLength, imageTypeCode, width, height, bpp, and imageDesc fields.

The idLength field corresponds to the length of an identifier string located after the header. Unless you are interested in reading the identifier, after loading the header you will probably want to skip over the number of bytes indicated by the idLength field.

The imageTypeCode tells you the type of Targa image you are loading. By looking at the type, you can determine the type of loading algorithm you should use. For instance, you will use different loading algorithms for loading an uncompressed Targa as compared to a compressed Targa. The possible values for imageTypeCode are listed in Table 6.4.

Table 6.4 Targa File Types

Code	Description
0	No image data
1	Uncompressed color-mapped image
2	Uncompressed RGB(A) true-color image
3	Uncompressed grayscale (black-and-white) image
9	Run-length encoded (compressed) color-mapped image
10	Run-length encoded (compressed) RGB(A) true-color image
11	Run-length encoded (compressed) grayscale image

The width, height, and bpp fields specify the width, height, and number of bits per pixel of the image, respectively.

Finally, the imageDesc field is a byte whose bits specify the number of attribute bits per pixel and the order in which pixel data is transferred from a file to the screen. For our purposes, we are interested in bits 4 and 5, which tell us how the image data needs to be rendered to the screen. Because we are using OpenGL and glDrawPixels(), we need to make sure the image data is stored in memory "upside-down." Given the possible values for bits 4 and 5 in Table 6.5, this means that you need to make sure the image origin is located at the bottom left. Some image tools like to save the Targa with the origin at the top left, which means you need to flip the Targa image data vertically to get a proper rendering with glDrawPixels().

Table 6.5 Targa Image Origin

First Pixel Destination	Bit 5	Bit 4	Hex Value
Bottom left	0	0	0x00
Bottom right	0	1	0x10
Top left	1	0	0x20
Top right	1	1	0x30

Loading Targa Files

On the CD you will find an example under the Chapter 6 folder entitled LoadTGA. In the example we have created a basic Targa loading class that will load 24-bit and 32-bit compressed and uncompressed Targa images. If you look at the CTargaImage.h header file, you will see the following class definition:

```
class CTargaImage
{
private:
    unsigned char   m_colorDepth;
    unsigned char   m_imageDataType;
    unsigned char   m_imageDataFormat;
    unsigned char  *m_pImageData;
    unsigned short m_width;
    unsigned short m_height;
    unsigned long   m_imageSize;

    // swap the red and blue components in the image data
    void SwapRedBlue();

public:
    CTargaImage();
    virtual ~CTargaImage();

    // loading and unloading
    bool Load(const char *filename);
    void Release();

    // flips image vertically
    bool FlipVertical();
```

```
        unsigned short GetWidth() { return m_width; }
        unsigned short GetHeight() { return m_height; }
        unsigned char  GetImageFormat() { return m_imageDataFormat; }

        // converts RGB format to RGBA format and vice versa
        bool ConvertRGBAToRGB();
        bool ConvertRGBToRGBA(unsigned char alphaValue);

        // returns the current image data
        unsigned char *GetImage() { return m_pImageData; }
};
```

As you can see, the CTargaImage class provides mechanisms for loading the Targa image, flipping it vertically, and converting the image data from one format to another. For space reasons, we are not going to show you the code for this class here in the book (look on the CD!), but we will show you how to use it with OpenGL to draw images on the screen.

In the CGfxOpenGL class Init() method, you will find code that creates two CTargaImage objects and loads the images. The two images included with this example are opengl_logo.tga, which is a compressed RGB image, and opengl_logo_un.tga, which is an uncompressed RGB image. Here is the code from the Init() method.

```
m_tga = new CTargaImage;
m_tgaUncompress = new CTargaImage;

if (!m_tga->Load("opengl_logo.tga"))
    return false;

if (!m_tgaUncompress->Load("opengl_logo_un.tga"))
    return false;
```

We draw the bitmaps in the Render() method using glDrawPixels(). Because we know that the images are 24-bit Targas, we use GL_RGB for the format parameter of glDrawPixels(). If we were using 32-bit images, we would specify GL_RGBA for the format parameter. Here is the code from the Render() method:

```
// draw compressed TGA at top of window
glRasterPos2i(250,400);
glDrawPixels(m_tga->GetWidth(), m_tga->GetHeight(), GL_RGB,
            GL_UNSIGNED_BYTE, m_tga->GetImage());

// draw uncompressed TGA at bottom of window
glRasterPos2i(250,100);
glDrawPixels(m_tgaUncompress->GetWidth(), m_tgaUncompress->GetHeight(), GL_RGB,
            GL_UNSIGNED_BYTE, m_tgaUncompress->GetImage());
```

Figure 6.5 A screenshot of the LoadTGA example. The top image is a compressed TGA. The bottom image is an uncompressed TGA.

Figure 6.5 is a screenshot of the LoadTGA example.

Summary

In this chapter, you learned about the OpenGL bitmap and how to load and draw Targa images. For OpenGL bitmaps, you learned how to set the current OpenGL raster position and draw the bitmaps. For images, or pixel maps, you learned how to draw the images, read image data from the screen, copy screen data from one region to another, and perform magnification, reduction, and flipping on image data. You also learned how to manage pixel storage.

What You Have Learned

- The term *bitmap* in the context of OpenGL is defined as a rectangular array of pixels, where one bit of information is stored about each pixel.
- When you draw a bitmap, every bit in the two-dimensional array that is set to 1 will correspond to a pixel in the current raster color on the screen. If a bit is set to 0, nothing is drawn.
- The `glRasterPos()` function specifies the current raster coordinates for drawing bitmaps in the OpenGL window. The coordinates sent to the function define the bottom-left corner of the bitmap's rectangle.

- If you want to specify the raster coordinates in screen coordinates, you need to set up a 2D viewport and projection matrix with the width and height of the viewport equal to the width and height of the OpenGL window.

- After you set the current raster position, you can draw your bitmap with the glBitmap() function.

- Sometimes you might want to read the pixels already on the screen so you can save them to disk as an image file or so you can manipulate them for special effects. You can do this with the OpenGL function glReadPixels().

- The glCopyPixels() function lets you copy pixel data from one portion of the screen to another.

- OpenGL also allows you to enlarge, reduce, and flip images with the glPixelZoom() function.

- The Targa image file format is a simple-to-use and understand image file that you can load into memory and display using OpenGL.

Review Questions

1. Write code to position and draw a 16 × 16 bitmap stored in the variable m_bitmapData at the location (150, 75) on the screen.

2. What function do you use to draw image (pixel map) data on the screen?

3. What function allows you to copy image data?

4. Write the line of code to double the size of image rasterizing operations.

On Your Own

1. Write a function to randomly place and display 100 8 × 8 bitmaps on the screen, given the following prototype:

```
void DrawRandomBitmaps(unsigned char *bitmapData);
```

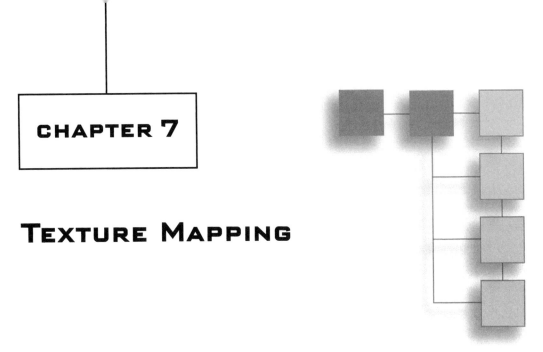

CHAPTER 7

TEXTURE MAPPING

Nothing we have discussed so far can bring as much realism to a 3D scene as texture mapping. Lighting comes close, but it doesn't have near the impact that a simple texture map can have when applied to a set of polygons. Instead of having multicolored polygons that seemingly come together to form a recognizable object, you can create photo-realistic worlds with texture mapping that can almost persuade the user that the objects being viewed on the screen are real. In this chapter, you'll learn how to achieve a high level of realism through an introduction to the concept and implementation of texture-mapping techniques in OpenGL.

In this chapter, you will learn about the following:

- The basics of texture mapping
- Texture coordinates
- Texture objects and texture binding
- Texture specification with 1D, 2D, 3D, and cube map textures
- Texture filtering
- Mipmaps and automatic mipmap generation
- Texture parameters, wrap modes, and level of detail
- Texture environments and texture functions

An Overview of Texture Mapping

In a nutshell, *texture mapping* allows you to attach images to polygons in order to provide more realistic graphics. As an example, you could apply an image of the front of this book to a rectangular polygon; the polygon would appear to be a visual representation of the front of the book. Another example would be to take a map of Earth and texture-map it onto a sphere. You then have a 3D visual representation of Earth. Nowadays, texture maps are used everywhere in 3D graphics. In fact, texture mapping is the first step in bringing the realism and authenticity desired in today's games.

Texture maps are composed of rectangular arrays of data; each element of these arrays is called a *texel*. Although they are rectangular arrays of data, texture maps can be mapped to non-rectangular objects, such as spheres, cylinders, and other 3D object models.

Usually, developers use the two-dimensional texture in their graphics; however, using one-dimensional and three-dimensional textures is not unheard of. The two-dimensional texture has both a width and a height, as seen in Figure 7.1. One-dimensional textures have a width and a height equal to only 1 pixel. Three-dimensional textures have a width, height, and depth and are sometimes called *volume textures*. In this chapter, we will be primarily concerned with two-dimensional textures.

When you map a texture onto a polygon, the texture will be transformed as the polygon is transformed. In other words, if you rotate the Earth example we just talked about, the texture map will rotate with the sphere and give the effect of a rotating Earth. Similarly, if you use translation and another rotation to rotate the Earth image around a sphere we'll call Sun, then the texture map will stay on the Earth sphere as it rotates around the Sun sphere. You can think of texture mapping as applying a sort of skin to a 3D object or polygon. You can move this skin around the object, stretch it, or shrink it, but no matter what, the skin, or texture map, stays with the polygons to which you apply it.

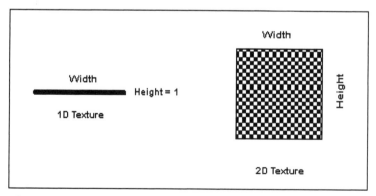

Figure 7.1 One-, two-, and three-dimensional textures.

Texture Coordinates

Before we cover how to specify textures with OpenGL, we first need to discuss how textures are mapped on to polygons through the use of texture coordinates.

Texture coordinates are used to determine exactly how to apply a texture map to a polygon. The lower-left corner of a texture is given the coordinates (0, 0), while the upper-right corner of a texture is given the coordinates (1, 1). Texture coordinates for 2D textures are given the notation (s, t), where s and t are equal to a value from 0 to 1. 1D, 3D, and 4D texture coordinates are given the notation (s), (s, t, r), and (s, t, r, q), respectively. Figure 7.2 illustrates 2D texture coordinate values for each vertex of a polygon.

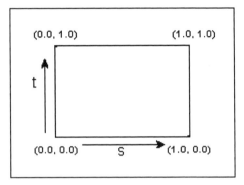

Figure 7.2 Texture coordinate values on a polygon.

Note

While texture coordinates are often in the range [0,1], there are some exceptions. Sometimes you will want to use texture coordinates with a value greater than 1 for *repeating* and *clamping*, which will be discussed in the "Texture Wrap Modes" section, later in this chapter.

Granted, you are not required to specify one texture per polygon. In fact, you can have a texture span as many polygons as you want, as long as you properly specify the texture coordinates across each polygon. As an example, we could divide the polygon shown in Figure 7.2 into two triangles by creating a diagonal for the polygon. If we kept the texture coordinates the same as the single polygon, then the two triangles would be textured exactly the same as the texture polygon. The lower-left corner of the texture is mapped to the lower-left corner of the left triangle, and the upper-right corner of the texture is mapped to the upper-right corner of the right triangle.

Texture coordinates are specified with the glTexCoord() function. This function specifies the current homogeneous texture coordinates (s, t, r, q) and is defined as:

```
void glTexCoord{1234}{sifd}(TYPE coords);
void glTexCoord{1234}{sifd}v(TYPE coords);
```

As an example, you would set a 2D texture coordinate to (0.2, 0.4) by executing the following line of code:

```
glTexCoord2f(0.2, 0.4);
```

Every time you specify a vertex with glVertex(), the current texture coordinate is applied to it. Typically, you'll change the texture coordinate every time you specify a new vertex. Given this functionality, the following code sets the 2D texture coordinates for a polygon:

```
glBegin(GL_POLYGON);
    glTexCoord2f(0.0f, 0.0f); glVertex3f(-0.5f, 0.5f, 0.5f);    // lower left
    glTexCoord2f(1.0f, 0.0f); glVertex3f(0.5f, 0.5f, 0.5f);     // lower right
    glTexCoord2f(1.0f, 1.0f); glVertex3f(0.5f, 0.5f, -0.5f);    // upper right
    glTexCoord2f(0.0f, 1.0f); glVertex3f(-0.5f, 0.5f, -0.5f);   // upper left
glEnd();
```

Now that you know how texture coordinates are assigned, it's time to learn how to actually create textures.

Using the Texture Map

As mentioned, textures are images that you apply to a polygon or set of polygons. These images can be loaded from an image file, or you can generate them procedurally in memory. Once you have your texture image data loaded into memory, to use it you need to specify it as a texture map with OpenGL. You accomplish this by first generating what is called a *texture object*, which you then use to store information about the texture, including the image data and how it is to be applied.

Note

You can use textures without using texture objects, in which case all texturing operations are applied using an internal default texture object. For anything beyond trivial examples, though, there are performance penalties involved with this, since you'll have to constantly reload the texture image data if you are using more than one texture. It's better to start using texture objects from the beginning.

Texturing is enabled and disabled through the use of the glEnable() and glDisable() functions discussed in Chapter 3, "OpenGL States and Primitives." The constants GL_TEXTURE_1D, GL_TEXTURE_2D, GL_TEXTURE_3D, and GL_TEXTURE_CUBE_MAP may be passed as the parameter to these functions to enabled or disable one-, two-, three-dimensional, or cube map texturing, respectively.

Now let's look at how you use texture objects.

Texture Objects

Texture objects are internal data structures that hold texture data and parameters. You never gain direct access to them, but instead you track them with a unique unsigned integer that acts as a handle. Each texture object has state associated with it that is unique to that texture. To facilitate the requirement of using unique identifiers for texture objects, OpenGL provides the glGenTextures() function:

```
void glGenTextures(GLsizei n, GLuint *textures);
```

This function returns n previously unused texture object identifiers in the textures array. The identifiers that are returned to you are marked as "used" by glGenTextures(), so each time you use the function, it returns unique texture object identifiers to you. Even though the identifier is marked as used, the texture object itself is not truly in use by OpenGL (meaning it acquires state and parameters) until it is first bound. Here's an example use of glGenTextures():

```
unsigned int textureObjects[3];

glGenTextures(3, textureObjects);
```

Texture Binding

The first time you bind a texture object, it acquires a new set of states with initial values, which you can then modify to suit your needs. The glBindTexture() function performs the binding operation:

```
void glBindTexture(GLenum target, GLuint texture);
```

target must be the desired target of the bound texture: GL_TEXTURE_1D, GL_TEXTURE_2D, GL_TEXTURE_3D, or GL_TEXTURE_CUBE_MAP. Each of these targets corresponds to a type of texture in OpenGL, which we will discuss in the section on "Specifying Textures." texture is simply the identifier for the texture object you want to bind.

A bound texture object remains bound to a target until it is deleted or another texture object is bound to the target. Calls to glBindTexture() after the initial call have the effect of selecting the texture object and binding it to the indicated target. In this way, texture objects can be used to store information about a texture that can quickly be retrieved and used by binding it.

While a texture object is bound to a target, OpenGL texturing operations on that target affect the texture object. Any texture queries to the target return state values from the bound texture object. For example, examine this code:

```
glBindTexture(GL_TEXTURE_2D, textureObjects[0]);

// all texture operations using GL_TEXTURE_2D now affect textureObjects[0]

glBindTexture(GL_TEXTURE_3D, textureObjects[1]);
```

```
// all texture operations using GL_TEXTURE_2D target still affect textureObjects[0]
// all texture operations using GL_TEXTURE_3D target now affect textureObjects[1]

glBindTexture(GL_TEXTURE_2D, textureObjects[2]);
// all texture operations using GL_TEXTURE_3D target still affect textureObjects[1]
// all texture operations using GL_TEXTURE_2D target now affect textureObjects[2]
```

Note

> You can have multiple texture targets enabled at one time, but when rendering starts, only the target with the highest dimensionality will be used, with GL_TEXTURE_CUBE_MAP being the highest and GL_TEXTURE_1D being the lowest.

Deleting Texture Objects

When you create texture objects, OpenGL internally allocates memory to store them, so to prevent resource leaks you need to delete them when you're done using them. Texture objects are deleted by calling the glDeleteTextures() function:

```
void glDeleteTextures(GLsizei n, GLuint *textures);
```

The textures parameter contains *n* texture object identifiers to be deleted. After a texture object has been deleted, it has no contents and is considered unused. Any texture objects in the textures array that are already unused are simply ignored, as is the value zero.

Resident Textures

All video cards have a limited amount of memory in which they can store texture data. When this limit is exceeded, some textures (usually the least recently used ones) need to be moved to system memory. This can cause a performance hit when they are used again, since they must then be moved back into video memory. You can determine whether a texture object is currently a part of the working set of texture objects in video memory by calling the function glAreTexturesResident():

```
GLboolean glAreTexturesResident(GLsizei n, GLuint *textures, GLboolean *residences);
```

This function returns GL_TRUE if all of the texture objects identified in textures are resident in the working set or if the OpenGL implementation does not concern itself with a working set. If at least one of the textures identified in textures is not resident in the working set, the function returns GL_FALSE with the status of each texture object in residences. GL_FALSE is also returned if any unused texture objects are identified in textures.

Texture Priority

You can guide OpenGL in determining which texture objects should be resident (if it supports a texture object working set) by specifying a priority for each texture object with the glPrioritizeTextures() function:

```
void glPrioritizeTextures(GLsizei n, GLuint *textures, GLclampf *priorities);
```

This function sets the priorities of *n* texture objects identified in the *textures* parameter to the values specified in *priorities*. Priority values are clamped to the range [0, 1] before being assigned to a texture object. A value of zero indicates the lowest priority, and one indicates the highest priority. glPrioritizeTextures() ignores specified texture objects that are unused or zero.

Specifying Textures

OpenGL provides three main functions for specifying a texture: glTexImage1D(), glTexImage2D(), and glTexImage3D(). Each function corresponds to the dimensionality of the texture. For instance, if the texture is a 3D texture, then you use glTexImage3D() to specify the 3D texture. OpenGL provides cube map texture functionality through special parameters to the glTexImage2D() function. Let's take a look at these functions.

2D Textures

The glTexImage2D() function is defined as:

```
void glTexImage2D(GLenum target, GLint level, GLint internalFormat, GLsizei width,
                  GLsizei height, GLint border, GLenum format, GLenum type,
                  const GLvoid* texels);
```

The target parameter must be either GL_TEXTURE_2D for a two-dimensional texture or GL_PROXY_TEXTURE_2D for a two-dimensional proxy texture. We won't be discussing proxy textures in detail, but they're used to test whether a given texture size and format can be supported without actually creating the texture data. Several other values may be used for the target parameter, as we will discuss with cube maps.

The level parameter specifies the level of detail of the texture map and is used when working with mipmaps. The base texture image has a level of detail of 0, which is what we will use until we discuss mipmaps.

The internalFormat parameter describes the base internal format of how the texture is stored in video memory and can be any of the values listed in Table 7.1. For backward compatibility with OpenGL 1.0, internalFormat may also take on a value of 1, 2, 3, or 4, which are respectively equivalent to the constants LUMINANCE, LUMINANCE_ALPHA, RGB, and RGBA.

Table 7.1 Texture Internal Formats

Format	Description
GL_ALPHA	Alpha values
GL_DEPTH_COMPONENT*	Depth values
GL_LUMINANCE	Grayscale values
GL_LUMINANCE_ALPHA	Grayscale and alpha values
GL_INTENSITY	Intensity values
GL_RGB	Red, green, and blue values
GL_RGBA	Red, green, blue, and alpha values

* Available only via the ARB_depth_texture extension under Windows

Tip

In addition to the values listed in Table 7.1, OpenGL provides several values that allow you to specify both the format and the desired number of bits per channel. These have the general form of *formatN* or formatN_ALPHAM, where format is one of the values in Table 7.1, N is the number of bits per channel, and *M* is the number of alpha bits. There are over 30 of these values, many of which aren't particularly useful, so we won't list them all here. The two most important ones are GL_RGB8 and GL_RGBA8, which request 8 bits for each color channel. By default, some graphics cards use less than 8 bits per channel for RGBA textures, so using GL_RGBA8 or GL_RGB8 instead of GL_RGBA or GL_RGB can result in noticeably higher texture quality. Note that these values are treated as requests; OpenGL may ignore the requested number of bits per channel.

The width and height parameters define the width and height of the texture map. Like glDrawPixels(), the width and height of a texture map must be equal to a power of 2 (though there are some extensions that allow you to get around this limitation), but the texture does not have to be square.

The border parameter indicates whether there is a border around the texture. This parameter is equal to either 0, for no border, or 1, for drawing a border in the color set with the GL_TEXTURE_BORDER_COLOR parameter (see the section "Texture Parameters" later in the chapter).

The format parameter is used to define the format of the image data contained in the texels array. It can be equal to any of the values listed in Table 7.2.

The type parameter defines the data type of the texture image data. This parameter can be any of the values listed in Table 7.3.

Looking at Table 7.3, you may notice the section of "packed" data formats and wonder how these work. Let's use the type GL_UNSIGNED_BYTE_3_3_2 as an example. In this case, all of the red, green, and blue (and alpha if available) components are packed into a single

Table 7.2 Texture Pixel Formats

Format	Description
GL_COLOR_INDEX	Color index values
GL_DEPTH_COMPONENT*	Depth values
GL_RED	Red pixel values (R)
GL_GREEN	Green pixel values (G)
GL_BLUE	Blue pixel values (B)
GL_ALPHA	Alpha values (A)
GL_RGB	Red, green, and blue values (RGB)
GL_RGBA	Red, green, blue, and alpha values (RGBA)
GL_BGR**	Blue, green, and red values (BGR)
GL_BGRA**	Blue, green, red, and alpha values (BGRA)
GL_LUMINANCE	Grayscale values (luminance)
GL_LUMINANCE_ALPHA	Grayscale values with alpha (luminance with alpha)

* Available only via the ARB_depth_texture extension under Windows
* Available only the EXT_bgra extension under Windows

Table 7.3 Texture Data Types

Format	Description
GL_BITMAP	A single bit (0 or 1)
GL_BYTE	Signed 8-bit integer (1 byte)
GL_UNSIGNED_BYTE	Unsigned 8-bit integer (1 byte)
GL_SHORT	Signed 16-bit integer (2 bytes)
GL_UNSIGNED_SHORT	Unsigned 16-bit integer (2 bytes)
GL_INT	Signed 32-bit integer (4 bytes)
GL_UNSIGNED_INT	Unsigned 32-bit integer (4 bytes)
GL_FLOAT	Single-precision floating point (4 bytes)
GL_UNSIGNED_BYTE_3_3_2	Packed into unsigned 8-bit integer. R3, G3, B2
GL_UNSIGNED_BYTE_2_3_3_REV	Packed into unsigned 8-bit integer. B2, G3, R3
GL_UNSIGNED_SHORT_5_6_5	Packed into unsigned 16-bit integer. R5, G6, B5
GL_UNSIGNED_SHORT_5_6_5_REV	Packed into unsigned 16-bit integer. B5, G6, R5
GL_UNSIGNED_SHORT_4_4_4_4	Packed into unsigned 16-bit integer. R4, G4, B4, A4
GL_UNSIGNED_SHORT_4_4_4_4_REV	Packed into unsigned 16-bit integer. A4, B4, G4, R4
GL_UNSIGNED_SHORT_5_5_5_1	Packed into unsigned 16-bit integer. R5, G5, B5, A1
GL_UNSIGNED_SHORT_1_5_5_5_REV	Packed into unsigned 16-bit integer. A1, B5, G5, R5
GL_UNSIGNED_INT_8_8_8_8	Packed into unsigned 32-bit integer. R8, G8, B8, A8
GL_UNSIGNED_INT_8_8_8_8_REV	Packed into unsigned 32-bit integer. A8, B8, G8, R8
GL_UNSIGNED_INT_10_10_10_2	Packed into unsigned 32-bit integer. R10, G10, B10, A2
GL_UNSIGNED_INT_2_10_10_10_REV	Packed into unsigned 32-bit integer. A2, B10, G10, R10

Packed pixel formats are available only via the ARB_packed_pixels extension under Windows

unsigned byte. Since this example packed format is defined as 3_3_2, the components available are red, green, and blue. If we were looking at a different data type format, say GL_UNSIGNED_SHORT_4_4_4_4, we would be dealing with red, green, blue, and alpha components packed into an unsigned short.

Normally components are packed with the first component in the most significant bits of the data type, with the successive components occupying the less significant bits. So for data type GL_UNSIGNED_BYTE_3_3_2 with the format being GL_RGB, the red component is in bits 5–7, the green component is in bits 2–4, and the blue component is in bits 0–1. Figure 7.3 illustrates the bit layout of the type GL_UNSIGNED_BYTE_3_3_2.

You may also notice that there is a GL_UNSIGNED_BYTE_2_3_3_REV listed in Table 7.3. In fact, all of the packed data types have a complementary type whose token name ends in _REV. With these types, the component packing order reverses from least to most significant bit locations. This means that the red component is in bits 0–2, the green component bits 3–5, and the blue component bits 6–7. Figure 7.4 illustrates the component packing for GL_UNSIGNED_BYTE_2_3_3_REV.

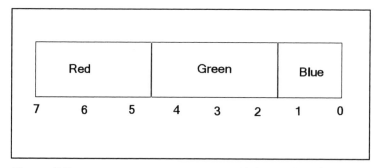

Figure 7.3 GL_UNSIGNED_BYTE_3_3_2 type with bit numbers for each component.

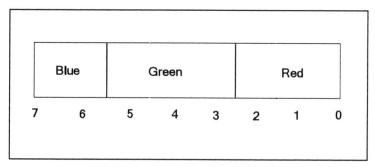

Figure 7.4 GL_UNSIGNED_BYTE_2_3_3_REV type with bit numbers for each component.

texels, the last parameter, is a pointer to the actual texture image data that you either generated or loaded from an image file. OpenGL will read the image data in the format you specified for the type parameter.

As an example, say you have loaded an RGBA image into the variable textureData that has a width and height of textureWidth and textureHeight, respectively, and you want to specify a texture with it. You simply use the glTexImage2D() function like so:

```
glTexImage2D(GL_TEXTURE_2D, 0, GL_RGBA, textureWidth, textureHeight, 0,
             GL_RGBA, GL_UNSIGNED_BYTE, textureData);
```

After this function is called, the texture is loaded and ready to use.

1D Textures

1D textures are essentially 2D textures with a height equal to 1. These textures are often used for drawing color bands or for performing shading techniques that would otherwise require an excessive number of polygons. To create a 1D texture, you use the glTexImage1D() function, which is defined as:

```
void glTexImage1D(GLenum target, GLint level, GLint internalFormat, GLsizei width,
                  GLint border, GLenum format, GLenum type, const GLvoid *texels);
```

All of the parameters for glTexImage1D() are the same as those for glTexImage2D(). The only difference between the two functions is the height parameter, which is not present in the glTexImage1D() function. For the target parameter, you now specify the value GL_TEXTURE_1D, which tells OpenGL that you are creating a 1D texture.

Here is a short code snippet creating a 32-texel–wide RGBA texture using the glTexImage1D() function:

```
unsigned char imageData[128];
...
glTexImage1D(GL_TEXTURE_1D, 0, GL_RGBA, 32, 0, GL_RGBA, GL_UNSIGNED_BYTE, imageData);
```

3D Textures

Extension

Extension name: EXT_texture3D

Name string: GL_EXT_texture3D

Promoted to core: OpenGL 1.2

Function names: glTexImage3DEXT()

Tokens: GL_TEXTURE_3D_EXT

3D textures can produce some amazing visual effects, but they consume an enormous amount of memory for even the modestly sized textures. Although the medical field already uses 3D textures for applications such as MRI, widespread use in 3D gaming remains to be seen. With advancements in graphics hardware, however, 3D textures may soon become more commonplace.

To create a 3D texture, you use the `glTexImage3D()` function:

```
glTexImage3D(GLenum target, GLint level, GLint internalFormat, GLsizei width,
             GLsizei height, GLsizei depth, GLint border, GLenum format, GLenum type,
             const GLvoid *texels);
```

The parameters for this function are essentially the same as those for `glTexImage1D()` and `glTexImage2D()`. The difference here is the `depth` parameter, which specifies the third dimension of the texture.

Here is a short code snippet creating a 16 × 16 × 16–texel RGB texture using the `glTexImage3D()` function:

```
unsigned char imageData[16*16*16*3];
...
glTexImage3D(GL_TEXTURE_3D, 0, GL_RGB, 16, 16, 16, 0, GL_RGB,
             GL_UNSIGNED_BYTE, imageData);
```

Cube Map Textures

Extension

Extension name: ARB_texture_cube_map

Name string: GL_ARB_texture_cube_map

Promoted to core: OpenGL 1.3

Function names: None

Tokens: GL_TEXTURE_CUBE_MAP_ARB, GL_TEXTURE_CUBE_MAP_POSITIVE_X_ARB, GL_TEXTURE_CUBE_MAP_NEGATIVE_X_ARB, GL_TEXTURE_CUBE_MAP_POSITIVE_Y_ARB, GL_TEXTURE_CUBE_MAP_NEGATIVE_Y_ARB, GL_TEXTURE_CUBE_MAP_POSITIVE_Z_ARB, GL_TEXTURE_CUBE_MAP_NEGATIVE_Z_ARB

A cube map texture is a set of six two-dimensional texture images. You specify a cube map texture by using the `glTexImage2D()` function with the `target` parameter equal to one of the following: GL_TEXTURE_CUBE_MAP_POSITIVE_X, GL_TEXTURE_CUBE_MAP_NEGATIVE_X, GL_TEXTURE_CUBE_MAP_POSITIVE_Y, GL_TEXTURE_CUBE_MAP_NEGATIVE_Y, GL_TEXTURE_CUBE_MAP_POSITIVE_Z, or GL_TEXTURE_CUBE_MAP_NEGATIVE_Z.

Cube map dimensions must not only be powers of two, but also of equal width and height, meaning they must be square. The six cube map texture targets listed previously form a single cube map texture, although each target corresponds to a distinct face of the cube map. Cube maps are generally used with 3D texture coordinates, with the (s, t, r) values treated as a direction vector coming from the center of a cube. When a texel is to be obtained from the cube map, the largest magnitude coordinate in the (s, t, r) vector determines which cube face is selected. A new set of coordinates, (s, t), is then calculated by dividing the two smaller magnitude coordinates by the largest magnitude coordinate. The new (s, t) vector is then used to look up the texel in the two-dimensional texture image representing that face of the cube map.

Notice that while the targets listed above are used when specifying, updating, or querying one of the cube map's six two-dimensional images, enabling cube map texturing or binding a cube map texture object requires use of the GL_TEXTURE_CUBE_MAP target.

Texture Filtering

Texture mapping a polygon is the act of mapping from texture image space to frame buffer image space. Typically, this mapping requires reconstruction of the texture image, which can result in a distortion of the image as it is applied to the polygon. After a texture map has been applied to a transformed polygon, a single screen pixel can represent a fraction of a texel if the viewpoint is close to the texture, or a pixel can represent a collection of texels when the viewpoint is further away. *Texture filtering* tells OpenGL how it should map the texels to pixels when calculating the final image.

In texture filtering, *magnification* refers to when a screen pixel represents a small portion of a texel. *Minification* refers to when a pixel contains a number of texels. You can tell OpenGL how to handle both of these filtering cases with the glTexParameter() function:

```
void glTexParameter{if}(GLenum target, GLenum pname, T param);
void glTexParameter{if}v(GLenum target, GLenum pname, T params);
```

Note

We will discuss more about the glTexParameter() function in the "Texture Parameters" section later in this chapter, so the parameter values discussed here apply strictly to texture filtering.

The value of the target parameter refers to the texture target and can be equal to GL_TEXTURE_1D, GL_TEXTURE_2D, GL_TEXTURE_3D, or GL_TEXTURE_CUBE_MAP. Specifying the texture magnification filter parameter requires the pname parameter to be GL_TEXTURE_MAG_FILTER; the texture minification filter parameter is specified with GL_TEXTURE_MIN_FILTER.

When specifying the GL_TEXTURE_MAG_FILTER, the param parameter may be equal to either GL_NEAREST or GL_LINEAR. Using GL_NEAREST for the magnificiation filter tells OpenGL to use the texel nearest to the center of the pixel being rendered. This is sometimes referred to as *point sampling*. Using GL_LINEAR tells OpenGL to use the weighted average of the four texels closest to the center of the pixel being rendered. This is known as *bilinear filtering*.

The minification filter allows a few more legal values than the magnification filter. Table 7.4 lists all of the values you may use when specifying GL_TEXTURE_MIN_FILTER. Note that the values listed in the table are in order of increasing rendering quality.

Table 7.4 Texture Minification Filter Values

Filter	Description
GL_NEAREST	Use the texel nearest to the center of the pixel being rendered.
GL_LINEAR	Use bilinear interpolation.
GL_NEAREST_MIPMAP_NEAREST	Use the mipmap level closest to the polygon resolution, and use GL_NEAREST filtering on that level.
GL_NEAREST_MIPMAP_LINEAR	Use the mipmap level closest to the polygon resolution, and use GL_LINEAR filtering on that level.
GL_LINEAR_MIPMAP_NEAREST	Use GL_NEAREST sampling on the two levels closest to the polygon resolution, and then linearly interpolate between the two values.
GL_LINEAR_MIPMAP_LINEAR	Use bilinear filtering to obtain samples from the two levels closest to the polygon resolution, and then linearly interpolate between the two values. This is also known as *trilinear filtering*.

You will notice that four of the legal values to GL_TEXTURE_MIN_FILTER deal with *mipmaps*. Ignore them for now, as we will discuss mipmaps in this chapter under the section aptly entitled "Mipmaps."

By default, the magnification filter is set to GL_LINEAR, and the minification is set to GL_NEAREST_MIPMAP_LINEAR.

Tip

When rendering with textures, OpenGL first checks to see if the current texture is complete. Among other things, this includes verifying that all levels of the mipmap have been defined if one of the mipmap modes has been chosen as the minification filter. If the texture is not complete, texturing is disabled. Because the default value for the minification filter uses mipmapping, you should be sure to either specify all of the mipmap levels or change the minification filter to GL_LINEAR or GL_NEAREST.

Basic Texture Example

Now that we have the minimum requirements for texture mapping covered, let's take a look at a basic example that does nothing more than apply a texture to two polygons. In the Chapter 7 folder on the CD, you will find an example entitled TextureBasics. This example moves two polygons along the z-axis to show how the minification and magnification texture filter settings affect the visual quality of a texture map. Figure 7.5 is a screenshot of this example.

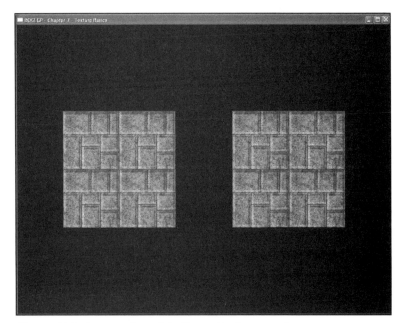

Figure 7.5 A screenshot of the TextureBasics example.

The polygon on the left uses GL_LINEAR for both minification and magnification. As such, the texture is linearly interpolated as it moves closer to and further from the viewpoint, resulting in a smooth transition.

The polygon on the right uses GL_LINEAR for minification and GL_NEAREST for magnification. As the polygon approaches the camera, you will notice that the texture's visual quality changes slightly when it passes through the threshold for OpenGL to switch from minification filtering to magnification filtering.

The code to set up the texture objects and filtering modes is in the Init() method:

```
bool CGfxOpenGL::Init()
{
    glClearColor(0.0, 0.0, 0.0, 0.0);
```

```
    // enable 2D texturing
    glEnable(GL_TEXTURE_2D);

    m_textureOne = new CTargaImage;

    // load texture image data
    if (!m_textureOne->Load("rock.tga"))
        return false;

    // retrieve "unused" texture object
    glGenTextures(1, &m_textureObjectOne);

    // bind the texture object
    glBindTexture(GL_TEXTURE_2D, m_textureObjectOne);

    // set the min and mag texture filters
    glTexParameteri(GL_TEXTURE_2D, GL_TEXTURE_MAG_FILTER, GL_LINEAR);
    glTexParameteri(GL_TEXTURE_2D, GL_TEXTURE_MIN_FILTER, GL_LINEAR);

    // specify a texture for the texture object
    glTexImage2D(GL_TEXTURE_2D, 0, GL_RGB, m_textureOne->GetWidth(),
                m_textureOne->GetHeight(), 0, GL_RGB, GL_UNSIGNED_BYTE,
                m_textureOne->GetImage());

    // create the second texture object
    glGenTextures(1, &m_textureObjectTwo);
    glBindTexture(GL_TEXTURE_2D, m_textureObjectTwo);

    glTexParameteri(GL_TEXTURE_2D, GL_TEXTURE_MAG_FILTER, GL_NEAREST);
    glTexParameteri(GL_TEXTURE_2D, GL_TEXTURE_MIN_FILTER, GL_LINEAR);

    glTexImage2D(GL_TEXTURE_2D, 0, GL_RGB, m_textureOne->GetWidth(),
                m_textureOne->GetHeight(), 0, GL_RGB, GL_UNSIGNED_BYTE,
                m_textureOne->GetImage());

    // initialize movement variables
    m_zPos = -5.0f;
    m_zMoveNegative = true;

    return true;
}
```

In the Init() method, we first enable 2D texturing and then load the texture image data using the CTargaImage class we created in Chapter 6, "Bitmaps and Images with OpenGL." We then get an unused texture object through glGenTextures(), bind the texture object, specify the minification and magnification for the texture object as GL_LINEAR, and finally specify the texture with glTexImage2D(). We then repeat the process for the second texture object, while using the same texture image data and applying GL_NEAREST to magnification filtering and GL_LINEAR to minification filtering.

The other two methods of interest in this example are the DrawPlane() and Render() methods, shown here:

```
void CGfxOpenGL::DrawPlane()
{
    glBegin(GL_TRIANGLE_STRIP);
        glTexCoord2f(1.0, 0.0); glVertex3f(2.0, -2.0, -2.0);
        glTexCoord2f(0.0, 0.0); glVertex3f(-2.0, -2.0, -2.0);
        glTexCoord2f(1.0, 1.0); glVertex3f(2.0, -2.0, 2.0);
        glTexCoord2f(0.0, 1.0); glVertex3f(-2.0, -2.0, 2.0);
    glEnd();
}


void CGfxOpenGL::Render()
{
    // clear screen and depth buffer
    glClear(GL_COLOR_BUFFER_BIT | GL_DEPTH_BUFFER_BIT);

    // load the identity matrix (clear to default position and orientation)
    glLoadIdentity();

    // draw the left polygon
    glPushMatrix();
        // translate the world coordinate system along the z-axis
        glTranslatef(-3.0, 0.0, m_zPos);
        glRotatef(90.0, 1.0, 0.0, 0.0);

        // bind the texture
        glBindTexture(GL_TEXTURE_2D, m_textureObjectOne);

        // draw the plane at the world origin
        DrawPlane();
    glPopMatrix();

    // do it all again for the right polygon
```

```
glPushMatrix();
    glTranslatef(3.0, 0.0, m_zPos);
    glRotatef(90.0, 1.0, 0.0, 0.0);
    glBindTexture(GL_TEXTURE_2D, m_textureObjectTwo);
    DrawPlane();
glPopMatrix();
}
```

In DrawPlane(), we are specifying the texture coordinates and drawing the vertices of the textured polygon. In the Render() method, notice that before rendering each polygon with DrawPlane(), we first bind the texture object that we want to use to texture the polygon we are drawing. Binding a texture object selects it for the current texture unit, where it can then be processed by any texturing commands that follow.

Mipmaps

The term *mipmap* stems from a Latin phrase meaning "many in one." It's used to refer to a texture that is composed of many different levels. Each level has dimensions that are half of the previous one. For example, if we start with a base image with dimensions 64×64, then the next mipmap level image will have a resolution of 32×32. The next image after that will be 16×16, then 8×8, 4×4, 2×2, and finally 1×1, resulting in a set of seven mipmap levels.

Mipmaps were introduced to combat a visual artifact known as *swimming*. Swimming is the result of two adjacent pixels sampling from widely separated portions of the texture map. This is common for polygons that are far away from the viewer, where you might have for example a triangle that is represented as only five pixels sampling from a 512×512 texture. For static scenes, this isn't a problem, but as soon as you introduce motion, the portions of the texture being sampled change, resulting in different colors appearing. Mipmaps reduce this problem because levels with lower resolutions are used for distant polygons, leading to more consistent sampling. Mipmaps have the additional benefit of reducing texture cache misses, since the smaller levels are more likely to remain in limited but high-speed video memory for as long as they are needed. Figure 7.6 illustrates the concept of mipmaps.

OpenGL performs mipmapping by determining which texture image to use based on the size of the fragment relative to the size of the texels being applied to it. OpenGL chooses the mipmap level that allows as close to one-to-one mapping as possible.

Each level in a mipmap is defined using glTexImage3D(), glTexImage2D(), or glTexImage1D(). The level parameter of these functions specifies the level of detail, or resolution level, of the image being specified.

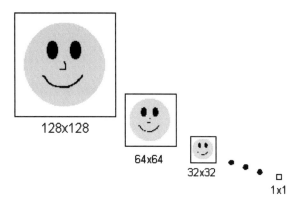

128x128

64x64

32x32

1x1

Figure 7.6 Mipmaps help control the level of detail for textured objects.

By default, you have to specify all levels starting from level 0 to the level at which the texture becomes 1×1 (which is equivalent to $\log_2$ of the largest dimension of the base texture). You can, however, change these limits by using the glTexParameter() function with its pname parameter set to GL_TEXTURE_BASE_LEVEL or GL_TEXTURE_MAX_LEVEL, respectively. The value passed to either of these parameters must be a positive integer.

Mipmapping is first enabled by specifying one of the mipmapping values for texture minification. Once the texture minification filter has been set, you then only need to specify the texture mipmap levels with one of the glTexImage3D(), glTexImage2D(), or glTexImage1D() functions, depending on your texture dimensionality. The following example code sets up a seven-level mipmap with a minification filter of GL_NEAREST_MIPMAP_LINEAR and starting at a 64×64 base texture:

```
glTexParameteri(GL_TEXTURE_2D, GL_TEXTURE_MAG_FILTER, GL_LINEAR);
glTexParameteri(GL_TEXTURE_2D, GL_TEXTURE_MIN_FILTER, GL_NEAREST_MIPMAP_LINEAR);
glTexImage2D(GL_TEXTURE_2D, 0, GL_RGB, 64,64,0, GL_RGB, GL_UNSIGNED_BYTE, texImage0);
glTexImage2D(GL_TEXTURE_2D, 1, GL_RGB, 32,32,0, GL_RGB, GL_UNSIGNED_BYTE, texImage1);
glTexImage2D(GL_TEXTURE_2D, 2, GL_RGB, 16,16,0, GL_RGB, GL_UNSIGNED_BYTE, texImage2);
glTexImage2D(GL_TEXTURE_2D, 3, GL_RGB, 8, 8, 0, GL_RGB, GL_UNSIGNED_BYTE, texImage3);
glTexImage2D(GL_TEXTURE_2D, 4, GL_RGB, 4, 4, 0, GL_RGB, GL_UNSIGNED_BYTE, texImage4);
glTexImage2D(GL_TEXTURE_2D, 5, GL_RGB, 2, 2, 0, GL_RGB, GL_UNSIGNED_BYTE, texImage5);
glTexImage2D(GL_TEXTURE_2D, 6, GL_RGB, 1, 1, 0, GL_RGB, GL_UNSIGNED_BYTE, texImage6);
```

Mipmaps and the OpenGL Utility Library

The GLU library provides the gluBuild2DMipmaps() and gluBuild1DMipmaps() functions to build mipmaps automatically for two- and one-dimensional textures, respectively. These functions replace the set of function calls you would normally make to the `glTexImage2D()` and `glTexImage1D()` functions to specify mipmaps.

```
int gluBuild2DMipmaps(GLenum target, GLint components, GLint width, GLint height,
  GLenum format, GLenum type, const void *data);
int gluBuild1DMipmaps(GLenum target, GLint components GLint width, GLenum format,
  GLenum type, const void *data);
```

One of the nice features about these functions is that you do not have to pass a power-of-2 image because `gluBuild2DMipmaps()` and `gluBuild1DMipmaps()` automatically rescale your images' width and height to the closest power of 2 for you.

The following code uses the `gluBuild2DMipmaps()` function to specify mipmaps in the same way as the previous mipmap example using `glTexImage2D()`:

```
glTexParameteri(GL_TEXTURE_2D, GL_TEXTURE_MAG_FILTER, GL_LINEAR);
glTexParameteri(GL_TEXTURE_2D, GL_TEXTURE_MIN_FILTER, GL_NEAREST_MIPMAP_LINEAR);
gluBuild2DMipmaps(GL_TEXTURE_2D, GL_RGB, 64, 64, GL_RGB, GL_UNSIGNED_BYTE, texImage0);
```

Automatic Mipmap Generation

Extension

Extension name: SGIS_generate_mipmap

Name string: GL_SGIS_generate_mipmap

Promoted to core: OpenGL 1.4

Function names: None

Tokens: GL_GENERATE_MIPMAP_SGIS

As of Version 1.4, OpenGL has introduced a new method for automatically generating mipmaps with the texture parameter GL_GENERATE_MIPMAP. Setting this parameter to GL_TRUE will induce a mechanism that automatically generates all mipmap levels higher than the base level. The internal formats and border widths of the derived mipmap images all match those of the base level image, and each increasing mipmap level reduces the size of the image by half. The actual contents of the mipmap images are computed by a repeated, filtered reduction of the base mipmap level.

One of the nice features of this parameter is that if you change the texture image data, the mipmap data is calculated automatically, which makes it extremely useful for textures you're changing on the fly.

We are actually discussing texture parameters in the next section. This means you should read on to find out how to use the automatic mipmap generation functionality of OpenGL!

Texture Parameters

OpenGL provides several parameters to control how textures are treated when specified, changed, or applied as texture maps. Each parameter is set by calling the glTexParameter() function (as mentioned in the section "Texture Filtering"):

```
void glTexParameter{if}(GLenum target, GLenum pname, TYPE param);
void glTexParameter{if}v(GLenum target, GLenum pname, TYPE params);
```

As mentioned before, the value of the target parameter refers to the texture target and can be equal to GL_TEXTURE_1D, GL_TEXTURE_2D, GL_TEXTURE_3D, or GL_TEXTURE_CUBE_MAP. The pname parameter is a constant indicating the parameter to be set, a list of which is shown in Table 7.5. In the first form of the glTexParameter() function, param is a single-valued parameter; in the second form, params is an array of parameters whose type depends on the parameter being set.

Table 7.5 Texture Parameters

Name	Type	Values
GL_TEXTURE_WRAP_S	integer	GL_CLAMP, GL_CLAMP_TO_EDGE*, GL_REPEAT, GL_CLAMP_TO_BORDER*, GL_MIRRORED_REPEAT*
GL_TEXTURE_WRAP_T	integer	GL_CLAMP, GL_CLAMP_TO_EDGE*, GL_REPEAT, GL_CLAMP_TO_BORDER*, GL_MIRRORED_REPEAT*
GL_TEXTURE_WRAP_R	integer	GL_CLAMP, GL_CLAMP_TO_EDGE*, GL_REPEAT, GL_CLAMP_TO_BORDER*, GL_MIRRORED_REPEAT*
GL_TEXTURE_MIN_FILTER	integer	GL_NEAREST, GL_LINEAR, GL_NEAREST_MIPMAP_NEAREST, GL_NEAREST_MIPMAP_LINEAR, GL_LINEAR_MIPMAP_NEAREST, GL_LINEAR_MIPMAP_LINEAR
GL_TEXTURE_MAG_FILTER	integer	GL_NEAREST, GL_LINEAR
GL_TEXTURE_BORDER_COLOR	4 floats	any 4 values from 0 to 1
GL_TEXTURE_PRIORITY	float	any value from 0 to 1
GL_TEXTURE_MIN_LOD*	float	any value
GL_TEXTURE_MAX_LOD*	float	any value
GL_TEXTURE_BASE_LEVEL*	integer	any non-negative integer
GL_TEXTURE_MAX_LEVEL*	integer	any non-negative integer
GL_TEXTURE_LOD_BIAS*	float	any value
GL_DEPTH_TEXTURE_MODE**	enum	GL_LUMINANCE, GL_INTENSITY, GL_ALPHA
GL_TEXTURE_COMPARE_MODE**	enum	GL_NONE, GL_COMPARE_R_TO_TEXTURE
GL_TEXTURE_COMPARE_FUNC**	enum	GL_LEQUAL, GL_GEQUAL, GL_LESS, GL_GREATER, GL_EQUAL, GL_NOTEQUAL, GL_ALWAYS, GL_NEVER
GL_GENERATE_MIPMAP*	boolean	GL_TRUE or GL_FALSE

* Available only via extensions under Windows. See the explanation of the parameter in this chapter for details.

** Available only via the ARB_depth_texture and ARB_shadow extensions under Windows.

Texture parameters for a cube map texture apply to the entire cube map; the six individual texture images cannot be controlled separately.

Texture Wrap Modes

Texture wrap modes allow you to modify how OpenGL interprets texture coordinates outside of the range [0, 1] and at the edge of textures. Using the glTexParameter() function with GL_TEXTURE_WRAP_S, GL_TEXTURE_WRAP_T, or GL_TEXTURE_WRAP_R, you can specify how OpenGL interprets the *s, t,* and *r* texture coordinates, respectively.

OpenGL provides five wrap modes: GL_REPEAT, GL_CLAMP, GL_CLAMP_TO_EDGE, GL_CLAMP_TO_BORDER, and GL_MIRRORED_REPEAT. Let's discuss these individually.

Wrap Mode GL_REPEAT

The GL_REPEAT wrap mode is the default behavior of OpenGL for texture coordinates. In this mode, OpenGL essentially ignores the integer portion of texture coordinates and uses only the fractional part. For example, if you specify the 2D texture coordinates (2.0, 2.0), then the texture will be placed twice in the *s* and *t* directions, as compared to the texture being placed once with texture coordinates of (1.0, 1.0) in the same polygon space. This essentially means GL_REPEAT allows you to create a tiled effect. Figure 7.7 illustrates how the GL_REPEAT wrap mode with texture coordinates (2.0, 2.0) affects the TextureBasics example presented earlier.

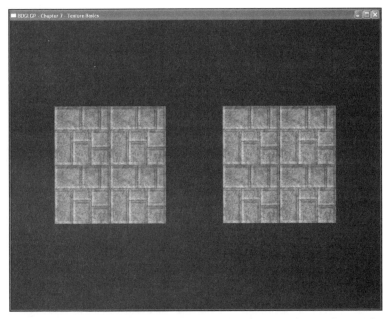

Figure 7.7 Result of using GL_REPEAT with texture coordinates (2.0, 2.0) with the TextureBasics example.

While GL_REPEAT is OpenGL's default behavior, you can force it by specifying GL_REPEAT as the value for GL_TEXTURE_WRAP_S, GL_TEXTURE_WRAP_T, or GL_TEXTURE_WRAP_R. The following line of code will force GL_REPEAT on the currently bound texture object's *s* coordinate:

```
glTexParameteri(GL_TEXTURE_2D, GL_TEXTURE_WRAP_S, GL_REPEAT);
```

Wrap Mode GL_CLAMP

The GL_CLAMP wrap mode simply clamps texture coordinates in the range 0.0 to 1.0. If you specify texture coordinates outside this range, then OpenGL will take the edge of the texture and extend it to the remainder of the textured surface. Figure 7.8 illustrates how the GL_CLAMP wrap mode with texture coordinates (2.0, 2.0) affects the TextureBasics example presented earlier (look at the right polygon).

The following example line of code tells OpenGL to use GL_CLAMP on the currently bound texture object's *t* coordinate:

```
glTexParameteri(GL_TEXTURE_2D, GL_TEXTURE_WRAP_T, GL_CLAMP);
```

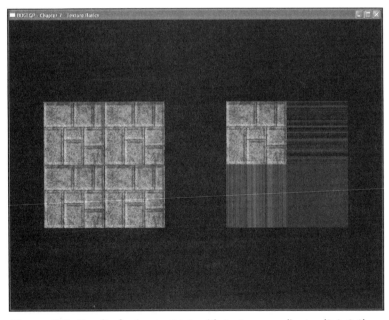

Figure 7.8 Result of using GL_CLAMP with texture coordinates (2.0, 2.0) in the TextureBasics example.

Wrap Mode GL_CLAMP_TO_EDGE

The GL_CLAMP_TO_EDGE wrap mode clamps texture coordinates such that the texture filter never samples a border texel. Normally, OpenGL clamps such that the texture coordinates are limited to *exactly* the range 0 to 1. This means that when GL_CLAMP is used, OpenGL straddles the edge of the texture image, taking half of its color sample values from within the texture image and the other half from the texture border.

When GL_CLAMP_TO_EDGE is used, however, OpenGL never takes color samples from the texture border. The color used for clamping is taken only from the texels at the edge of the texture image. This can be used to prevent seams between textures.

The following line of code tells OpenGL to use GL_CLAMP_TO_EDGE on the currently bound texture object's *s* coordinate:

```
glTexParameteri(GL_TEXTURE_2D, GL_TEXTURE_WRAP_S, GL_CLAMP_TO_EDGE);
```

Extension

Extension name: SGIS_texture_edge_clamp

Name string: GL_SGIS_texture_edge_clamp

Promoted to core: OpenGL 1.2

Function names: None

Tokens: GL_CLAMP_TO_EDGE_SGIS

Wrap Mode GL_CLAMP_TO_BORDER

The GL_CLAMP_TO_BORDER wrap mode clamps texture coordinates in such a way that mirrors the behavior of GL_CLAMP_TO_EDGE. Instead of sampling only the edge of the texture image, GL_CLAMP_TO_BORDER only samples the texture border for its clamp color.

The following line of code tells OpenGL to use GL_CLAMP_TO_BORDER on the currently bound texture object's *s* coordinate:

```
glTexParameteri(GL_TEXTURE_2D, GL_TEXTURE_WRAP_S, GL_CLAMP_TO_BORDER);
```

Extension

Extension name: ARB_texture_border_clamp

Name string: GL_ARB_texture_border_clamp

Promoted to core: OpenGL 1.3

Function names: None

Tokens: GL_CLAMP_TO_BORDER_ARB

Wrap Mode GL_MIRRORED_REPEAT

The GL_MIRRORED_REPEAT wrap mode essentially defines a texture map twice as large as the original texture image. The additional texture map area created contains a mirror image of the original texture. You can use this wrap mode to achieve seamless tiling of a surface.

The following line of code tells OpenGL to use GL_MIRRORED_REPEAT on the currently bound texture object's *s* coordinate:

```
glTexParameteri(GL_TEXTURE_2D, GL_TEXTURE_WRAP_S, GL_MIRRORED_REPEAT);
```

Extension

Extension name: ARB_texture_mirrored_repeat

Name string: GL_ARB_texture_mirrored_repeat

Promoted to core: OpenGL 1.4

Function names: None

Tokens: GL_MIRRORED_REPEAT_ARB

Texture Level of Detail

The decision to use the minification filtering mode or the magnification filtering mode on a texture is determined by a set of parameters controlling the texture level of detail calculations. By manipulating these parameters, you can control the transition of textures from minification filtering to magnification filtering and vice versa.

Two of these parameters, GL_TEXTURE_MIN_LOD and GL_TEXTURE_MAX_LOD, allow you to control the level of detail range. By default, the range is [−1000.0, 1000.0], which essentially guarantees that the level of detail will never be clamped. The following code sets the level of detail range to [−10.0, 10.0] for a two-dimensional texture:

```
glTexParameterf(GL_TEXTURE_2D, GL_TEXTURE_MIN_LOD, -10.0);
glTexParameterf(GL_TEXTURE_2D, GL_TEXTURE_MAX_LOD, 10.0);
```

Another parameter, GL_TEXTURE_LOD_BIAS, allows you to control the level of detail bias level, causing it to change levels sooner or later than it normally would. The bias level is used in the computation for determining the mipmap level of detail selection, providing a means to blur or sharpen textures. This functionality can lead to special effects such as depth of field, blurring, or image processing. Here's an example:

```
glTexParameterf(GL_TEXTURE_2D, GL_TEXTURE_LOD_BIAS, 3.0);
```

Extension

Extension name: EXT_texture_lod_bias

Name string: GL_EXT_texture_lod_bias

Promoted to core: OpenGL 1.4

Function names: None

Tokens: GL_TEXTURE_LOD_BIAS_EXT

Texture Environments and Texture Functions

OpenGL's glTexEnv() function allows you to set parameters of the texture environment that determine how texture values are applied when texturing:

```
void glTexEnv{if}(GLenum target, GLenum pname, T param);
void glTexEnv{if}v(GLenum target, GLenum pname, T params);
```

For this function, the target parameter must be either GL_TEXTURE_ENV or GL_TEXTURE_FILTER_CONTROL. The pname parameter tells OpenGL which parameter you wish to set with the value passed to param (or params for an array of values).

To better explain the purpose of texture environments, let's review how OpenGL texturing works. Texturing is enabled and disabled with the glEnable()/glDisable() functions by specifying the dimensionality of the texture you wish to use. For instance, you may specify GL_TEXTURE_1D, GL_TEXTURE_2D, GL_TEXTURE_3D, or GL_TEXTURE_CUBE_MAP to enable the one-, two-, or three-dimensional, or cube map texture mapping, respectively. The rule of texture dimensionality follows that the highest enabled dimensionality (1D, 2D, 3D, cube) is enabled and used for texture mapping. If all texturing is disabled, any fragments coming through the pipeline are simply passed to the next stage.

If texturing is enabled, a texture is determined based on the texture parameters and dimensionality (1D, 2D, 3D, or cube map) of the incoming fragment. The texture environment is then used to determine the texture function applied to the texture, whose red, green, blue, and alpha values are then replaced with freshly computed ones. These RGBA values are finally passed on to further OpenGL operations in the pipeline.

OpenGL includes one or more *texture units* representing stages in the texture mapping process that are enabled and have texture objects bindings independently from each other. Each unit has its own set of states, including those related to the texture environment.

Figure 7.9 illustrates how each texture unit is paired with a texture environment function. Note that in the figure each texture unit passes its results on to the next texture unit. This

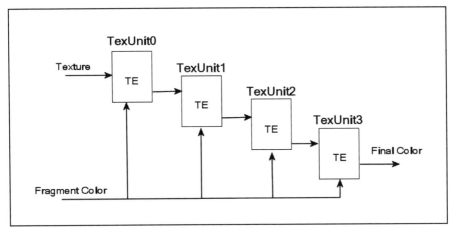

Figure 7.9 Texture environments operate on all textures passed through their associated texture units.

functionality is called *multitexturing*, which will be discussed in Chapter 9, "More on Texture Mapping." Only the first texture unit (typically texture unit zero) is used when using basic texture mapping techniques as described in this chapter. The important concept to understand right now is that a texture environment is tied to a texture unit and affects all textures passing through that texture unit. This is contrary to the common misconception among newcomers to OpenGL that each texture object maintains states related to the texture environment.

Now that we have that down, let's discuss how we modify the texture environment.

Specifying the Texture Environment

Looking back at the glTexEnv() function, if the target is equal to GL_TEXTURE_FILTER_CONTROL, then pname must be set equal to GL_TEXTURE_LOD_BIAS. The value parameter passed must then be a single floating-point value that sets the level of detail bias for the currently active texture unit. This functionality is equivalent to the texture object level of detail bias described in the section "Texture Level of Detail" in this chapter.

When target is equal to GL_TEXTURE_ENV, pname can be set to GL_TEXTURE_ENV_MODE, GL_TEXTURE_ENV_COLOR, GL_COMBINE_RGB, or GL_COMBINE_ALPHA.

If GL_TEXTURE_ENV_COLOR is used, then OpenGL expects four floating-point values in the range from 0 to 1 representing an RGBA color to be passed to the params parameter. You may also pass four integers, and OpenGL will convert them to floating-point values as necessary. This color is used in conjunction with the GL_BLEND environment mode.

If pname is GL_TEXTURE_ENV_MODE, then you are specifying the *texture function*. The result of a texture function is dependent on the texture itself and the fragment it is being applied to. The exact texture function that is used depends on the internal format of the texture that was specified. For reference, the base internal formats are listed in Table 7.6. Acceptable values for GL_TEXTURE_ENV_MODE are GL_REPLACE, GL_MODULATE, GL_DECAL, GL_BLEND, GL_ADD, and GL_COMBINE.

Table 7.6 Texture Internal Formats

Format	Texture Source Color
GL_ALPHA	$C_s = (0, 0, 0); A_s = A_t$
GL_LUMINANCE	$C_s = (L_t, L_t, L_t); A_s = 1$
GL_LUMINANCE_ALPHA	$C_s = (L_t, L_t, L_t); A_s = A_t$
GL_INTENSITY	$C_s = (I_t, I_t, I_t); A_s = I_t$
GL_RGB	$C_s = (R_t, G_t, B_t); A_s = 1$
GL_RGBA	$C_s = (R_t, G_t, B_t); A_s = A_t$

Note

You may notice subscripts being used in the following tables. A subscript of t indicates a filtered texture value, s indicates the texture source color, f denotes the incoming fragment value, c refers to the values assigned with GL_TEXTURE_ENV_COLOR, and v refers to the final computed value. For regular-sized text, C refers to the RGB triplet, A is the alpha component value, L is a luminance component value, and I is an intensity component value.

The color values listed in the following tables are all in the range [0, 1]. Each table shows how the texture functions use colors from the texture value, texture source color, incoming fragment color, and texture environment value to determine the final computed value. Table 7.7 includes the calculations for GL_REPLACE, GL_MODULATE, and GL_DECAL. Table 7.8 includes the calculations for GL_BLEND and GL_ADD.

Table 7.7 GL_REPLACE, GL_MODULATE, GL_DECAL

Format	GL_REPLACE	GL_MODULATE	GL_DECAL
GL_ALPHA	$C_v = C_f$ $A_v = A_s$	$C_v = C_f$ $A_v = A_f A_s$	undefined
GL_LUMINANCE	$C_v = C_s$ $A_v = A_s$	$C_v = C_f C_s$ $A_v = A_f$	undefined
GL_LUMINANCE_ALPHA	$C_v = C_s$ $A_v = A_s$	$C_v = C_f C_s$ $A_v = A_f A_s$	undefined
GL_INTENSITY	$C_v = C_s$ $A_v = A_s$	$C_v = C_f C_s$ $A_v = A_f A_s$	undefined
GL_RGB	$C_v = C_s$ $A_v = A_f$	$C_v = C_f C_s$ $A_v = A_f$	$C_v = C_s$ $A_v = A_f$
GL_RGBA	$C_v = C_s$ $A_v = A_s$	$C_v = C_f C_s$ $A_v = A_f A_s$	$C_v = C_f(1 - A_s) + C_s A_s$ $A_v = A_f$

Table 7.8 GL_BLEND and GL_ADD

Format	GL_BLEND	GL_ADD*
GL_ALPHA	$C_v = C_f$	$C_v = C_f$
	$A_v = A_f A_s$	$A_v = A_f A_s$
GL_LUMINANCE	$C_v = C_f(1 - C_s) + C_c C_s$	$C_v = C_f + C_s$
	$A_v = A_f$	$A_v = A_f$
GL_LUMINANCE_ALPHA	$C_v = C_f(1 - C_s) + C_c C_s$	$C_v = C_f + C_s$
	$A_v = A_f A_s$	$A_v = A_f A_s$
GL_INTENSITY	$C_v = C_f(1 - C_s) + C_c C_s$	$C_v = C_f + C_s$
	$A_v = A_f(1 - A_s) + A_c A_s$	$A_v = A_f A_s$
GL_RGB	$C_v = C_f(1 - C_s) + C_c C_s$	$C_v = C_f + C_s$
	$A_v = A_f$	$A_v = A_f$
GL_RGBA	$C_v = C_f(1 - C_s) + C_c C_s$	$C_v = C_f + C_s$
	$A_v = A_f A_s$	$A_v = A_f A_s$

* Available only via the ARB_texture_env_add extension under Windows.

Since we know these tables can be a little overwhelming for the uninitiated, let's step through a couple of these formulas and figure out what exactly is going on. We'll start with one of the easy ones and look at GL_REPLACE with the format GL_RGBA.

Looking at the table, you will see $C_v = C_s$ and $A_v = A_s$. That's not too bad, right? But what is it saying? As noted prior to the tables, the s subscript indicates the texture source color, and the v subscript indicates our final color output. So, $C_v = C_s$ says that the texture source RGB values will be transferred straight to the final color output. Similarly, $A_v = A_s$ says that the alpha component will be copied to the final alpha output value. So if we have an RGBA color value of (0.5, 0.3, 0.8, 0.5), then the final RGBA output value will be (0.5, 0.3, 0.8, 0.5). How about a slightly more difficult equation, like GL_MODULATE on the GL_RGBA format?

In the table you will see $C_v = C_f C_s$ and $A_v = A_f A_s$. It's not a terribly complicated set of functions, but the results are much different. So, what are these equations saying? Well, you know what the s and v subscript are, and if you look at the prior note you will see that the f subscript denotes the incoming fragment value. $C_v = C_f C_s$ is saying that the fragment color is multiplied by the texture source color. $A_v = A_f A_s$ is saying the same, except with the alpha component values. As an example, these formulas are saying that if the polygon we are texturing has a solid color of red without transparency, (1.0, 0.0, 0.0, 1.0), and we reach a texture color value of (0.2, 1.0, 0.7, 0.5), then the final color output for the texture fragment will be equal to (1.0 × 0.2, 0.0 × 1.0, 0.0 × 0.7, 1.0 × 0.5), or (0.2, 0.0, 0.0, 0.5). That's not too bad, right? One more example: GL_BLEND with GL_RGB.

GL_RGB doesn't work with an alpha component value, so we can focus on the equation given in the table for the RGB values: $C_v = C_f(1 - C_s) + C_c C_s$. In English (or at least our best dialect of the language), this means that the final color value is equal to the incoming fragment color multiplied by the result of one minus the texture source color. The result of this multiplication is then added to the result of the texture environment color multiplied by the texture source color. In other words, given a texture source color of (0.2, 0.5, 1.0), a fragment color of (1.0, 0.5, 0.8), and a texture environment color of (0.3, 0.4, 0.9), the formula gives a final value of (1.4, 0.45, 0.9). However, 1.4 is beyond the [0, 1] range that color values are limited to, so OpenGL clamps the final color value to (1.0, 0.45, 0.9).

If the value of GL_TEXTURE_ENV_MODE is GL_COMBINE, then the texture function OpenGL selects depends on the values of GL_COMBINE_RGB and GL_COMBINE_ALPHA. This is directly related to multitexturing, it will be covered in Chapter 9.

Textured Terrain

In *OpenGL Game Programming*, we provided an example in the texture chapter that rendered and textured a simple heightfield terrain. We are going to revisit that example and hopefully make it better!

In its most basic form, a *heightfield terrain* is a virtual representation of a landscape whose data points are a two-dimensional set of evenly spaced height values. When you render these data points as a mesh on the screen, you see what resembles a landscape.

Keep in mind that the method we are about to show you is only one way to develop a simple landscape. Terrain rendering is a fairly large area of computer graphics, with plenty of research and interest. Do a search for the topic on your favorite search engine, and you will find enough information to keep you busy for years.

Building the Mesh

Keeping in mind our definition of heightfield terrain, you are going to create a grid of vertices that are spaced evenly apart but have varying height values based on the height of the terrain data at each vertex's grid location.

You will be determining the height values by loading a 32 × 32 grayscale Targa image into memory with each color value in the image representing a height value mapped to a grid location in the heightfield. Since we will be using a grayscale image, the color values and effectively the height values will range from 0 to 255.

After loading the height values into an array in memory, you will have a set of data points that represent the height of the terrain. Next you need to determine the distance between each height vertex, which we will call the *map scale*. We will use the map scale to programmatically increase or decrease the actual width and height of the terrain in world units.

When you assign the 3D vertex coordinates for each height value, you will need to multiply the map scale factor by the height value's (x, y) index location in the heightfield array. For example, when you are defining the x coordinate for a vertex, you will determine the height value's x-axis location in the heightfield array and multiply that value by the map scale factor.

To render the terrain map, you will use a GL_TRIANGLE_STRIP for each row of height values along the z-axis. You will need to render the points of the triangle strip in a specific order so the heightfield terrain is rendered properly. Each row is drawn by specifying vertices in a *Z* pattern along the x-axis, as shown in Figure 7.10. For texturing, you will texture every group of 16 vertices. Once you reach the end of the row, you move on to the next row of heightfield data and repeat the process until the terrain is complete. As an added bonus, water is added into the terrain by rendering a textured quadrilateral at a "water level" height.

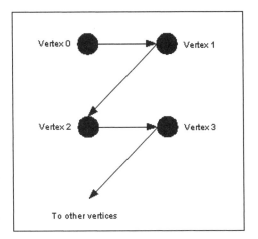

Figure 7.10 Process the vertices in a *Z* pattern for each row in the terrain.

This example also includes a *skybox*, which is a large cube whose inside faces are textured with images representing the distant horizon. Skyboxes provide a good, simple way to enhance the environment of an outdoor graphics scene. The position of the camera is used as the origin of the skybox, with all six sides of the skybox remaining centered around the camera even as it moves around the world. Maintaining the origin of the skybox at the camera position helps keep the illusion of distance for the viewer.

Finally, we added mouse input control for the camera, so you can rotate and set the height of the camera with the mouse.

You can see the source code in the CD included with this book, under Chapter 7, and the folder Terrain. We aren't going to dump all of the code here for you, but let's take a look at the most important function, DrawTerrain():

```
void CGfxOpenGL::DrawTerrain()
{
    // draw the terrain
    glBindTexture(GL_TEXTURE_2D, m_grassTexture);
    glTexEnvf(GL_TEXTURE_ENV, GL_TEXTURE_ENV_MODE, GL_MODULATE);
    for (int z = 0; z < TERRAIN_SIZE - 1; ++z)
    {
        glBegin(GL_TRIANGLE_STRIP);
```

```
        for (int x = 0; x < TERRAIN_SIZE; ++x)
        {
            // render two vertices of the strip at once
            float scaledHeight = heightmap[z * TERRAIN_SIZE + x] / SCALE_FACTOR;
            float nextScaledHeight = heightmap[(z + 1)* TERRAIN_SIZE + x] / SCALE_FACTOR;
            float color = 0.5f + 0.5f * scaledHeight / MAX_HEIGHT;
            float nextColor = 0.5f + 0.5f * nextScaledHeight / MAX_HEIGHT;

            glColor3f(color, color, color);
            glTexCoord2f((GLfloat)x/TERRAIN_SIZE*8, (GLfloat)z/TERRAIN_SIZE*8);
            glVertex3f(static_cast<GLfloat>(x - TERRAIN_SIZE/2), scaledHeight,
                    static_cast<GLfloat>(z - TERRAIN_SIZE/2));

            glColor3f(nextColor, nextColor, nextColor);
            glTexCoord2f((GLfloat)x/TERRAIN_SIZE*8, (GLfloat)(z+1)/TERRAIN_SIZE*8);
            glVertex3f(static_cast<GLfloat>(x - TERRAIN_SIZE/2), nextScaledHeight,
                    static_cast<GLfloat>(z + 1 - TERRAIN_SIZE/2));
        }
        glEnd();
    }


    //draw the water
    glBindTexture(GL_TEXTURE_2D, m_waterTexture);
    glTexEnvf(GL_TEXTURE_ENV, GL_TEXTURE_ENV_MODE, GL_REPLACE);
    glBegin(GL_QUADS);
        glTexCoord2f(0.0, 0.0);
        glVertex3f(-TERRAIN_SIZE/2.1f, WATER_HEIGHT, TERRAIN_SIZE/2.1f);

        glTexCoord2f(TERRAIN_SIZE/4.0f, 0.0);
        glVertex3f(TERRAIN_SIZE/2.1f, WATER_HEIGHT, TERRAIN_SIZE/2.1f);

        glTexCoord2f(TERRAIN_SIZE/4.0f, TERRAIN_SIZE/4.0f);
        glVertex3f(TERRAIN_SIZE/2.1f, WATER_HEIGHT, -TERRAIN_SIZE/2.1f);

        glTexCoord2f(0.0, TERRAIN_SIZE/4.0f);
        glVertex3f(-TERRAIN_SIZE/2.1f, WATER_HEIGHT, -TERRAIN_SIZE/2.1f);
    glEnd();
}
```

The first half of the DrawTerrain() method draws the actual terrain. First we bind the terrain's grass texture, and then we loop through every row in the terrain heightfield data and draw each row two vertices at a time for the GL_TRIANGLE_STRIP. We also apply a color to the terrain based on the height of each vertex as a simple way to make the terrain shaded.

Notice how we use the texture function GL_MODULATE to allow the shading color we apply to mix in with the texture colors.

The second half of the DrawTerrain() method draws the water level. The water texture is bound, and the texture function GL_REPLACE is used.

A screenshot of the Terrain example is shown in Figure 7.11.

Figure 7.11 A screenshot of the Terrain example.

Summary

In this chapter you learned the basics of texture mapping, including texture objects, how to specify textures (1D, 2D, 3D, and cube maps), how to use texture coordinates, and how to set up texture filtering modes. You also learned the concept of mipmaps and how to create them with OpenGL. And finally you learned about texture parameters and texture environments and how they affect the final output of your OpenGL texturing.

What You Have Learned

- Texture mapping allows you to attach images to polygons to create realistic objects.
- Texture maps are composed of rectangular arrays of data; each element of these arrays is called a texel.
- Texture coordinates are used to map textures onto primitives.
- Texture objects represent texture data and parameters and are accessed through unique unsigned integers.

- Each texture object has a state associated with it that is unique to that texture.
- The first time you bind a texture, the texture object acquires a new state with initial values, which you can then modify to suit your needs. After that, binding effectively selects the texture.
- OpenGL provides three main functions for specifying a texture: `glTexImage1D()`, `glTexImage2D()`, and `glTexImage3D()`.
- Texture filtering tells OpenGL how it should map the pixels and texels when calculating the final image.
- Magnification refers to when a screen pixel represents a small portion of a texel.
- Minification refers to when a pixel represents a collection of texels.
- A mipmap is a texture consisting of levels of varying resolutions taken from the same texture image. Each level in the texture has a resolution lower than the previous one.
- OpenGL provides several parameters to control how textures are treated when specified, changed, or applied as texture maps. Each parameter is set by calling the `glTexParameter()` function.
- The decision to use the minification filtering mode or the magnification filtering mode on a texture is determined by a set of parameters controlling the texture level of detail calculations.
- OpenGL's `glTexEnv()` function allows you to set parameters of the texture environment that determines how texture values are interpreted when texturing.

Review Questions

1. How is 2D texturing enabled in OpenGL?
2. What is a texture object?
3. Write the line of code to specify a 64 × 64 2D RGBA texture whose pixel data is stored in unsigned bytes.
4. If the base texture level size is 128 × 128, what are the dimensions of the mipmaps?
5. What is the default OpenGL texture wrap mode?
6. True or false: Each texture unit maintains its own texture environment.

On Your Own

1. Given a pointer to 2D image data, `imageData`, whose dimensions are 256 × 256 and type is RGBA, write code to create a texture object, specify the 2D texture with mipmaps, and texture a polygon with that texture.
2. Modify the Terrain example to texture the higher elevations of the terrain with a snow texture.

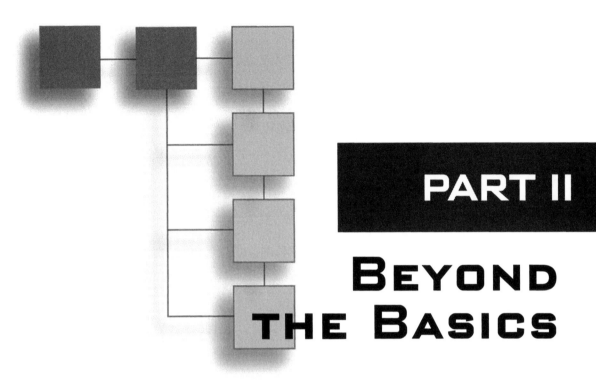

PART II

BEYOND THE BASICS

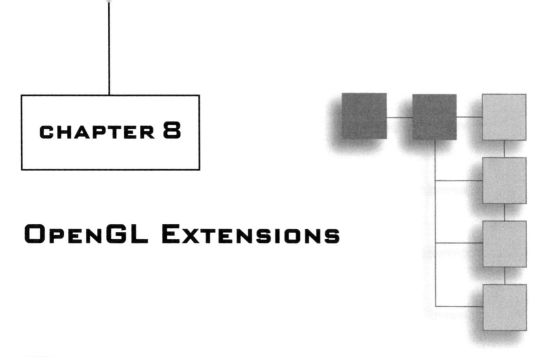

CHAPTER 8

OpenGL Extensions

B ack in Chapter 1, "The Exploration Begins . . . Again," we mentioned that the OpenGL extension mechanism exists so that hardware vendors can easily innovate and add features that graphics and game developers can immediately access through OpenGL. The most useful and ubiquitous of these extensions eventually become part of the OpenGL core specification.

In this chapter you'll learn more about extensions and how to use them. Specifically, you'll learn:

- Exactly what an extension is
- Why extensions are particularly important on Windows platforms
- How to use extensions under Windows
- How to use GLee to manage extensions easily and quickly

Anatomy of an Extension

Fundamentally, an extension is—just like OpenGL itself—a specification. When a new extension is created, it is documented and released through several channels, most importantly the official OpenGL Extension Registry, which can be found online at:

http://oss.sgi.com/projects/ogl-sample/registry/

The specification for an extension includes a great deal of information about the extension, including a brief justification for its existence, other extensions it depends on or interacts with, updates to the OpenGL specification that need to be made to accommodate it, and a revision history. It also includes the name of the extension, the extension name string, and new functions and tokens introduced by the extension. Because these are the things you'll be dealing with most often, let's look at each one of them in detail.

Extensions Under Windows

Given the bleeding edge nature of extensions, they may seem out of place in a beginners' text, a sentiment with which we'd normally agree. However, if you're using OpenGL on any Windows platforms, extensions are absolutely necessary because they are the only current means of using anything beyond OpenGL 1.1.

To understand why, let's review what you need in order to program using any precompiled library, including OpenGL. First of all, you need the appropriate header files. The headers contain function prototypes, constant definitions, and macros. Second, you need the libraries containing the implementations of functions defined in the header. Most libraries get updated from time to time, adding new features, and possibly changing existing ones. To be able to take advantage of these new features in a program you're writing, you need to have the latest headers and libraries.

That's where the problem lies. The latest commercial headers and libraries for OpenGL available on Windows platforms are for OpenGL 1.1. That's right, the latest OpenGL headers and libraries for Windows are four versions and almost 10 years out of date.

Fortunately, even though Microsoft has not been keeping up with the latest OpenGL specification, the major graphics hardware vendors have been. The latest OpenGL features are implemented in their hardware and drivers and just waiting to be tapped—through the extension mechanism.

Extension Names

Every OpenGL extension has a name by which it can be precisely and uniquely identified. They use the following naming convention:

`PREFIX_extension_name`

The `PREFIX` identifies the vendor who developed the extension or, in the case of EXT and ARB, the extension's level of promotion. Table 8.1 lists the most important prefixes currently in use and their associated meaning. The `extension_name` identifies the extension. Note that the name cannot contain any spaces. Some example extension names are `ARB_shading_language_100`, `EXT_packed_pixels`, `NV_blend_square`, and `ATI_texture_float`.

Tip

Some extensions share a name but have a different prefix. These extensions may not be interchangeable because their semantics may differ slightly. For example, `ARB_texture_env_combine` is not the same thing as `EXT_texture_env_combine`. Rather than making assumptions, be sure to consult the extension specifications when you're unsure.

Table 8.1 Subset of OpenGL Extension Prefixes

Prefix	Meaning/Vendor
ARB	Extension approved by OpenGL's Architectural Review Board (first introduced with OpenGL 1.2)
EXT	Extension agreed upon by more than one OpenGL vendor
ATI	ATI Technologies
ATIX	ATI Technologies (experimental)
NV	NVIDIA Corporation
SGI	Silicon Graphics
SGIS	Silicon Graphics (specialized)
SUN	Sun Microsystems
WIN	Microsoft

Name Strings

Each extension defines a name string that, when used in conjunction with `glGetString(GL_EXTENSIONS)`, is used to identify whether or not an implementation supports the extension. We'll discuss the details of how to use this in the "Using Extensions" section later in this chapter.

Name strings are generally the name of the extension preceded by another prefix. For most OpenGL name strings, this is `GL_` (e.g., `GL_ARB_shadow`). When the name string is tied to a particular windows system however, the prefix will reflect which system that is (e.g., Win32 uses `WGL_`).

Note

Some extensions may define more than one name string. This would be the case if the extension provided both core OpenGL functionality and functionality specific to the windowing system.

Functions

Many (but not all) extensions introduce one or more new functions to OpenGL. To use these functions, you'll have to obtain a pointer to their entry point, which requires that you know the name of the function. This process is described in detail in the "Using Extensions" section.

The functions defined by the extension follow the naming convention used by the rest of OpenGL, namely `glFunctionName()`, with the addition of a suffix using the same letters as the extension name's prefix. For example, the `NV_fence` extension includes the functions `glGetFencesNV()`, `glSetFenceNV()`, `glTestFenceNV()`, and so on.

Tokens

An extension may define one or more tokens or enumerants. In some extensions, these tokens are intended for use in the new functions defined by the extension (which may be able to use existing enumerants as well). In other cases, they are intended for use with existing OpenGL functions, thereby adding new functionality. For example, the ARB_texture_env_add extension defines a new enumerant, GL_ADD. This enumerant can be passed as the params parameter of the various glTexEnv() functions when the pname parameter is GL_TEXTURE_ENV_MODE.

The new enumerants follow the normal OpenGL naming convention (i.e., GL_WHATEVER), except that they are suffixed by the letters used in the extension name's prefix, such as GL_VERTEX_SOURCE_ATI.

Using new enumerants is much simpler than using new functions, since they are simply numeric values. These values appear in the spec, so you can define the tokens yourself or use a third-party header, such as the one provided by SGI at the following URL:

http://oss.sgi.com/projects/ogl-sample/ABI/glext.h

In addition to definitions for new tokens, this file also contains prototypes and function pointer typedefs for extension functions. Similar headers are available from the NVIDIA and ATI Web sites.

Tip

Though most extensions add either functions or tokens (or both), some don't. The ones that don't simply allow existing functions and tokens to be used together in ways that previously weren't allowed.

Using Extensions

Now that you have a better understanding of what an extension is, it's time to learn how to use them. The process can be described in a few simple steps:

1. Determine whether or not the extension is supported.

2. Obtain the entry point for any of the extension's functions that you want to use.

3. Define any tokens you're going to use.

Note

Before checking for extension availability and obtaining pointers to functions, you MUST have a current rendering context.

Checking the Name String

Calling glGetString() with GL_EXTENSIONS returns a string containing a list of all of the name strings for all extensions supported by the implementation. You can then parse this string to determine whether the extension you want is present. The code will look something like this:

```
char* extensionsList = (char*) glGetString(GL_EXTENSIONS);
```

After this executes, extensionsList points to a null-terminated buffer. The name strings in it are separated by spaces, including a space after the last name string.

Note

> We're casting the value returned by glGetString() because the function actually returns an array of unsigned chars. Because most of the string manipulation functions require signed chars, we do the cast once now instead of doing it many times later.

When parsing the extension string, some care needs to be taken to avoid accidentally matching a substring. For example, if you're trying to use the NV_texture_shader extension and the implementation doesn't support it but it does support NV_texture_shader3, calling something like:

```
strstr("GL_NV_texture_shader", extensionsList);
```

is going to give you positive results, making you think that the EXT_texture_env extension is supported, when it's really not. The CheckExtension() function shown below demonstrates one way to avoid this problem.

```
bool CheckExtension(char* extensionName)
{
  // get the list of supported extensions
  char* extensionList = (char*) glGetString(GL_EXTENSIONS);

  if (!extensionName || !extensionList)
    return false;

  while (*extensionList)
  {
    // find the length of the first extension substring
    unsigned int firstExtensionLength = strcspn(extensionList, " ");


    if (strlen(extensionName) == firstExtensionLength &&
        strncmp(extensionName, extensionList, firstExtensionLength) == 0)
    {
```

```
        return true;
    }

    // move to the next substring
    extensionList += firstExtensionLength + 1;
}

return false;
}
```

If an extension you'd like to use isn't supported, you need to take appropriate action. This may be disabling that particular feature, trying a similar extension instead, or even exiting gracefully. The important thing is to not assume that the extension exists. Doing so can lead to crashes or weird behavior, especially if you're using new or vendor-specific extensions.

Obtaining the Function's Entry Point

Because you do not have the implementation of extension functions available to you when you compile your program, you need to dynamically link to them at runtime. This merely involves obtaining a function pointer.

The first step is to declare a function pointer. If you've worked with function pointers before, you know that they can be pretty ugly. If not, here's an example:

```
void (APIENTRY * pglCopyTexSubImage3DEXT) (GLenum, GLint, GLint,
    GLint, GLint, GLint, GLint, GLsizei, GLsizei) = NULL;
```

The next step is attempting to assign an entry point to the function pointer. The function used to do this varies, depending on the platform you're using. For Windows, it's wglGetProcAddress():

```
PROC wglGetProcAddress(LPCSTR lpszProcName);
```

The only parameter is the name of the function you want to get the address of. The return value is the entry point of the function if it exists, or NULL otherwise. Because the value returned is a generic pointer, you need to cast it to the appropriate function pointer type.

Let's look at an example, using the function pointer we declared above:

```
pglCopyTexSubImage3DEXT =
    (void (APIENTRY *) (GLenum, GLint, GLint, GLint, GLint,
                        GLint, GLint, GLsizei, GLsizei))
    wglGetProcAddress("glCopyTexSubImage3DEXT");
```

And you thought the function pointer declaration was ugly.

You can make life easier on yourself by using typedefs. As mentioned earlier, the glext.h header already contains typedefs for most of the extension functions, making your life easier. Using this header, the previous code improves to:

```
PFNGLCOPYTEXSUBIMAGE3DEXTPROC pglCopyTexSubImage3DEXT = NULL;
pglCopyTexSubImage3DEXT = (PFNGLCOPYTEXSUBIMAGE3DEXTPROC)
    wglGetProcAddress("glCopyTexSubImage3DEXT");
```

As long as wglGetProcAddress() doesn't return NULL, you can then freely use the function pointer as if it were a normal OpenGL function.

Tip

You may notice that in the example code we've added a p to the beginning of the function name. When declaring OpenGL function pointers, it's a good idea to avoid using the same name as the function because this can cause linking conflicts when using shared libraries. One way to get around having to use the prefixed function in your code is to use an alias, such as #define glCopyTexSubImage3DEXT pglCopyTexSubImage3DEXT.

Declaring Enumerants

If you are using glext.h or some other third-party header, all the tokens you need are already defined for you. Otherwise, you can look up the values in the spec and define them yourself. For example, the spec for EXT_texture_lod_bias says that GL_TEXTURE_LOD_BIAS_EXT should have a value of 0x8501, so you'd use the following:

```
#define GL_TEXTURE_LOD_BIAS_EXT    0x8501
```

WGL Extensions

In addition to the standard OpenGL extensions, there are some extensions that are specific to the Windows system. These extensions provide additions that are very specific to the windowing system and the way it interacts with OpenGL, such as additional options related to pixel formats. These extensions are easily identified by their use of "WGL" instead of "GL" in their names. The name strings for these extensions normally aren't included in the buffer returned by glGetString(GL_EXTENSIONS), although a few are. To get all of the Windows-specific extensions, you'll have to use another function, wglGetExtensionsStringARB(). As the ARB suffix indicates, it's an extension itself (ARB_extensions_string), so you'll have to get the address of it yourself using wglGetProcAddress(). Note that some drivers identify this as wglGetExtensionsStringEXT() instead, so if you fail to get a pointer to one, try the other. The format of this function is as follows:

```
const char* wglGetExtensionsStringARB(HDC hdc);
```

Its sole parameter is the handle to your rendering context. The function returns a buffer similar to that returned by `glGetString(GL_EXTENSIONS)`, with the only difference being that it contains only the names of WGL extensions.

Tip

Most of the time, it's good practice to check for an extension by examining the buffer returned by `glGetString()` before trying to obtain function entry points. However, it's not strictly necessary to do so. If you try to get the entry point for a non-existent function, `wglGetProcAddress()` will return `NULL`, and you can simply test for that. The reason for mentioning this is because to use `wglGetExtensionsStringARB()`, that's exactly what you have to do. It appears that with most drivers, the name string for this extension doesn't appear in the buffer returned by `glGetString()`. Instead, it is included in the buffer returned by `wglGetExtensionsStringARB()`! Go figure.

Note

Some WGL extension string names appear in the buffer returned by `wglGetExtensionsStringARB()` as well as the buffer returned by `glGetString()`. This is due to the fact that those extensions existed before the creation of `ARB_extensions_string`, and so their name strings appear in both places to avoid breaking existing software.

Just as there is a `glext.h` header for core OpenGL extensions, so is there a `wglext.h` for WGL extensions. You can find it at the following link:

http://oss.sgi.com/projects/ogl-sample/ABI/wglext.h

Introduction to GLee

Throughout the book, many of the demos have used one or two extensions to get around the Windows OpenGL 1.1 limitation. As you can see from the code, managing a few extensions isn't particularly difficult. However, as you begin to develop more complex games, you may find yourself managing dozens of extensions, which can be painful. For this reason, many people have developed libraries to automatically manage extensions. Some of them have even released these libraries to the public.

The best publicly available OpenGL extension library we've found is the OpenGL Easy Extension library, or GLee, developed and maintained by Ben Woodhouse. GLee is currently available for Windows and Linux, is updated automatically from the OpenGL Extension Registry, and is released under an unrestrictive modified BSD license. We've included the latest version of GLee on the CD, but you can check for updates at:

http://elf-stone.com/downloads.php#GLee

Setting Up GLee

Before using GLee, you need to install it appropriately on your system. For Linux, this is as easy as unpacking the tarball and running the install script included with it. For Windows, you need to extract the files and copy GLee.h to the same location as the OpenGL headers (which are in your compiler's header directory in the gl_ subdirectory) and GLee.lib to your compiler's library directory. Alternatively, you can use the GLee source code directly by extracting GLee.cpp someplace convenient for later use.

Once GLee is installed, you can use it in your projects by including the header and linking to the library or including GLee.cpp in your project. GLee.h should be included instead of gl.h, which it includes internally.

Using GLee

Before using GLee in your project, you have to initialize it. This should be done after you've initialized the rest of OpenGL and is done by calling the following function:

```
GLboolean GLeeInit();
```

If this call returns GL_TRUE, GLee has been successfully started, and you will then be able to use it to access the full core and extended functionality of OpenGL—well, insofar as your video card supports it. If GLeeInit() returns GL_FALSE, you can call the following function:

```
const char* GLeeGetErrorString();
```

which returns a descriptive string explaining the problem.

GLee includes a global Boolean variable for each extension that you can check to see whether that particular extension is supported. The names of these flags are the extension names prefixed by GLEE_. To check to see whether point sprites are available, you would use:

```
if (GLEE_ARB_point_sprite)
{
    glEnable(GL_POINT_SPRITE_ARB);
    ...
}
```

Platform-specific (WGL/GLX) extensions are handled slightly differently. The Boolean variables for them are named GLEE_ followed by the full name string, including the WGL or GLX portion (for example, GLEE_WGL_ARB_pbuffer).

You can also test to see which OpenGL version is supported by checking the value of GLEE_VERSION_x_y where x is the major and y is the minor OpenGL version. To check to see if OpenGL 1.4 is supported, you would use:

```
if (GLEE_VERSION_1_4)
{
    glSecondaryColor3f(0.5f, 0.3f, 1.0f);
    ...
}
```

That's all there is to it. As you can see from even these brief code snippets, GLee has already defined all the tokens and set up the necessary function pointers for you.

Using GLee with Core Extensions

There are many extensions that are now part of core OpenGL. GLee allows you to use these features without using suffixes on the functions. For example, you can use:

```
glFogCoordf(...);
```
instead of:
```
glFogCoordfEXT(...);
```

If you choose to use the former approach, be sure that you're testing the GLEE_VERSION_x_y flag to see if the OpenGL implementation supports the version number and that the extension was promoted to the core. Testing only the extension-specific flag could result in a false positive. For example, if you are using fog coordinates, you might be tempted to use something like the following code:

```
if (GLEE_EXT_fog_coord)
  glFogCoordf(...);
```

However, on systems with OpenGL 1.3 or earlier, glFogCoordf is an invalid pointer, even though GLEE_EXT_fog_coord may be true. This is because fog coordinates weren't promoted to the core until OpenGL 1.4. The following code avoids this problem and provides a more robust solution:

```
if (GLEE_VERSION_1_4)
  glFogCoordf(...)
else if (GLEE_EXT_fog_coord)
  glFogCoordfEXT(...)
```

Extensions in Action

Because the demos for this book were written for Windows, and many of them make use of post-OpenGL 1.1 features, there are plenty of examples of using extensions available on the CD. Rather than picking some arbitrary extension to use as an example for this chapter, we've taken the fog demo from Chapter 5 and rewritten it using GLee instead of directly obtaining function pointers. As you can see from Figure 8.1, textures have also been added, contributing to the realism.

Figure 8.1 Chapter 5's Fog demo, rebuilt using GLee and textures.

Summary

OpenGL extensions are essential to anyone doing development for Windows. You should now understand why they are important and how you can use them to take advantage of the latest features offered by modern video cards. You've also seen how libraries such as GLee can make managing extensions easier. In addition to the core extensions used throughout this book, you're encouraged to explore and experiment with extensions on your own to see the latest and greatest coming in the world of graphics.

What You Have Learned

- Extensions exist to enable hardware vendors to innovate and add new features quickly.
- The primary elements of extensions that you deal with when programming are functions, tokens, and the extension string.
- Libraries such as GLee make it easy to manage a large number of extensions.

Review Questions

1. What does the ARB extension prefix indicate?

2. Why are extensions particularly important on Windows platforms?

3. How can you check to see whether an extension is supported (without using GLee)?

4. When should you check GLEE_VERSION_x_y instead of checking extension-specific flags such as GLEE_ARB_point_parameters?

On Your Own

1. Write a program to display a list of all the extensions supported by your OpenGL implementation. If you're using Windows, check for Windows-specific extensions as well.

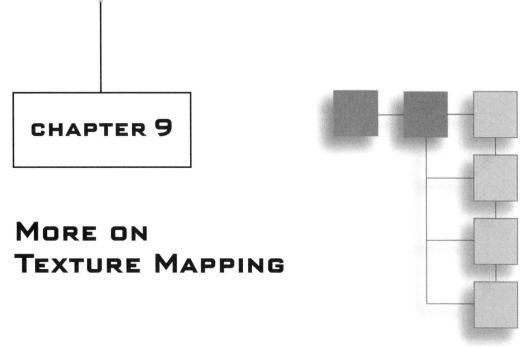

CHAPTER 9

MORE ON TEXTURE MAPPING

In Chapter 7, "Texture Mapping," you learned about all of the basic elements involved in texture mapping, but there is still much to learn. Texture mapping is one of the most important components of 3D graphics, and we've only scratched the surface of what OpenGL has to offer to support texture mapping. In this chapter, we'll dive a little deeper, exploring such topics as:

- Alternative methods of specifying texture data
- How to use the texture matrix
- How to have OpenGL generate texture coordinates for you
- What multitexturing is, and how to use it
- How to use texture combiners

More on Texture Specification

In Chapter 7, you learned about the glTexImage() functions. These functions each take an array of data—either loaded from an image file or generated procedurally—that is used to form the entire texture image. This is how you'll use textures most of the time, but there may be instances where you'll only want to update a sub-region of an existing texture. Perhaps you would like to create a texture from an image that you rendered from the screen. You'll learn how to do both in this section.

Sub-Images

Every time you create a new texture using one of the glTexImage() functions, OpenGL has to internally allocate memory and perform other operations, which can be expensive. An alternative to this is to reuse an existing texture—either because it's no longer being used or because it's being updated dynamically—by simply modifying the existing texture image data. Given a texture that has already been successfully created, you can modify all or part of it using one of the following APIs:

```
void glTexSubImage1D(GLenum target, GLint level, GLint xoffset, GLsizei width,
                     GLenum format, GLenum type, const GLvoid* pixels);
void glTexSubImage2D(GLenum target, GLint level, GLint xoffset, GLint yoffset,
                     GLsizei width, GLsizei height, GLenum format, GLenum type,
                     const GLvoid* pixels);
void glTexSubImage3D(GLenum target, GLint level, GLint xoffset, GLint yoffset,
                     GLint zoffset, GLsizei width, GLsizei height,
                     GLsizei depth, GLenum format, GLenum type,
                     const GLvoid* pixels);
```

Extension

Extension name: EXT_texture3D

Name string: GL_EXT_texture3D

Promoted to core: OpenGL 1.2

Function names: glTexSubImage3DEXT(), glCopyTexSubImage3DEXT()

Most of the parameters should look familiar to you from the glTexImage() functions in Chapter 7. There are two new sets of parameters. xoffset, yoffset, and zoffset are used to specify the left, bottom, and front (respectively) coordinates of the area that you want to place a sub-image in. width, height, and depth are the dimensions of this area. The are defined by these values and must fit within the boundaries of the existing texture.

You'll notice that there are no internalformat, width, height, or border parameters. This is because these parameters were all established when the texture was originally created, and changing them would require reallocating memory, which would defeat the purpose of using glTexSubImage() in the first place.

Copying from the Color Buffer

Being able to render something to the screen and then use the rendered image as a texture can be used for many different procedural and dynamic effects, such as reflection. This can be done using one of the following:

```
void glCopyTexImage1D(GLenum target, GLint level, GLint internalformat, GLint x,
                      GLint y, GLsizei width, GLint border);
void glCopyTexImage2D(GLenum target, GLint level, GLint internalformat, GLint x,
                      GLint y, GLsizei width, GLsizei height, GLint border);
```

The target, level, internalformat, and border parameters are the same as for the glTexImage() functions. The major difference is that instead of passing an array containing the texture image data, the texture is created by copying pixels from the color buffer. The x and y parameters are used to specify the bottom left corner of the rectangle to copy from, and width and height are the dimensions of the rectangle. The dimensions of the rectangle must be powers of two.

You'll notice that there is no 3D version of glCopyTexImage(). This is because these functions create a complete new texture, just like glTexImage(). It's impossible to create a complete 3D texture from a 2D image.

It is also possible to update all or a portion of an existing texture by copying from the screen. This is similar to glTexSubImage() and has the same advantages. The APIs for doing this are as follows:

```
void glCopyTexSubImage1D(GLenum target, GLint level, GLint xoffset, GLint x,
                         GLint y, GLsizei width);
void glCopyTexSubImage2D(GLenum target, GLint level, GLint xoffset,
                         GLint yoffset, GLint x, GLint y, GLsizei width,
                         GLsizei height);
void glCopyTexSubImage3D(GLenum target, GLint level, GLint xoffset,
                         GLint yoffset, GLint zoffset, GLint x, GLint y,
                         GLsizei width, GLsizei height);
```

The target and level parameters have the same purpose that you've seen in many texture functions. xoffset, yoffset, and zoffset are used to specify the bottom-left-front corner of the region of the texture that you want to update. x and y indicate the bottom left corner of the screen rectangle you are copying from, and width and height are the dimensions of the rectangle.

Tip

When using glTexSubImage() or glCopyTexSubImage() with mipmaps, you can make your life much easier by using automatic mipmap generation, as described in Chapter 7. Doing so, you only need to modify the base level, and all the other levels will be updated automatically.

In the "Environment Mapping" section of this chapter, you'll see an example that uses glCopyTexImage2D() and glCopyTexSubImage2D() to dynamically generate cube map textures. The code that does this is shown here:

```
void CGfxOpenGL::GenerateEnvTexture()
{
  static bool s_initialized = false;

  glViewport(0, 0, ENV_TEX_SIZE, ENV_TEX_SIZE);
```

```
glMatrixMode(GL_PROJECTION);
glLoadIdentity();

gluPerspective(90, 1, 0.1, 500);

glMatrixMode(GL_MODELVIEW);
for (int i = 0; i < 6; ++i)
{
  glClear(GL_DEPTH_BUFFER_BIT);

  glLoadIdentity();
  gluLookAt(0.0, 0.0, 0.0,
            ENV_ROTATION[i][0], ENV_ROTATION[i][1], ENV_ROTATION[i][2],
            ENV_ROTATION[i][3], ENV_ROTATION[i][4], ENV_ROTATION[i][5]);

  // draw the scene
  m_skybox.Render(0.0, 0.0, 0.0);
  DrawBalls();

  glBindTexture(GL_TEXTURE_CUBE_MAP, m_envTexID);

  if (s_initialized)
  {
    glCopyTexSubImage2D(GL_TEXTURE_CUBE_MAP_POSITIVE_X + i, 0, 0, 0, 0, 0,
                        ENV_TEX_SIZE, ENV_TEX_SIZE);
  }
  else
  {
    glCopyTexImage2D(GL_TEXTURE_CUBE_MAP_POSITIVF_X + i, 0, GL_RGB, 0, 0,
                     ENV_TEX_SIZE, ENV_TEX_SIZE, 0);
  }
}

s_initialized = true;

SetupProjection(m_windowWidth, m_windowHeight);
}
```

This code generates the faces of a cube map texture by rendering the scene six times, rotating the camera by 90 degrees each time to capture all views. The scene is rendered into a viewport that matches the size of the texture. The screen is then copied into the texture for the appropriate cube face. The first time through this loop, glCopyTexImage2D() is used to properly initialize and create the texture. After that, `glCopyTexSubImage2D()` is used to update the entire texture.

Note

Copying from the screen is a slow operation. Using `glCopyTexImage()` is better than using `glReadPixels()`/`glTexImage()`, and `glCopyTexSubImage()` is even better, but they still may cause a performance bottleneck if you're making heavy use of them for texture generation. There are a couple of extensions that provide faster alternatives, but they are beyond the scope of this book.

The Texture Matrix Stack

In Chapter 4, "Coordinate Transformations and OpenGL Matrices," we talked about how you can transform vertices with translation, rotation, and scaling by modifying the modelview matrix. We also mentioned the matrix stack and how you can push and pop matrices to achieve hierarchical modeling.

You can do these same things with textures through the use of texture matrices and the *texture matrix stack*. For instance, you can use the `glTranslatef()` function to move a texture across a surface. Similarly, you can use the `glRotatef()` function to rotate texture coordinates on a surface, which, in effect, rotates the texture. The game *American McGee's Alice*, by Electronic Arts and Rogue Entertainment, made great use of the effects produced by manipulating the texture matrix when they created the psychedelic world of Wonderland.

Manipulating the texture matrix is very easy. You can use any of the standard matrix-manipulation functions that OpenGL provides, such as `glMultMatrix()`, `glPushMatrix()`, `glPopMatrix()`, and the transformation functions. You just need to select the texture matrix stack as the current stack using `glMatrixMode()`:

```
glMatrixMode(GL_TEXTURE);
```

Then you can perform any transformations you want on the texture matrix and the texture matrix stack. All texture coordinates are multiplied by the texture matrix in exactly the same way vertices are multiplied by the projection and modelview matrices.

Following is some sample code that shows how you can rotate a texture on a surface:

```
// clear screen and depth buffer
glClear(GL_COLOR_BUFFER_BIT | GL_DEPTH_BUFFER_BIT);
glLoadIdentity();

// set current matrix mode to texture matrix mode
glMatrixMode(GL_TEXTURE);
```

```
glLoadIdentity();
glRotatef(angle, 0.0f, 0.0f, 1.0f);        // rotate the texture
glMatrixMode(GL_MODELVIEW);                  // go back to modelview matrix

glBindTexture(GL_TEXTURE_2D, texID);        // set current texture

// draw textured quad
glBegin(GL_QUADS);
    glTexCoord2f(0.0f, 0.0f);
    glVertex3f(-20.0f, -20.0f, -40.0f);
    glTexCoord2f(1.0f, 0.0f);
    glVertex3f(20.0f, -20.0f, -40.0f);
    glTexCoord2f(1.0f, 1.0f);
    glVertex3f(20.0f, 20.0f, -40.0f);
    glTexCoord2f(0.0f, 1.0f);
    glVertex3f(-20.0f, 20.0f, -40.0f);
glEnd();
```

As you can see, you set the current matrix mode to the texture matrix mode. You then load the identity matrix, which is the default texture matrix to begin with (before you apply the glRotatef() function to the texture matrix), which will rotate your texture at some angle around the positive z-axis. After you've performed your rotation, you tell OpenGL to go back to the modelview matrix mode, where you draw a textured quadrilateral. Not too difficult, is it?

Note

The texture matrix will be applied to *all* texture coordinates, so if you're using it to animate a few textures, be sure to reset it to identity before you render any textures that you don't want animated. Better yet, use glPush/PopMatrix().

Try playing around with the texture matrix stack on your own. You might find some awesome effects to use in your games!

Texture Coordinate Generation

In Chapter 7, we talked about what texture coordinates are and how to use them, but we didn't say much about how you come up with appropriate texture coordinates in the first place. If you're loading a model from a file, it will usually include texture coordinates if the model includes a texture, so that's what you'll use most of the time. For some texture applications, however, you can have OpenGL automatically generate texture coordinates for you. This works in situations where the texture coordinates can be determined using well-defined mathematical steps. Examples include reflections, contouring, and projective texturing. We'll be discussing a couple of specific examples here.

Texture coordinate generation is controlled independently for each coordinate. To use it, you must first enable it by passing GL_TEXTURE_GEN_S, GL_TEXTURE_GEN_T, GL_TEXTURE_GEN_R, or GL_TEXTURE_GEN_Q (each corresponding to the indicated coordinate) to glEnable().

To specify how texture coordinates are generated, you use one of the following:

```
void glTexGen{ifd}(GLenum coord, GLenum pname, TYPE param);
void glTexGen{ifd}v(GLenum coord, GLenum pname, const TYPE *params);
```

coord indicates which texture coordinate to apply the parameter to. Valid values are GL_S, GL_T, GL_R, and GL_Q, corresponding to the *s*, *t*, *r*, and *q* texture coordinates. The accepted values of pname and the param or params associated with them are listed in Table 9.1.

Table 9.1 Texture Generation Parameters

Parameter	Meaning
GL_TEXTURE_GEN_MODE	param specifies the texture generation mode, which must be GL_OBJECT_LINEAR, GL_EYE_LINEAR, GL_SPHERE_MAP, GL_REFLECTION_MAP*, or GL_NORMAL_MAP*.
GL_OBJECT_PLANE	params is a pointer to a four-element array of values that are used as parameters for the texture coordinate generation function. Used in conjunction with GL_OBJECT_LINEAR.
GL_EYE_PLANE	Same as above, but used with GL_EYE_LINEAR.

* Available only via the ARB_texture_cube_map extension under Windows.

If the texture generation mode is GL_OBJECT_LINEAR, then the texture coordinates are generated using the following equation:

$$\text{texcoord} = p_1 * x_0 + p_2 * y_0 + p_3 * z_0 + p_4 * w_0$$

x_0, y_0, z_0, and w_0 are the object-space coordinates of the vertex the texture coordinate is being generated for. p_1, p_2, p_3, and p_4 are the four parameters provided via GL_OBJECT_PLANE. These are used to pass the *A*, *B*, *C*, and *D* coefficients of a plane, so this equation is in effect calculating the distance from the plane and using that as the texture coordinate.

The GL_EYE_LINEAR texture generation mode uses a similar equation, except that eye-space vertex coordinates are used, and the inverse modelview matrix is applied to the plane parameters when they are specified.

When using the GL_NORMAL_MAP mode, the (s, t, r) texture coordinates are generated by using the vertex's normal, transformed into eye-space. These are intended to be used with cube maps.

The remaining two texture generation modes will be covered in the next section, but for now, let's look at an example of generating texture coordinates based on the distance from a plane.

When rendering terrain, you can create a visually appealing effect by varying the color based on the height of the terrain. Areas close to sea level appear as sand; slightly higher areas appear as grass, and then dirt or rock, and finally snow on the highest peaks. One way to achieve this is to create a one-dimensional texture like the one shown in Figure 9.1. Then, you would enable texture generation based on the height above sea level by passing the coefficients for the sea level plane to glTexGen() and enable texture generation for the s coordinate. Later in this chapter, in the "Multitexturing" section, you'll see a demo that does exactly that, so let's look at the code that sets up and uses texture coordinate generation.

First, during initialization, texture coordinate generation is enabled, GL_OBJECT_LINEAR mode is selected, and the reference plane is passed via GL_OBJECT_PLANE:

```
glEnable(GL_TEXTURE_GEN_S);
glTexGeni(GL_S, GL_TEXTURE_GEN_MODE, GL_OBJECT_LINEAR);

GLfloat waterPlane[] = { 0.0, 1.0, 0.0, -WATER_HEIGHT };
glTexGenfv(GL_S, GL_OBJECT_PLANE, waterPlane);
```

Then, when actually rendering the terrain, the only thing that needs to be done is to scale the generated texture coordinate. This is because the generated coordinate is the distance from the plane, which could be any value. We want the texture coordinates to fall in the range [0, 1] so that the lowest points correspond to sand and the highest points correspond to snow. This is simply a matter of dividing the texture coordinate by the maximum terrain height. Using the texture matrix you learned about in the last section, this is done as follows:

```
glMatrixMode(GL_TEXTURE);
glLoadIdentity();
glScalef(1.0f/MAX_HEIGHT, 1.0, 1.0);
```

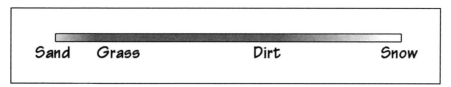

Figure 9.1 A 1D texture used to color terrain.

That's all there is to it. Similar methods can be used for creating contours or projective textures. Now let's look at the other two texture generation modes.

Environment Mapping

If you've ever tried to model things like chrome, polished metal, or glass, you know that no matter how you tweak the materials or what texture you use, it doesn't look very much like the real thing. This is because all of these things reflect the environment they are in, so to model them correctly, you need to use *environment mapping*. The GL_SPHERE_MAP and GL_REFLECTION_MAP texture generation modes can be used in conjunction with an appropriate texture map to create realistic reflections.

For the GL_SPHERE_MAP mode, or *sphere mapping*, the texture coordinates are generated using a vector from the eye to the point on the surface and the surface normal (transformed into eye space) to create a reflection vector. The reflection vector is used to calculate the texture coordinates. These coordinates are then used to index into a 2D texture map like that shown in Figure 9.2. The image is a picture of a sphere completely reflecting the world around it. Both the *s* and *t* coordinates need to be generated via sphere mapping to have it work correctly.

Sphere mapping comes with many drawbacks, one of the most significant being that it's view dependent, so viewing a reflective object from anywhere other than the center of projection can produce incorrect results. They also tend to not look very accurate on objects that aren't roughly spherical. Finally, obtaining the texture image in the first place presents a challenge. Traditionally, they were obtained by taking a photograph of a perfectly reflective sphere placed in the room that is being modeled. For this to be completely mathematically correct, the camera needs to be infinitely far away, but since this is impossible, a fish eye lens is used instead to get results that are reasonably close. This approach isn't really viable for game environments.

Figure 9.2 A typical texture used with GL_SPHERE_MAP.

Another drawback is that the reflection won't pick up any objects moving in the world, so it will be immediately obvious that the surface isn't really reflective.

An alternative way to generate the texture image is to render the world six times (once for each direction) from the reflective object's perspective. The results are then stored in the six faces of a cube map, which is then applied to a sphere. This is actually how the image in Figure 9.2 was generated. This approach is much better, since a reflection image can be generated anywhere in your world, and it can be updated dynamically to reflect objects in motion. However, as you're about to see, you can make use of the cube map directly, so the additional step of generating a sphere map is wasteful. Cube maps are also view independent and can be easily mapped onto any objects. For these reasons, sphere mapping is generally not used anymore.

When cube map textures were introduced to OpenGL, they brought with them the GL_REFLECTION_MAP texture coordinate generation mode. The texture coordinates are generated in a manner similar to GL_SPHERE_MAP, except that instead of creating *s* and *t* coordinates for a 2D texture, *s*, *t*, and *r* coordinates are generated that are used to index into the faces of the cube map. Cube maps are much easier to update dynamically and do a better job of capturing the entire environment. The example in the next section shows you how cube maps can be used for reflections.

Example: Reflective Cube Mapping

On the CD, you'll find an example program for this chapter entitled EnvironmentMapping, that puts reflective cube maps to use. As you can see from Figure 9.3, this program shows a reflective sphere that is being orbited by two colored balls, placed in an outdoor environment. In the "Copying from the Color Buffer" section earlier in this chapter, you saw the portion of this code that creates the faces of the cube map texture by

Figure 9.3 A reflective sphere, made possible with cube maps and reflection mapping.

rendering the scene six times from the perspective of the sphere. The cube map is then applied to the sphere using texture coordinate generation. To do this, the texture generation mode is first set up during initialization, as follows:

```
glTexGenf(GL_S, GL_TEXTURE_GEN_MODE, GL_REFLECTION_MAP);
glTexGenf(GL_T, GL_TEXTURE_GEN_MODE, GL_REFLECTION_MAP);
glTexGenf(GL_R, GL_TEXTURE_GEN_MODE, GL_REFLECTION_MAP);
```

Then, to actually apply the texture to the sphere, texture coordinate generation for the *s*, *t* and *r* coordinates has to be enabled. This happens in the Render() method, as shown below:

```
void CGfxOpenGL::Render()
{
  GenerateEnvTexture();

  glClear(GL_DEPTH_BUFFER_BIT);

  glLoadIdentity();

  m_skybox.Render(0.0, 0.0, 0.0);

  glTranslatef(0.0, 0.0, -5.0);

  GLfloat lightPos[] = { 0.5f, 0.5, 1.0, 0.0 };
  glLightfv(GL_LIGHT0, GL_POSITION, lightPos);

  glEnable(GL_TEXTURE_GEN_S);
  glEnable(GL_TEXTURE_GEN_T);
  glEnable(GL_TEXTURE_GEN_R);

  glEnable(GL_TEXTURE_CUBE_MAP);
  glBindTexture(GL_TEXTURE_CUBE_MAP, m_envTexID);
  glTexEnvf(GL_TEXTURE_ENV, GL_TEXTURE_ENV_MODE, GL_MODULATE);

  glColor3f(1.0f, 1.0f, 1.0f);
  gluSphere(m_pObj, 1.0, 64, 64);
  glDisable(GL_TEXTURE_CUBE_MAP);

  glDisable(GL_TEXTURE_GEN_S);
  glDisable(GL_TEXTURE_GEN_T);
  glDisable(GL_TEXTURE_GEN_R);

  DrawBalls();
}
```

As you can see, creating dynamic reflections with cube maps is quite easy. The cost involved is not trivial because it requires that the scene be rendered an additional six times per reflective object. When used in moderation however, the visual payoff is worth it.

Multitexturing

Extension

Extension name: `ARB_multitexture`

Name string: `GL_ARB_multitexture`

Promoted to core: OpenGL 1.2.1

Function names: `glActiveTextureARB(),_glMultiTexCoord{1234}{sifd}[v]ARB()`

Tokens: `GL_TEXTUREn_ARB`, `GL_MAX_TEXTURE_UNITS_ARB`

In the examples you've seen so far, when you texture-map a polygon, you apply only one texture to it. It's actually possible to apply several textures to the same polygon through a series of texture operations. This is called *multitexturing*.

Up to this point, the textures you've seen assign colors to the polygons they are applied to. Textures used in this way are often referred to as *diffuse maps*. When using multitexturing, typically only one of the textures will be used in this way. The other textures will be used to either modify the diffuse map values or provide additional information. For example, grayscale images can be used to modulate the diffuse color to simulate per pixel lighting or to vary the details. A texture may include normals or other parameters encoded as RGBA values that are used to perform calculations to simulate bumpy surfaces. You'll see some specific examples of multitexturing in this section, but we'll be giving you only a small taste of the many possibilities they offer.

Multitexturing makes use of a series of *texture units*. Each texture unit represents a single texture application, and when you perform multitexturing, each texture unit passes its results to the next texture unit as shown in Figure 9.4. You've actually been making use of texture units all along; everything you've done so far has used the default texture unit (which is texture unit 0). Let's look more closely at what texture units represent and see how to use them.

Texture Units

Each texture unit has a set of states associated with it that allows it to keep settings separate from the other texture units. Each texture unit has its own texture environment, texture matrix stack, texture coordinate generation states, and texture image and filtering

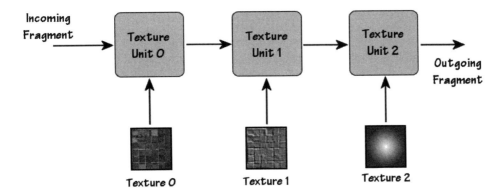

Figure 9.4 Texture unit pipeline.

parameters. The latter two are usually derived from the texture object that is bound to the texture unit. In addition, each of the texture targets (GL_TEXTURE_1D, GL_TEXTURE_2D, GL_TEX- TURE_3D, and GL_TEXTURE_CUBE_MAP) are enabled or disabled on a per–texture-unit basis.

You use the glActiveTexture() function to change the currently active texture unit. It is defined as:

```
void glActiveTexture (GLenum texUnit);
```

After this function is called, all calls to glTexImage() (including the copy and subimage ver- sions), glTexParameter(), glTexEnv(), glTexGen(), and glBindTexture() affect the texture unit defined in texUnit. The texUnit parameter is of the form GL_TEXTURE*n*, where *n* is equal to any integer between 0 and 1 less than the number of supported texture units. For example, GL_TEXTURE0 is for the first texture unit available. You can find out how many texture units are supported by your OpenGL implementation by using GL_MAX_TEXTURE_UNITS, as follows:

```
int maxTexUnits;      // holds the maximum number of supported texture units
glGetIntegerv(GL_MAX_TEXTURE_UNITS, &maxTexUnits);
```

If glGetIntegerv() returns 1, then the OpenGL implementation does not support multitexturing.

Any texture object can be used with any texture unit. When you make a call to glBindTexture(), the texture object gets bound to the currently active texture unit, and its parameters and image data become the texture unit's parameters and texture data. To enable a texture unit, you simply have to assign valid texture data to it and then enable the appropriate texture target. To later disable it, you need to make sure that all texture tar- gets are disabled. Always remember that OpenGL is a state machine, so the current tex- ture unit will always be whatever you set it to the last time you called glActiveTexture().

Take care to always be aware of what the active texture unit is when making calls to any texture related functions.

The following example should help you to better understand how to use texture units. Assuming that texture1 and texture2 are handles to valid texture objects for 2D textures, the following code binds them to texture units 0 and 1:

```
glActiveTexture(GL_TEXTURE0);
glEnable(GL_TEXTURE_2D);
glBindTexture(GL_TEXTURE_2D, texture1);
glTexEnvi(GL_TEXTURE_ENV, GL_TEXTURE_ENV_MODE, GL_REPLACE);
glActiveTexture(GL_TEXTURE1);
glEnable(GL_TEXTURE_2D);
glBindTexture(GL_TEXTURE_2D, texture2);
glTexEnvi(GL_TEXTURE_ENV, GL_TEXTURE_ENV_MODE, GL_MODULATE);
```

Pay particular attention to the calls to glTexEnv(). The first one causes the color from texture1 to replace the incoming fragment color. This value is then used as the input to texture unit 1, which modulates the value with the color in texture2.

Specifying Texture Coordinates

Now that you know how to assign textures to each texture unit and configure the texture units' states, you need to define how to apply the textures to polygons. Because you are applying more than one texture to a single polygon, you'll need to define more than one set of texture coordinates as well. In fact, you'll need one set of texture coordinates for each texture unit that you create. glTexCoord() isn't up to the task, because it only specifies coordinates for texture unit 0—it completely ignores the active texture unit. Instead, you'll need to use glMultiTexCoord():

```
void glMultiTexCoord{1234}{sifd}(GLenum texUnit, TYPF coords);
void glMultiTexCoord{1234}{sifd}v(GLenum texUnit, const TYPE *coords);
```

texUnit is used to indicate which texture unit this coordinate is for. It uses the same GL_TEXTUREn values as glActiveTexture(). The parameters are otherwise the same as glTexCoord(). In fact, using glTexCoord() is equivalent to using glMutliTexCoord() with GL_TEXTURE0.

Example: Multitextured Terrain

It's time to take a look at a real example of using multitexturing. On the CD, you'll find a demo for this chapter entitled MultitexTerrain, shown in Figure 9.5. This example uses one texture to color the terrain based on the height above sea level, as described earlier under "Texture Coordinate Generation." This is combined with a second grayscale texture that contains grass-like detail.

Figure 9.5 Terrain demo modified to use multitexturing.

This is the how the textures are initialized:

```
image.Load("grass.tga");
glGenTextures(1, &m_grassTexture);
glBindTexture(GL_TEXTURE_2D, m_grassTexture);
gluBuild2DMipmaps(GL_TEXTURE_2D, GL_RGB, image.GetWidth(), image.GetHeight(),
                  GL_RGB, GL_UNSIGNED_BYTE, image.GetImage());
image.Release();

image.Load("water.tga");
glGenTextures(1, &m_waterTexture);
glBindTexture(GL_TEXTURE_2D, m_waterTexture);
gluBuild2DMipmaps(GL_TEXTURE_2D, GL_RGB, image.GetWidth(), image.GetHeight(),
                  GL_RGB, GL_UNSIGNED_BYTE, image.GetImage());
image.Release();

image.Load("height.tga");
glGenTextures(1, &m_heightTexture);
glBindTexture(GL_TEXTURE_1D, m_heightTexture);
glTexParameteri(GL_TEXTURE_1D, GL_TEXTURE_MIN_FILTER, GL_LINEAR);
glTexParameteri(GL_TEXTURE_1D, GL_TEXTURE_WRAP_S, GL_CLAMP);
glTexImage1D(GL_TEXTURE_1D, 0, GL_RGB, image.GetWidth(), 0, GL_RGB,
```

```
                        GL_UNSIGNED_BYTE, image.GetImage());
image.Release();

glActiveTexture(GL_TEXTURE1);
glEnable(GL_TEXTURE_GEN_S);
glTexGeni(GL_S, GL_TEXTURE_GEN_MODE, GL_OBJECT_LINEAR);

GLfloat waterPlane[] = { 0.0, 1.0, 0.0, -WATER_HEIGHT };
glTexGenfv(GL_S, GL_OBJECT_PLANE, waterPlane);
glActiveTexture(GL_TEXTURE0);
```

The interesting thing to notice here is that most of the texture creation code doesn't have to concern itself with the currently active texture unit. This is because the parameters and images are being bound to texture objects, which will later be bound to texture units as they are needed. The texture unit matters only at the end, when texture coordinate generation is enabled.

Next up is the code that draws the terrain:

```
glBindTexture(GL_TEXTURE_2D, m_grassTexture);
glTexEnvf(GL_TEXTURE_ENV, GL_TEXTURE_ENV_MODE, GL_REPLACE);

glActiveTexture(GL_TEXTURE1);
glBindTexture(GL_TEXTURE_1D, m_heightTexture);

glMatrixMode(GL_TEXTURE);
glLoadIdentity();
glScalef(1.0f/MAX_HEIGHT, 1.0, 1.0);
glMatrixMode(GL_MODELVIEW);

glTexEnvf(GL_TEXTURE_ENV, GL_TEXTURE_ENV_MODE, GL_MODULATE);
glEnable(GL_TEXTURE_1D);
for (int z = 0; z < TERRAIN_SIZE - 1; ++z)
{
  glBegin(GL_TRIANGLE_STRIP);
  for (int x = 0; x < TERRAIN_SIZE; ++x)
  {
    GLfloat scaledHeight = heightmap[z * TERRAIN_SIZE + x] / SCALE_FACTOR;
    GLfloat nextScaledHeight = heightmap[(z + 1)*TERRAIN_SIZE + x]/SCALE_FACTOR;

    glMultiTexCoord2f(GL_TEXTURE0, x * TC_SCALE, z * TC_SCALE);
    glVertex3f((GLfloat)x - TERRAIN_SIZE/2, scaledHeight,
               (GLfloat)z - TERRAIN_SIZE/2);
```

```
        glMultiTexCoord2f(GL_TEXTURE0, x * TC_SCALE, (z+1) * TC_SCALE);
        glVertex3f((GLfloat)x - TERRAIN_SIZE/2, nextScaledHeight,
                    (GLfloat)(z + 1) - TERRAIN_SIZE/2);
    }
    glEnd();
}
glDisable(GL_TEXTURE_1D);
glActiveTexture(GL_TEXTURE0);

//draw the water
glBindTexture(GL_TEXTURE_2D, m_waterTexture);
glTexEnvf(GL_TEXTURE_ENV, GL_TEXTURE_ENV_MODE, GL_REPLACE);
//render water
```

The grass texture is first bound to texture unit 0. Then texture unit 1 is activated, and the height texture is bound to it. The texture matrix is selected and set to scale the *s* coordinate, which applies only to texture coordinates for texture unit 1, since each texture unit has its own texture matrix stack. 1D textures are enabled, and the terrain is rendered. The texture coordinates for texture unit 0 are specified using glMutiTexCoord2f(), and the texture coordinates for texture unit 1 are being automatically generated. Once rendering is complete, 1D textures are enabled, and since they were the only enabled texture target for texture unit 1, it is effectively disabled. Finally texture unit 0 is activated again, and the water is rendered with only one texture.

Texture Combine

Note

Texture combiners are available only via extensions under Windows. The ARB_texture_env_combine and ARB_texture_env_dot3 extensions were added in OpenGL 1.3, and ARB_texture_env_crossbar was added in OpenGL 1.4.

In Chapter 7, you learned about various texture modes that can be selected by using glTexEnv(). In addition to the modes you've been using such as GL_MODULATE and GL_REPLACE, OpenGL supports a number of functions that were introduced in 1.3 and 1.4 for use with multitexturing. Because these functions are typically used to combine two or more textures, they're often referred to as *texture combiners*. When you set GL_TEXTURE_ENV_MODE to GL_COMBINE, additional glTexEnv() parameters become valid. These parameter names are listed in Table 9.2 along with the parameters that can be used with them. Note that for all of the parameters discussed in this section, the target parameter must be set to GL_TEXTURE_ENV. As a reminder, glTexEnv() has the following form:

```
void glTexEnv{if}(GLenum target, GLenum pname, TYPE param);
```

Table 9.2 Texture Combiner glTexEnv() Parameters

pname	Valid params
GL_COMBINE_RGB	GL_REPLACE, GL_MODULATE, GL_ADD, GL_ADD_SIGNED, GL_INTERPOLATE, GL_SUBTRACT, GL_DOT3_RGB, or GL_DOT3_RGBA
GL_COMBINE_ALPHA	GL_REPLACE, GL_MODULATE, GL_ADD, GL_ADD_SIGNED, GL_INTERPOLATE, or GL_SUBTRACT
GL_RGB_SCALE	Floating point constant scaling factor for RGB
GL_ALPHA_SCALE	Floating point constant scaling factor for alpha

GL_RGB_SCALE and GL_RGB_ALPHA are used to set floating point factors that the final fragment RGB and alpha values are scaled by after all textures have been applied. GL_COMBINE_RGB and GL_COMBINE_ALPHA are used to specify what function to use to combine textures. These functions are defined in Table 9.3.

You'll notice that GL_DOT3_RGB and GL_DOT3_RGBA share the same function. The difference between the two is that with the former, the result of the function is stored in the RGB components; with the latter, the result is stored in the alpha component as well, in which case the result of the GL_COMBINE_ALPHA function is ignored. These modes are used for bump mapping.

Each of the functions listed in Table 9.3 takes up to three arguments. The real power of texture combiners stems from the fact that you are in complete control of what those arguments are. They may come from a texture (from any texture unit, not just the current one), the results of the previous texture unit, the color of the incoming fragment prior to any texture application, or a constant color (specifically, the color set via GL_TEXTURE_ENV_COLOR). These arguments are set by passing one of the values from Table 9.4 to glTexEnv(). Arguments for the RGB and alpha components are set independently of each other.

Table 9.3 Combiner Functions

Name	Function
GL_REPLACE	$Arg0$
GL_MODULATE	$Arg0 * Arg1$
GL_ADD	$Arg0 + Arg1$
GL_ADD_SIGNED	$Arg0 + Arg1 + 0.5$
GL_INTERPOLATE	$Arg0 * Arg2 + Arg1 * (1 - Arg2)$
GL_SUBTRACT	$Arg0 - Arg1$
GL_DOT3_RGB, GL_DOT3_RGBA	$4 * (Arg0_r - 0.5) * (Arg1_r - 0.5) + (Arg0_g - 0.5) * (Arg1_g - 0.5) + (Arg0_b - 0.5) * (Arg1_b - 0.5)$. GL_COMBINE_RGB only.

Table 9.4 Combiner Argument Specification

pname	Valid params
GL_SOURCEi_RGB, GL_SOURCEi_ALPHA	GL_TEXTURE, GL_TEXTUREn, GL_CONSTANT, GL_PRIMARY_COLOR, or GL_PREVIOUS.
GL_OPERANDi_RGB	GL_SRC_COLOR, GL_ONE_MINUS_SRC_COLOR, GL_SRC_ALPHA, or GL_ONE_MINUS_SRC_ALPHA.
GL_OPERANDi_ALPHA	GL_SRC_ALPHA, or GL_ONE_MINUS_SRC_ALPHA.

i is the argument number and can be 0, 1, or 2, corresponding to the arguments in Table 9.3. The arguments can be set to any of the following:

GL_TEXTURE is used to indicate the texture image associated with the current texture unit.

GL_TEXTUREn is used to indicate the texture image associated with texture unit n.

GL_CONSTANT is for the texture environment color of the current texture unit.

GL_PRIMARY_COLOR indicates the primary color of the incoming fragment used as input for texture unit 0.

GL_PREVIOUS indicates the output of the previous texture unit. For texture unit 0 this is equivalent to GL_PRIMARY_COLOR.

The GL_OPERANDi parameters are used to further specify which components to use from the indicated argument. So if you wanted to use the complement of the RGB values of the current texture unit's texture image as argument 0, you would use the following:

```
glTexEnvf(GL_TEXTURE_ENV, GL_SOURCE0_RGB, GL_TEXTURE);
glTexEnvf(GL_TEXTURE_ENV, GL_OPERAND0_RGB, GL_ONE_MINUS_SRC_COLOR);
```

To bring this all together, let's look at an example of setting up a combiner. To keep things simple, we'll set up the combiner to perform the same operation as GL_MODULATE. You'd never do this in practice of course, but using a well-understood operation should make the example quite clear. As you'll recall, modulation determines the result by multiplying the incoming fragment color by the texture color. The following code shows how to do the same thing with a combiner.

```
// Set the texture mode to GL_COMBINE. This must be done to use combiners.
glTexEnvf(GL_TEXTURE_ENV, GL_TEXTURE_ENV_MODE, GL_COMBINE);

// Set both the RGB and alpha combiners to modulate
glTexEnvf(GL_TEXTURE_ENV, GL_COMBINE_RGB, GL_MODULATE);
glTexEnvf(GL_TEXTURE_ENV, GL_COMBINE_ALPHA, GL_MODULATE);
```

```
// Set Arg0 to be the incoming fragment color for both RGB and alpha
glTexEnvf(GL_TEXTURE_ENV, GL_SOURCE0_RGB, GL_PRIMARY_COLOR);
glTexEnvf(GL_TEXTURE_ENV, GL_SOURCE0_ALPHA, GL_PRIMARY_COLOR);

// Set Arg1 to be the current texture color for both RGB and alpha
glTexEnvf(GL_TEXTURE_ENV, GL_SOURCE1_RGB, GL_TEXTURE);
glTexEnvf(GL_TEXTURE_ENV, GL_SOURCE1_ALPHA, GL_TEXTURE);

// Use the unmodified source color and alpha for both Arg0 and Arg1
glTexEnvf(GL_TEXTURE_ENV, GL_OPERAND0_RGB, GL_SRC_COLOR);
glTexEnvf(GL_TEXTURE_ENV, GL_OPERAND0_ALPHA, GL_SRC_ALPHA);
glTexEnvf(GL_TEXTURE_ENV, GL_OPERAND1_RGB, GL_SRC_COLOR);
glTexEnvf(GL_TEXTURE_ENV, GL_OPERAND1_ALPHA, GL_SRC_ALPHA);
```

This example is completely impractical, but it should help you better understand how to set up texture combiners. We'll look at a more practical example in the next section.

Example: Image Interpolation

The interpolation combiner mode is in some ways the most complex because it's the only one that takes three parameters. The CD includes an example of using combiner interpolation. You'll find it in the Combiner folder for this chapter. This program takes two images and gradually interpolates between them over time, creating a crossfading effect. It does this by loading one image into texture unit 0 and the other into texture unit 1. During initialization, the two texture units are set up as follows:

```
CTargaImage image;

glGenTextures(2, m_texID);

glActiveTexture(GL_TEXTURE0);
glBindTexture(GL_TEXTURE_2D, m_texID[0]);
image.Load("2.tga");
gluBuild2DMipmaps(GL_TEXTURE_2D, 3, image.GetWidth(), image.GetHeight(), GL_RGB,
                  GL_UNSIGNED_BYTE, image.GetImage());
image.Release();
glEnable(GL_TEXTURE_2D);
// pass the texture through to the next unit
glTexEnvf(GL_TEXTURE_ENV, GL_TEXTURE_ENV_MODE, GL_REPLACE);

glActiveTexture(GL_TEXTURE1);
glBindTexture(GL_TEXTURE_2D, m_texID[1]);
image.Load("1.tga");
gluBuild2DMipmaps(GL_TEXTURE_2D, 3, image.GetWidth(), image.GetHeight(), GL_RGB,
```

```
                        GL_UNSIGNED_BYTE, image.GetImage());
image.Release();
glEnable(GL_TEXTURE_2D);

// set the combine mode
glTexEnvf(GL_TEXTURE_ENV, GL_TEXTURE_ENV_MODE, GL_COMBINE);

// use the interpolate combiner function
glTexEnvf(GL_TEXTURE_ENV, GL_COMBINE_RGB, GL_INTERPOLATE);

// set Arg0 to be the output of texture unit 0
glTexEnvf(GL_TEXTURE_ENV, GL_SOURCE0_RGB, GL_PREVIOUS);

// set Arg1 to be the current texture image
glTexEnvf(GL_TEXTURE_ENV, GL_SOURCE1_RGB, GL_TEXTURE);

// set Arg2 to be the texture env color for tex unit 1
glTexEnvf(GL_TEXTURE_ENV, GL_SOURCE2_RGB, GL_CONSTANT);

// use the constant alpha to modify the rgb components
glTexEnvf(GL_TEXTURE_ENV, GL_OPERAND2_RGB, GL_SRC_ALPHA);
```

Texture unit 0 doesn't really need to do anything; it just needs to be active and enabled so that the texture bound to it will be available to texture unit 1. Because the texture environment mode is set to GL_REPLACE, texture unit 1 will be able to access the texture using either GL_PREVIOUS or GL_TEXURE0.

Texture unit 1 is set up to use the texture from unit 0 as Arg0 and its own texture as Arg1. The alpha component of the constant color will be used as Arg2, which acts as the interpolator. The constant color is updated over time so that the first image gradually fades into the second image. This can be see in the Prepare() and Render() routines:

```
void CGfxOpenGL::Prepare(float dt)
{
  m_interpol += dt/TOTAL_TIME;
  if (m_interpol > 1.0)
    m_interpol = 1.0;
}


void CGfxOpenGL::Render()
{
  glClear(GL_COLOR_BUFFER_BIT | GL_DEPTH_BUFFER_BIT | GL_STENCIL_BUFFER_BIT);

  GLfloat texEnvColor[] = { 0.0, 0.0, 0.0, 0.0 };
```

```
   texEnvColor[3] = m_interpol;
   glActiveTexture(GL_TEXTURE1);
   glTexEnvfv(GL_TEXTURE_ENV, GL_TEXTURE_ENV_COLOR, texEnvColor);

   glBegin(GL_QUADS);
     glMultiTexCoord2f(GL_TEXTURE0, 0.0, 0.0);
     glMultiTexCoord2f(GL_TEXTURE1, 0.0, 0.0);
     glVertex3f(-1.0, -1.0f, -2.0);
     glMultiTexCoord2f(GL_TEXTURE0, 1.0, 0.0);
     glMultiTexCoord2f(GL_TEXTURE1, 1.0, 0.0);
     glVertex3f(1.0, -1.0f, -2.0);
     glMultiTexCoord2f(GL_TEXTURE0, 1.0, 1.0);
     glMultiTexCoord2f(GL_TEXTURE1, 1.0, 1.0);
     glVertex3f(1.0, 1.0f, -2.0);
     glMultiTexCoord2f(GL_TEXTURE0, 0.0, 1.0);
     glMultiTexCoord2f(GL_TEXTURE1, 0.0, 1.0);
     glVertex3f(-1.0, 1.0f, -2.0);
   glEnd();
}
```

Figure 9.6 shows this example in the middle of the interpolation.

Figure 9.6 Image interpolation using texture combiners.

Summary

You've now seen just how powerful OpenGL's texturing support really is. You can update textures dynamically, even using the screen as an image source. You can apply transformations to texture coordinates to move, scale, or rotate them on the fly. You can have OpenGL generate texture coordinates automatically for reflections and other effects. Most importantly, you can apply multiple textures to a single object, with tremendous control over how the textures are used and combined.

What You Have Learned

- You can update all or a part of an existing texture using `glTexSubImage()`.
- You can create textures from the screen using `glCopyTexImage()` or `glCopyTexSubImage()`.
- A texture matrix is applied to texture coordinates just as the modelview and projection matrices are applied to vertex coordinates.
- OpenGL can automatically generate texture coordinates for you with `glTexGen()`.
- Environment mapping enables you to create complex reflective surfaces.
- Multitexturing is the process of applying more than one texture to a polygon in a single pass.
- Multitexturing is controlled through the use of texture units, each of which represents a single texture application. The current texture unit can be changed with `glActiveTexture()`.
- Texture combiners provide a wide range of additional methods for applying textures.

Review Questions

1. Why is updating an existing texture better than creating a new one?
2. How many texture matrix stacks are there?
3. Which two texture generation modes require additional parameters?
4. How do you enable and disable a texture unit?
5. What texture environment mode (`GL_TEXTURE_ENV_MODE`) do you need to set to be able to use texture combiners?

On Your Own

1. Write the code to set up a texture combiner that does the same thing as the `GL_ADD` environment mode described in Chapter 7.

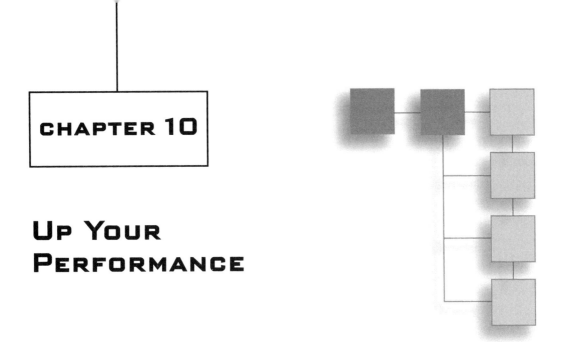

CHAPTER 10

UP YOUR PERFORMANCE

In many graphics applications, and in virtually all games, maintaining an interactive frame rate and smooth animation is of utmost importance. Although rapid advancements in graphics hardware have lessened the need to optimize every single line of code, programmers still need to focus on writing efficient code that, through the graphics API, harnesses the full power of the underlying hardware. In this chapter, you'll learn several methods for improving your game's performance.

- Display lists
- Vertex arrays
- Frustum culling

Display Lists

After you've been writing OpenGL code for a while, you'll probably notice that there are sections of code that you are calling frequently, with the same state machine settings every time. Wouldn't it be nice if you could process those commands in advance (maybe at initialization) and then send the preprocessed commands down the graphics pipeline, storing them on the video card for future use, rather than processing them all from scratch every time? That's exactly the idea behind OpenGL's display lists.

As you'll see momentarily, display lists are quite easy to create and use; the only catch to using them is that it's not always obvious when they will help improve performance. In addition, some vendors do a better job than others in the implementation of display lists, so your mileage may vary. In the worst case, though, they should never hurt performance.

To see how display lists are created and used, let's look at an example. Suppose you have a program in which you draw a bunch of pyramids, which you're representing as four triangles (the bottom isn't drawn, because you can't see it). You'd probably create a function to do it, and it might look something like this (because all four triangles share a single common central point, you can use a triangle fan):

```
void DrawPyramid()
{
  glBegin(GL_TRIANGLE_FAN);
    glVertex3f(0.0, 1.0, 0.0);
    glVertex3f(-1.0, 0.0, 1.0);
    glVertex3f(1.0, 0.0, 1.0);
    glVertex3f(1.0, 0.0, -1.0);
    glVertex3f(-1.0, 0.0, -1.0);
  glEnd();
}
```

Because this function is getting called all the time, it's a good candidate to consider for a display list (in truth, it probably won't benefit much from being in a display list, because it's not doing anything else particularly expensive, but it illustrates the point). So, how do you put these calls into a display list?

Creating a Display List

First of all, before you can place items in a display list, you must get a name for one, much as you got a name for a texture object in Chapter 7, "Texture Mapping." This is done by using glGenLists():

```
GLuint glGenLists(GLsizei range);
```

Here, range is the number of display lists you need. The function returns an unsigned integer representing the first display list in the range requested. The next list in the range can be accessed by adding one to this value, and so on. You can think of the values returned by glGenLists() as the names, or IDs, of your display lists. They just provide a unique handle that allows you to tell OpenGL which display list you are currently working with.

You should always check the return value of glGenLists() to make sure that it is not 0. This is not a valid list name, and it indicates that some error has occurred, such as there not being range contiguous names available. As an additional precaution, at any time you can check to see whether a list name is valid by using glIsList():

```
GLboolean glIsList(GLuint listName);
```

This function returns GL_TRUE if listName is a valid name for a display list and GL_FALSE otherwise.

Filling a Display List with Commands

After you have a valid list name, the next step is to place commands in the display list associated with it. This is done in a manner very similar to the way you use glBegin()/glEnd() to surround primitive drawing commands. First, you call a function that specifies the display list you want to fill, and when you're finished, you call another function completing the list. These functions are glNewList() and glEndList(), respectively:

```
void glNewList(GLuint listName, GLenum mode);
void glEndList();
```

Here, listName is the name of the display list you want to fill. Note that it can be a new list you just created with glGenLists(), or it can be a list that you've been using but are ready to clear out and fill with new commands. mode is the compilation mode, and it can be either GL_COMPILE or GL_COMPILE_AND_EXECUTE. The second option executes the commands as it compiles them, whereas the first just compiles them.

Although you can place any OpenGL commands you want between glNewList() and glEndList(), some commands cannot be compiled into a display list. These will instead be executed immediately. These functions are glGenLists(), glDeleteLists(), glFeedbackBuffer(), glSelectBuffer(), glRenderMode(), glColorPointer(), glFogCoordPointer(), glEdgeFlagPointer(), glIndexPointer(), glNormalPointer(), glTexCoordPointer(), glSecondaryColorPointer(), glVertexPointer(), glClientActiveTexture(), glInterleavedArrays(), glEnableClientState(), glDisableClientState(), glPushClientAttrib(), glPopClientAttrib(), glReadPixels(), glPixelStore(), glGenTextures(), glDeleteTextures(), glAreTexturesResident(), glGenQueries(), glDeleteQueries(), glBindBuffer(), glDeleteBuffers(), glGenBuffers(), glBufferData(), glBufferSubData(), glMapBuffer(), glUnmapBuffer(), glFlush(), and glFinish(). Some of these functions are not covered in this volume but are included here for completeness.

In addition, each of the glGet() and glIs() commands executes immediately, as do the glTexImage() functions if a proxy texture is being created (if you're not using a proxy texture, you can safely use the glTexImage() functions, though there are better ways to handle textures, as we'll discuss later in "Display Lists and Textures").

Executing Display Lists

After you have a display list, you can then use it in any place you would have used the code compiled into it. This is done with:

```
void glCallList(GLuint listName);
```

This causes the commands in the list indicated by listName to immediately be executed in order, just as if they were inserted into your code.

So, what if you want to call several display lists at once? Well, conveniently, OpenGL provides direct support for this:

```
void glCallLists(GLsizei num, GLenum type, const GLvoid *lists);
```

Here, num is the total number of lists to be executed, and lists is a pointer to an array of display list names. Although the value returned by glGenLists() is an unsigned integer, and that's the type expected by most other display list functions, in reality, you could cast the name to some other data type that's more convenient for your use. And that's why lists is a void pointer and why the type member is present to indicate the actual data type stored in the array. Table 10.1 lists the values that can be used, though typically, you'll just use integers.

Table 10.1 glCallLists() Types

Constant	Type
GL_BYTE	Signed 1-byte integer
GL_UNSIGNED_BYTE	Unsigned 1-byte integer
GL_SHORT	Signed 2-byte integer
GL_UNSIGNED_SHORT	Unsigned 2-byte integer
GL_INT	Signed 4-byte integer
GL_UNSIGNED_INT	Unsigned 4-byte integer
GL_FLOAT	4-byte floating-point value

When glCallLists() is used, OpenGL will iterate over list, from 0 to num −1, calling the display list name indicated at each index in the iteration. If any of the display lists' names in the list array are not valid, they'll simply be ignored.

There may be times in doing this (such as when using display lists for text output) that you don't want the iteration to start at zero, but rather at some offset. You can set the offset at which the iteration begins using the following.

```
void glListName(GLuint offset);
```

This causes the iteration to begin at offset and end at offset + num −1. The value of the offset is 0 by default. Remember, because OpenGL is a state machine, if you change the offset, it will remain at the value you set it to until you change it again. If you want to restore it to its original value after you're finished, before changing the offset, you can use glGet() with GL_LIST_BASE to find the original offset value.

Display List Gotchas

There are a number of things to be aware of when using display lists. For starters, you can use glCallList() or glCallLists() within display lists—it's perfectly legal to include them within a glNewList()/glEndList() block. To prevent the possibility of infinite recursion caused by two lists calling each other, however, the commands within the display list executed by glCallList() are not made part of the new display list.

Another thing to keep in mind is that display lists can contain calls that change the current OpenGL server-side state, and there is no built-in mechanism to save and restore the state over display list calls. Therefore, you want to be sure to save and restore state information yourself using `glPush/PopMatrix()` and/or `glPush/PopAttrib()`.

Destroying Display Lists

Creating a display list allocates memory in which to store the commands, so after you are finished using a display list—either at program termination or beforehand—you need to explicitly destroy it to avoid resource leaks. Doing so is quite straightforward via `glDeleteLists()`:

```
void glDeleteLists(GLuint listName, GLsizei range);
```

This frees the memory associated with the display lists starting with `listName` and proceeding to `listName + range` −1. If any name within the range refers to a nonexistent list, it will simply be ignored. If `range` is 0, the call is ignored, and if `range` is negative, it generates an error.

Now that you know how to create, fill, call, and destroy display lists, let's see what you have to do to rewrite the previous pyramid routine using them. First, of course, you need to create the list, as follows:

```
GLuint pyramidList = glGenLists(1);
```

Next, you need to fill this list with commands. To do this, you'll rewrite the `DrawPyramid()` function from earlier. Because you'll only be calling it once now (at startup), you'll rename it `InitializePyramid()`. Because the list creation also needs to happen only once, you'll move the creation code into the function as well and have it take a reference to a `GLuint` as a parameter (so that you can pass the list handle in and have it be set). The new function appears here:

```
void InitializePyramid(GLuint &pyramidList)
{
  pyramidList = glGenLists(1);

  glNewList(pyramidList, GL_COMPILE);
  glBegin(GL_TRIANGLE_FAN);
    glVertex3f(0.0, 1.0, 0.0);
    glVertex3f(-1.0, 0.0, 1.0);
    glVertex3f(1.0, 0.0, 1.0);
    glVertex3f(1.0, 0.0, -1.0);
    glVertex3f(-1.0, 0.0, -1.0);
  glEnd();
  glEndList();
}
```

Now, when you need to draw a pyramid, you just translate, rotate, and scale as needed, and then use this:

```
glCallList(pyramidList);
```

to actually draw the pyramid. When you finish using the pyramid list (probably when exiting the program), you free the list with:

```
glDeleteLists(pyramidList, 1);
```

And that's it. Again, remember that in this example, you're probably not going to gain much from using a display list, but you should at least have a pretty good idea of how to use them now.

Display Lists and Textures

Because any of the texture functions can be used within display lists, you might be tempted to create lists that encapsulate the process of defining texture parameters and loading texture data into them. If texture objects didn't exist, this would probably be a good way to go about it. Texture objects do exist, however, and in addition to being quite easy to use, they provide a much greater performance boost than you could get by using display lists for the same purpose. The best approach, then, is to create and initialize your textures once, bind them to a texture object, and then when you need them, select them with appropriate calls to glBindTexture(). Note that there is nothing wrong with putting the calls to glBindTexture(), glTexCoord(), and even glTexEnv() within display lists, because these are involved with using the texture as opposed to creating it, and they are not tied to an individual texture object.

Vertex Arrays

Thus far in the examples presented in this book, you have been using the glBegin()/glEnd() model, often referred to as immediate mode. Immediate mode is useful for simple applications and for prototype code, since it is easy to understand and visualize. However, it comes with some performance challenges that make it less useful for applications with lots of geometry that needs to be rendered at a high frame rate, such as games.

For example, let's say you're rendering a model containing 2,000 lit and textured triangles using immediate mode. Assume that you're able to pack all of the vertex data into a single triangle strip (a "best case" scenario that's not often practical). Your rendering code may look something like the following:

```
glBegin(GL_TRIANGLE_STRIP);

for (int n = 0; n < model.m_numVertices; ++n) // m_numVertices is 2002
{
```

```
    glNormal3fv(myModel.m_normals[n]);
    glTexCoord2f(myModel.m_texCoords[n]);
    glVertex3f(myModel.m_vertices[n]);
}
glEnd();
```

There are several problems with this code. The first is that 6,008 function calls are made. Every time you make a function call, there is a small amount of overhead required to push parameters on the stack and to make the jump to the function. With over 6,000 calls being made, this overhead adds up.

The second and third problems are illustrated in Figure 10.1. Assuming that this mesh represents a triangle strip (perhaps a portion of the mesh in the example above), each of the circled vertices is a redundant vertex. In other words, each of these vertices is shared by more than three triangles, but since a triangle strip can represent, at most, three triangles per vertex, each of the circled vertices needs to be sent to the video card more than once. This results in using additional bandwidth to send the data to the video card. In addition, the vertex is likely to be transformed and lit more than once. These two operations waste bandwidth and processing cycles.

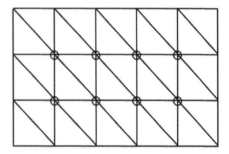

Figure 10.1 A mesh with redundant vertices.

To address these issues, OpenGL includes vertex arrays. Vertex arrays offer the following advantages:

- Large batches of data can be sent with a small number of function calls. As you'll see by the end of this section, the example above could be reduced to four function calls (and possibly even two!) using vertex arrays.
- Through the use of indexed vertex arrays, vertices can be sent exactly once per triangle mesh, reducing bandwidth and potentially avoiding redundant transformation and lighting.

TIP

Even with vertex arrays, a single vertex may be transformed and lit more than once due to the fact that video cards have a limited vertex cache. The vertex cache stores transformed and lit vertices so that if they are needed again, they can be fetched from the cache rather than reprocessed. However, as new vertices are moved into the cache, old ones are pushed out, so if two triangles that use a single vertex are far apart in the data, the cached vertex from the first probably won't still be around when the second one is processed. Therefore, it's often a good idea to keep your data as localized as possible.

Now that you understand the reasons for using vertex arrays, it's time to learn how they are used.

Array-Based Data

So far, we've been using relatively simple objects in our demos, and thus, we've been able to describe them explicitly in the code. In a real game, however, you'll be working with models containing hundreds or even thousands of polygons, and describing such complicated models directly in the code just isn't practical—even if you manage to create decent-looking results, it's going to be a nightmare to maintain. Instead, one of the following two approaches is usually taken:

- **Load the model from a file.** Dozens of great modeling packages enable you to create a model visually and then export the geometric data to a file, which can be read by your program. This approach offers the greatest flexibility. Model loading will be discussed in much greater detail later in the book.

- **Generate the model procedurally.** Some things you want to represent can be implicitly described with equations due to patterns they contain or because they possess some random properties that you can generate on the fly. A good example of this is fractals. Geometric data for fractals can be created by a procedure that produces the same values every frame.

Whichever approach is used, it should be fairly obvious that you don't want to repeat all the work every frame—you certainly don't want to be constantly reading a model from disk, and even procedural methods can have enough overhead to have an adverse effect on performance. Instead, you'll take the geometric data these methods generate and store it in arrays, which you can then access as needed.

This process can be summarized in the following steps:

1. Generate the data you need, either procedurally or from a model file on disk.
2. Save this data in an array or set of arrays (for example, you could put the position of each vertex in one array, the vertex normal in another, color in another, and so on).

With your data stored in arrays, it's ready for use by OpenGL's vertex array functions.

Enabling Vertex Arrays

Like most OpenGL features, to be able to use vertex arrays, you must first enable them. You might expect this to be done with glEnable(), but it's not. OpenGL provides a separate pair of functions to control vertex array support:

```
void glEnableClientState(GLenum array);
void glDisableClientState(GLenum array);
```

The array parameter is a flag indicating which type of array you're enabling (or disabling). Each type of vertex attribute you want to use (for example, position, normal, color) can be stored in an array, and you need to enable whichever attributes you are using individually, using one of the flags listed in Table 10.2.

Table 10.2 Array Type Flags

Flag	Meaning
GL_VERTEX_ARRAY	Enables an array containing the position of each vertex.
GL_NORMAL_ARRAY	Enables an array containing the vertex normal for each vertex
GL_COLOR_ARRAY	Enables an array containing color information for each vertex
GL_SECONDARY_COLOR_ARRAY	Enables an array containing color information for each vertex
GL_INDEX_ARRAY	Enables an array containing indices to a color palette for each vertex
GL_FOG_COORD_ARRAY**	Enables an array containing the fog coordinate for each vertex
GL_TEXTURE_COORD_ARRAY	Enables an array containing the texture coordinate for each vertex
GL_EDGE_FLAG_ARRAY	Enables an array containing an edge flag for each vertex

* Available only via the EXT_secondary_color extension under Windows.

** Available only via the EXT_fog_coord extension under Windows.

TIP

It is common in OpenGL documentation to refer to all these array types collectively as *vertex arrays*, which can be confusing because there is also a specific array type that is called a vertex array. That said, they are collectively referred to as vertex arrays because each array contains data that is referenced on a per-vertex basis. The array type containing positional information is specifically called a vertex array because the data stored in it is used internally as if calls to glVertex() were being made. If you'll notice, the name of each array type roughly corresponds to the name of the OpenGL call that will be made on the data it contains (color arrays mimic glColor(), texture coordinate arrays mimic glTexCoord(), and so on).

Working with Arrays

After you have enabled the array types that you will be using, the next step is to give OpenGL some data to work with. It's up to you to create arrays and fill them with the data you will be using (procedurally, from files, or by any other means, as we've already discussed). Then you need to tell OpenGL about these arrays so it can use them. The function used to do this depends on the type of array you're using. Let's look at each function in detail.

In each of the following functions, stride indicates the byte offset between array elements. If the data is tightly packed (meaning there is no padding between each element), you can set this to zero. Otherwise you can use the stride to compensate for padding or even to pack data for multiple attributes into a single array. pointer is a pointer to an array containing the vertex data or, more specifically, points to the first element you want to use within that array. The data type of the array is indicated by type. The other parameters will be explained with each individual function.

```
void glVertexPointer(GLint size, GLenum type, GLsizei stride, GLvoid *pointer);
```

This array contains positional data for the vertices. size is the number of coordinates per vertex, and it must be 2, 3, or 4. type can be GL_SHORT, GL_INT, GL_FLOAT, or GL_DOUBLE.

```
void glTexCoordPointer(GLint size, GLenum type, GLsizei stride, GLvoid *pointer);
```

This array contains texture coordinates for each vertex. size is the number of coordinates per vertex, and it must be 1, 2, 3, or 4. type can be set to GL_SHORT, GL_INT, GL_FLOAT, or GL_DOUBLE.

```
void glNormalPointer(GLenum type, GLsizei stride, GLvoid *pointer);
```

This array contains normal vectors for each vertex. Normals are always stored with exactly three coordinates (x, y, z) so there is no size parameter. type can be GL_BYTE, GL_SHORT, GL_INT, GL_FLOAT, or GL_DOUBLE.

```
void glColorPointer(GLint size, GLenum type, GLsizei stride, GLvoid *pointer);
```

This specifies the primary color array. size is the number of components per color, which should be either 3 or 4 (for RGB or RGBA). type can be GL_BYTE, GL_UNSIGNED_BYTE, GL_SHORT, GL_UNSIGNED_SHORT, GL_INT, GL_UNSIGNED_INT, GL_FLOAT, or GL_DOUBLE.

```
void glSecondaryColorPointer(GLint size, GLenum type, GLsizei stride, GLvoid *pointer);
```

This specifies the secondary color array. size is the number of components per color, which is always 3 (for RGB). The types allowed are identical to those for glColorPointer().

Extension

Extension name: EXT_secondary_color

Name string: GL_EXT_secondary_color

Promoted to core: OpenGL 1.4

Function names: glSecondaryColorPointerEXT()

Tokens: GL_SECONDARY_COLOR_ARRAY_EXT

```
void glIndexPointer(GLenum type, GLsizei stride, GLvoid *pointer);
```

This array represents color indices for use with palletized display modes. type can be set to GL_SHORT, GL_INT, GL_FLOAT, or GL_DOUBLE.

Extension

Extension name: EXT_fog_coord

Name string: GL_EXT_fog_coord

Promoted to core: OpenGL 1.4

Function names: glFogCoordPointerEXT()

Tokens: GL_FOG_COORD_ARRAY_EXT

```
void glFogCoordPointer(GLenum type, GLsizei stride, GLvoid *pointer);
```

This array is used to specify fog coordinates. type can be set to GL_FLOAT or GL_DOUBLE.

```
void glEdgeFlagPointer(GLsizei stride, GLboolean *pointer);
```

Edge flags become important when displaying polygons as lines, and this array allows you to specify which lines are edges. Unlike the other functions, pointer always points to an array of Boolean values, so there is no size or type parameter.

NOTE

For each vertex attribute, you can have only a single array specified at any one time. This means that if you want to represent more than one object in your game with vertex arrays, you have to either combine all the data for them into a single set of arrays or have each object have its own set of arrays that you switch between using gl*Pointer(). Although the former may be slightly faster because it doesn't require a lot of state changes, the latter is going to be easier to manage. In fact, a typical rendering loop will change the current arrays for every object, calling several gl*Pointer() functions and enabling or disabling vertex attributes as necessary.

After you've specified which arrays OpenGL should use for each vertex attribute, you can begin to have it access that data for rendering. There are several functions that you can choose from.

glDrawArrays()

When this function is called, OpenGL iterates over each of the currently enabled arrays, rendering primitives as it goes. To understand how it works, you need to look at the prototype:

```
void glDrawArrays(GLenum mode, GLint first, GLsizei count);
```

mode serves the same basic function as the parameter passed to glBegin(): It specifies which type of primitive the vertex data should be used to create. Valid values are GL_POINTS, GL_LINE_STRIP, GL_LINE_LOOP, GL_LINES, GL_TRIANGLE_STRIP, GL_TRIANGLE_FAN, GL_TRIANGLES, GL_QUAD_STRIP, GL_QUADS, and GL_POLYGON. first specifies the index at which the iteration should start, and count specifies the number of indices to process. It should be noted that after a call to glDrawArrays(), states related to the array types being used are undefined. For example, if using normal arrays, the current normal will be undefined after glDrawArrays() returns.

glMultiDrawArrays()

Extension

Extension name: EXT_multi_draw_arrays

Name string: GL_EXT_multi_draw_arrays

Promoted to core: OpenGL 1.4

Function names: glMultiDrawArraysEXT(), glMultiDrawElementsEXT()

OpenGL provides the ability to draw multiple arrays with a single call via glMultiDrawArrays(), which has the following prototype:

```
void glMultiDrawArrays(GLenum mode, GLint *first, GLsizei *count, GLsizei primcount);
```

This is similar to glDrawArrays(), except that the first and count parameters are now arrays, and there is an additional parameter primcount that indicates how many elements are in each array. Calling glMultiDrawArrays() is functionally equivalent to the following:

```
for (int i = 0; i < primcount; ++i)
{
  if (count[i] > 0)
    glDrawArrays(mode, first[i], count[i]);
}
```

At present, most OpenGL drivers implement this function exactly like the code above, so it serves more as a convenience than a performance improvement.

glDrawElements()

This function is very similar to glDrawArrays(), but it is even more powerful. With glDrawArrays(), your only option is to iterate sequentially over the list, which means that you can't reference the same element more than once; glDrawElements(), on the other hand, allows you to specify the array elements in any order, and access each of them as many times as necessary. Let's look at the prototype:

```
void glDrawElements(GLenum mode, GLsizei count, GLenum type, const GLvoid *indices);
```

mode and count are used just as in glDrawArrays(). type is the data type of the values in indices, and it should be GL_UNSIGNED_BYTE, GL_UNSIGNED_SHORT, or GL_UNSIGNED_INT. indices is an array containing indexes for the vertices you want to render.

To understand the value of this method, it must be reiterated that not only can you specify the indices in any order, you can also specify the same vertex repeatedly in the series. In games, most vertices will be shared by more than one polygon; by storing the vertex once and accessing it repeatedly by its index, you can save a substantial amount of memory. In addition, good OpenGL implementations will perform operations on the vertex only once and keep the results in a cache, so that all references after the first are virtually free—as long as the vertex is still in the cache. The performance advantages of this should be obvious.

glMultiDrawElements()

This function is to glDrawElements() what glMultiDrawArrays() is to glDrawArrays(). It has the following prototype:

```
void glMultiDrawElements(GLenum mode, GLsizei *count, GLenum type, GLvoid **indices,
GLsizei primcount);
```

Again, the differences here are that count and indices are lists of primcount elements. Calling this function is equivalent to the following:

```
for (int i = 0; i < primcount; ++i)
{
  if (count[i] > 0)
    glDrawElements(mode, count[i], type, indices[i]);
}
```

This can be useful for things like drawing multiple triangle strips from a single set of vertex arrays. As with glMultiDrawArrays(), this function is more for convenience than anything else.

glDrawRangeElements()

Extension

Extension name: EXT_draw_range_elements

Name string: GL_EXT_draw_range_elements

Promoted to core: OpenGL 1.2

Function names: glDrawRangeElementsARB()

This function is similar in use to glDrawElements(). The primary difference is that the values in the vertex array that you are accessing fall within a limited range. For example, if you have a vertex array containing 1,000 vertices, but you know that the object you're about to draw accesses only the first 100 vertices, you can use glDrawRangeElements() to tell OpenGL that you're not using the whole array at the moment. This may allow the OpenGL to more efficiently transfer and cache your vertex data. The prototype is as follows:

```
void glDrawRangeElements(GLenum mode, GLuint start, GLuint end, GLsizei count,
                         GLenum type, const GLvoid *indices);
```

mode, count, type, and indices have the same purpose as the corresponding parameters. start and end correspond to the lower and upper bounds of the vertex indices contained in indices.

glArrayElement()

This is perhaps the least-efficient method of accessing vertex array data. Rather than calling upon a range of data, it allows you to evaluate and render a single vertex, as follows:

```
void glArrayElement(GLint index);
```

index is, naturally, the vertex you want to render. Using glArrayElement() is only marginally more efficient than using immediate mode. For optimal efficiency when using vertex arrays, you should favor glDrawElements() or glDrawRangeElements().

Tip

OpenGL 1.5 added an even more efficient method for processing vertex data in the form of *vertex buffer objects*, the primary advantage being that they allow you to create and store data in memory on your video card rather than in your PC's main memory. We won't be covering vertex buffer objects in this volume, but we will in a future volume.

Quick Review

To be sure you understand how vertex arrays work, let's recap. First, you need the data with which you will fill the arrays, which can be loaded from a file, generated procedurally, or defined by some other method. This data consists of a set of vertices describing some object in your world. Each vertex can include information about its position, color, texture coordinates, fog coordinates, edge flags, and/or normal vectors. In addition to storing this data in one or more arrays, you need to enable vertex arrays for each data type you will be using. Then you tell OpenGL to use each array with corresponding calls to gl*Pointer().

When you want to evaluate and render the data stored in these arrays, you make a call to one of the functions listed above. For each vertex, OpenGL takes the data associated with each attribute type and, in essence, applies the appropriate OpenGL call to that data. For example, the color array data is used as if you had called glColor(), the normal data is used as if you had called glNormal(), and so on. Note that these functions are not actually called (after all, you could do that yourself and avoid the whole concept of vertex arrays entirely), but the results are the same.

Interleaved Arrays

With the methods we've discussed so far, your vertex arrays will look something like Figure 10.2, with each vertex attribute stored in a separate array. Each of these arrays is passed independently via one of the gl*Pointer() functions, and when a draw command is made, OpenGL assembles data from each array to form complete vertices.

Instead of storing data for each attribute in separate arrays, you may want to pack all of the data into a single array, as shown in Figure 10.3.

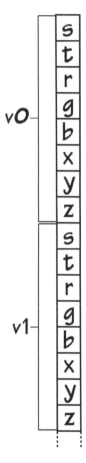

Figure 10.3 Position, color, and texture coordinate data stored in a single array.

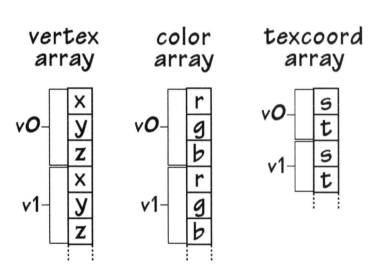

Figure 10.2 Arrays for position, color, and texture coordinate attributes.

To be able to use this type of array, you could use the methods we've been discussing so far by making use of the stride parameter. If the data from Figure 10.3 was in an array called vertexData, you could use the following code to set it up:

```
glVertexPointer(3, GL_FLOAT, 8 * sizeof(GLfloat), vertexData);
glColorPointer(3, GL_FLOAT, 8 * sizeof(GLfloat), &vertexData[3]);
glTexCoordPointer(2, GL_FLOAT, 8 * sizeof(GLfloat), &vertexData[6]);
```

You could then use glDrawElements() or any other draw functions just as you normally would.

OpenGL provides an alternative approach in the form of glInterleavedArrays():

```
void glInterleavedArrays(GLenum format, GLsizei stride, const GLvoid *pointer);
```

format is used to indicate exactly what data appears in the array pointed to by pointer. It can take on any of the values in Table 10.3. stride serves the same purpose as it does with the various gl*Pointer() functions. Note that the data should be ordered in a manner consistent with the ordering in the format parameter; i.e., texture coordinates are always first, followed by colors, then normals, then positions.

Table 10.3 Interleaved Array Formats

Plane	Description
GL_V2F	Position only, 2 elements (x,y)
GL_V3F	Position only, 3 elements (x,y,z)
GL_C4UB_V2F*	Color, 4 elements (r,g,b,a), and position, 2 elements (x,y)
GL_C4UB_V3F*	Color, 4 elements (r,g,b,a), and position, 3 elements (x,y,z)
GL_C3F_V3F	Color, 3 elements (r,g,b), and position, 3 elements (x,y,z)
GL_N3F_V3F	Normals, 3 elements, and position, 3 elements (x,y,z)
GL_C4F_N3F_V3F	Color, 4 elements (r,g,b,a), normals, 3 elements, and position, 3 elements (x,y,z)
GL_T2F_V3F	Texture coordinates, 2 elements (s,t), and position, 3 elements (x,y,z)
GL_T4F_V4F	Texture coordinates, 4 elements (s,t,r,q), and position, 4 elements (x,y,z,w)
GL_T2F_C4UB_V3F*	Texture coordinates, 2 elements (s,t), color, 4 elements (r,g,b,a), and position, 3 elements (x,y,z)
GL_T2F_C3F_V3F	Texture coordinates, 2 elements (s,t), color, 3 elements (r,g,b) and position, 3 elements (x,y,z)
GL_T2F_N3F_V3F	Texture coordinates, 2 elements (s,t), normals, 3 elements, and position, 3 elements (x,y,z)
GL_T2F_C4F_N3F_V3F	Texture coordinates, 2 elements (s,t), color, 4 elements (r,g,b,a), normals, 3 elements, and position, 3 elements (x,y,z)
GL_T4F_C4F_N3F_V4F	Texture coordinates, 4 elements (s,t,r,q), color, 4 elements (r,g,b,a), normals, 3 elements, and position, 4 elements (x,y,z,w)

* The C4UB type indicates colors represented as four floating point values stored in a single integer that is then cast to a float. This is necessary because other data types are floats, and it's not possible to have an array of multiple data types.

Using interleaved arrays, the code above could be rewritten as:

```
glInterleavedArrays(GL_T2F_C3F_V3F, 0, vertexData);
```

In addition to setting a pointer to the vertex attribute data, a call to `glInterleavedArrays()` will also enable any arrays indicated in the format parameter and disable those that aren't being used.

Unfortunately, interleaved arrays have some serious limitations. They don't support fog coordinates, secondary color, or edge flags. They also only work with the currently active texture unit, so multitexturing isn't possible. However, if you have data that consists only of position, color, normal, and/or texture coordinate information, interleaved arrays may be more convenient than the standard method.

Vertex Arrays and Multitexturing

Extension

Extension name: ARB_multitexture

Name string: GL_ARB_multitexture

Promoted to core: OpenGL 1.2.1

Function names: glClientActiveTextureARB()

Tokens: GL_MAX_TEXTURE_UNITS_ARB

Using multitexturing (see Chapter 9, "More on Texture Mapping") with vertex arrays requires some additional setup beyond what we have discussed so far. Each texture unit has its own set of states, and thus, vertex arrays can be enabled and disabled for each texture unit individually, and each has its own texture coordinate array pointer.

In OpenGL implementations supporting multitexturing, the texture unit that is active by default is the first one. Calls to `glTexCoordPointer()` and `glEnableClientState()`/`glDisableClientState()` with GL_TEXTURE_COORD_ARRAY affect only the currently active texture unit, so to use vertex arrays with other texture units, you have to switch to them by activating them. This is done with the following function:

```
void glClientActiveTexture(enum texture);
```

texture is a constant corresponding to the unit that you wish to make active, and it must be of the form GL_TEXTURE*i*, where *i* ranges from 0 to GL_MAX_TEXTURE_UNITS −1.

Caution

The state associated with `glClientActiveTexture()` is separate from the state associated with `glActiveTexture()`. When using multitexturing with vertex arrays, be sure to use the former, not the latter.

After you have activated the texture unit you wish to modify, you can then make calls to `glTexCoordPointer()` to assign an array of values or `glEnableClientState()`/`glDisable-ClientState()` to turn vertex arrays on or off for the current texture unit. Texture coordinate arrays for all texture units are disabled by default. To set up vertex arrays for the first two texture units, you'd use something like the following:

```
// Enable texture coordinate vertex arrays for texture unit 0
glClientActiveTexture(GL_TEXTURE0);
glEnableClientState(GL_TEXTURE_COORD_ARRAY);

// Specify an array (defined previously) to use with texture unit 0
glTexCoordPointer(2, GL_FLOAT, 0, (GLvoid *)texUnit0Vertices);

// Select and enable texture unit 1
glClientActiveTextureARB(GL_TEXTURE1);
glEnableClientState(GL_TEXTURE_COORD_ARRAY);

// Specify an array (defined previously) to use with texture unit 1
glTexCoordPointer(2, GL_FLOAT, 0, (GLvoid *)texUnit1Vertices);
```

After you've enabled and specified vertex arrays for each of the texture units you want to use, there is nothing else you need to do. Subsequent calls to `glDrawArrays()`, `glDrawElements()`, and so on will use them just like any other vertex arrays.

Locking Arrays

Many OpenGL implementations provide an extension that enables you to lock and unlock arrays. Locking the arrays lets the system know that, until they are unlocked, you won't be modifying the data in the arrays. Because OpenGL knows that the vertex array data is not changing, it may be able to cache the transformations or place the arrays in memory that can be accessed more quickly. This can lead to performance gains, especially if you're drawing the same geometry more than once. Because the vertex data is, in effect, compiled, the name of this extension is `EXT_compiled_vertex_array`. The functions associated with this extension are

```
void glLockArraysEXT(GLint first, GLsizei count);
void glUnlockArraysEXT();
```

The first parameter is the index of the first vertex you want to lock, and count is the total number of vertices to lock, starting at the first index.

Extension

Extension name: EXT_compiled_vertex_array

Name string: GL_EXT_compiled_vertex_array

Promoted to core: No

Function names: glLockArraysEXT(), glUnlockArraysEXT()

See the demo in the following section for sample code checking for and using this extension.

Marbles

We've provided a demo in the Marbles directory in the folder for this chapter on the CD. This demo draws a large number of marbles bouncing around inside a glass case with a mirrored floor. Each marble shares the same data but is colored and positioned independently. Immediate mode is used by default, but you can use the following keys to enable some of the features covered so far in this chapter:

<SPACE> Toggles vertex arrays for the marbles using glDrawElements().

<TAB> Toggles display lists for everything.

<C> Toggles compiled vertex arrays.

You should definitely see an improvement in frame rate when enabling vertex arrays. Display lists and compiled vertex arrays may or may not improve performance, depending on your hardware.

You'll notice that when display lists are enabled, the marbles freeze in place. This is due to the fact that each marble is positioned independently *inside* of the display list. Once the display list is compiled, the data within it can't be changed, so the marbles can't move relative to each other. You could, however, move the marbles as a group.

You'll also notice that when enabling compiled vertex arrays, the marble colors may change to a single color. This is because all of the marbles share the same base set of data. When the vertices get locked and cached away, the changes in the material may not get picked up.

Let's look at the most relevant code for the demo. First, after generating the data for the marbles, the vertex arrays are set up as follows:

```
bool CGfxOpenGL::Init()
{
  ...
  InitializeMarbles();
  glVertexPointer(3, GL_FLOAT, 0, m_positions);
  glNormalPointer(GL_FLOAT, 0, m_texCoords);
  glTexCoordPointer(3, GL_FLOAT, 0, m_texCoords);
  ...
}
```

The texture coordinate data is being used for both texture coordinates and normals because with cube-mapped spheres, the values are identical.

The relevant code for display lists happens in Render(), as shown below:

```
void CGfxOpenGL::Render()
{
  ...
  if (m_useList)
  {
    // use the existing list if there is one
    if (m_list)
    {
      glCallList(m_list);
      return;
    }
    else // otherwise, create a new one
    {
      m_list = glGenLists(1);
      glNewList(m_list, GL_COMPILE_AND_EXECUTE);
    }
  }

  glLightfv(GL_LIGHT0, GL_POSITION, LIGHT_POSITION);

  DrawFloor();
  DrawReflection();
  DrawMarbles(GL_FALSE);
  DrawBox();

  if (m_useList)
```

```
      glEndList();
}
```

Finally, the vertex arrays are put to use inside of DrawMarbles():

```
void CGfxOpenGL::DrawSphere()
{
  if (m_useVertexArrays)
  {
    for (int i = 0; i < m_numStrips; ++i)
    {
      glDrawElements(GL_TRIANGLE_STRIP, m_vertsPerStrip, GL_UNSIGNED_INT,
                     &m_indexArray[i * m_vertsPerStrip]);
    }
  }
  else // draw using immediate mode instead
  {
    for (int i = 0; i < m_numStrips; ++i)
    {
      glBegin(GL_TRIANGLE_STRIP);
      for (int j = 0; j < m_vertsPerStrip; ++j)
      {
        int index = m_indexArray[i * m_vertsPerStrip + j];
        glNormal3fv(m_texCoords[index].v);
        glTexCoord3fv(m_texCoords[index].v);
        glVertex3fv(m_positions[index].v);
      }
      glEnd();
    }
  }
}
```

A screenshot of the Marbles demo can be seen in Figure 10.4. Be sure to check out the source code on the CD to ensure that you fully understand how vertex arrays work.

Frustum Culling

One of the most basic rules in developing an efficient graphics engine is this: Don't draw what you can't see. For this reason, many algorithms have been developed to allow you to quickly identify large sets of data that can't possibly be seen by the viewer so that they can be discarded instead of sending them to the graphics hardware. We don't have space to even scratch the surface of the various methods available, but we will show you how to do something they almost all rely on: view-frustum culling.

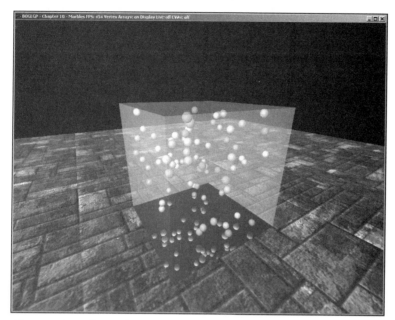

Figure 10.4 The Marbles demo.

As you'll recall, the view frustum defines the region of the world space that you can see. Usually, it is defined in terms of a camera, including the location of the viewer, field of view, and so on. In reality, this information is used to construct six planes that bound the view frustum. Anything within this frustum is visible (unless something else inside of the frustum is obstructing it). Anything outside of it can be discarded.

OpenGL automatically rejects any triangles that fall outside of the view frustum, so you don't *have* to do it yourself for rendering to work properly. However, OpenGL does frustum culling on a per-triangle basis. Although it does this extremely quickly and cheaply, when you're dealing with hundreds of thousands or even millions of triangles, this cost adds up and degrades performance. Fortunately, you know more about your game data than OpenGL does, and you can use this information to make rendering more efficient.

For example, your game generally consists of models made up of several thousand triangles. You can construct a simple bounding volume such as a box or a sphere for each model and then test that object against the view frustum yourself. If it is completely outside of it, you can discard it. With one simple check you can eliminate thousands of others.

If the object does not fall completely outside of the view frustum, there are two possibilities: It is either partially or completely contained by the view frustum. Continuing to test the partially visible object will probably be more expensive than letting OpenGL do it for you, so either way, you pass the object to OpenGL and move on to the next one.

You can imagine creating hierarchies of bounding volumes, each containing many smaller ones. By testing the top-level volumes, you can potentially eliminate huge amounts of data with a single test. When you encounter volumes that are partially contained, you can move down the hierarchy and test the sub-volumes, repeating the process. Eventually, the sub-volumes will be small enough that it'll be cheaper to have OpenGL test them for you, and you'll be done.

Now that you have an idea of what frustum culling is and how you can leverage it to improve performance, it's time to look at the details of how it's done.

Determining the View Frustum

The first step is determining the equations for the planes that describe the view frustum. Although it's possible to calculate them yourself, it's easier to simply extract that information from the current projection and modelview matrices, which you can do by passing GL_PROJECTION_MATRIX or GL_MODELVIEW_MATRIX to glGetFloatv(). But first, let's review the plane equation.

As you may recall from your geometry classes, the equation for a plane can be defined as follows:

$$Ax + By + Cz + D = 0$$

A, B, and C define the plane's normal vector, D is the distance from the origin to the plane, and x, y, and z are any points on the plane. You can take any point and plug it into the plane equation, and if the result is 0, the point lies on the plane. If the result is greater than 0, the point is in front of the plane, and if it is negative, it is behind the plane.

To extract the A, B, C, and D terms from the projection and modelview matrices, you first have to multiply the former by the latter. Then the plane values can be found by adding or subtracting one of the first three rows of the matrix with the fourth row. Table 10.4 shows which rows to use for each plane.

Table 10.4 Sources for Plane Equations

Plane	Row
Left	1
Right	1 (negated)
Bottom	2
Top	2 (negated)
Near	3
Far	3 (negated)

If PM contains the concatenated projection and modelview matrix, then the left and right planes can be extracted as follows:

```
left.A = PM[3] + PM[0];
left.B = PM[7] + PM[4];
left.C = PM[11] + PM[8];
left.D = PM[15] + PM[12];
```

```
right.A = PM[3] - PM[0];
right.B = PM[7] - PM[4];
right.C = PM[11] - PM[8];
right.D = PM[15] - PM[12];
```

These values aren't quite ready to use yet because they need to be normalized. You do this by finding the length of the normal vector and then dividing A, B, C, and D by the length. Note that the normals will point toward the center of the view frustum.

Testing Points

Once you have the plane equations for all six planes, the next step is to determine whether or not something is inside the frustum. We'll start off with the simplest object to test: a point. A point is completely contained within the view frustum if it is in front of all six planes. Simply plug the x, y, and z coordinates into each of the six plane equations, and if the results are all positive, the point is inside the frustum. If even one result is negative, the point is outside the frustum. Here's what this would look like in pseudocode:

```
function PointInFrustum(point)
{
  for each plane
    if (plane.A * point.x + plane.B * point.y + plane.C * point.z + plane.D) < 0
      return false

  return true
}
```

Testing Spheres

Points are easy to test but aren't very useful on their own. Spheres on the other hand are far more useful, since they can be used as bounding volumes for more complex objects. Testing spheres against the view frustum is almost as easy as testing points—in fact, the two are closely related. Remember that when you test a point against a plane, you don't just find out whether or not the point is in front or in back of the plane; you find out how far it is from the plane. If you represent a sphere as a point and a radius, you just need to test to see if the distance from the point to the plane is greater than or equal to the radius. If this is true for all six planes, the sphere is within the view frustum. This is shown in the following pseudocode:

```
function SphereInFrustum(sphere)
{
  for each plane
    dist = plane.A*sphere.x + plane.B*sphere.y + plane.C*sphere.z + plane.D
```

```
    if dist <= -sphere.radius
        return false

    return true
}
```

Notice that this code checks the distance against the negative radius, which means that the function returns `false` if the sphere is completely outside the view frustum. It returns `true` if the sphere is completely or partially inside the view frustum. If you would like to know whether the sphere is completely or partially contained, you'll have to modify the algorithm slightly. This is left for an exercise for the reader at the end of the chapter.

Frustum Culling Applied

To help you better understand the advantages of frustum culling and how to implement it, take a look at the FrustumCulling demo in the directory for this chapter on the CD. This demo, shown in Figure 10.5, revisits the terrain demo you've seen in previous chapters. Monsters—loaded from the popular *Quake 2* model format, have been added to the world. Although the camera is stationary, you can use the left and right arrows to spin around in place. When each model is loaded, a bounding sphere is calculated for it, which is then tested against the view frustum while rendering. Frustum culling can be toggled

Figure 10.5 An example of frustum culling.

on and off with the space bar to see the difference it makes to the frame rate. The following code is used to extract the view frustum:

```
void ExtractPlane(plane_t &plane, GLfloat *mat, int row)
{
  int scale = (row < 0) ? -1 : 1;
  row = abs(row) - 1;

  // calculate plane coefficients from the matrix
  plane.A = mat[3] + scale * mat[row];
  plane.B = mat[7] + scale * mat[row + 4];
  plane.C = mat[11] + scale * mat[row + 8];
  plane.D = mat[15] + scale * mat[row + 12];

  // normalize the plane
  float length = sqrtf(plane.A * plane.A +
                       plane.B * plane.B +
                       plane.C * plane.C);
  plane.A /= length;
  plane.B /= length;
  plane.C /= length;
  plane.D /= length;
}


void CGfxOpenGL::CalculateFrustum()
{
  // get the projection and modelview matrices
  GLfloat projection[16];
  GLfloat modelview[16];

  glGetFloatv(GL_PROJECTION_MATRIX, projection);
  glGetFloatv(GL_MODELVIEW_MATRIX, modelview);

  // use OpenGL to multiply them
  glPushMatrix();
  glLoadMatrixf(projection);
  glMultMatrixf(modelview);
  glGetFloatv(GL_MODELVIEW_MATRIX, modelview);
  glPopMatrix();

  // extract each plane
  ExtractPlane(m_frustum.l, modelview, 1);
```

```
  ExtractPlane(m_frustum.r, modelview, -1);
  ExtractPlane(m_frustum.b, modelview, 2);
  ExtractPlane(m_frustum.t, modelview, -2);
  ExtractPlane(m_frustum.n, modelview, 3);
  ExtractPlane(m_frustum.f, modelview, -3);
}
```

The test for view frustum intersection is done with the SphereInFrustum() function:

```
bool SphereInFrustum(sphere_t sphere, frustum_t frustum)
{
  GLfloat dist;
  for (int i = 0; i < 6; ++i)
  {
    dist = frustum.planes[i].A * sphere.center.x +
           frustum.planes[i].B * sphere.center.y +
           frustum.planes[i].C * sphere.center.z +
           frustum.planes[i].D;

    if (dist <= -sphere.radius)
      return false;
  }

  return true;
}
```

Summary

You've now learned how to use two features included with OpenGL—display lists and vertex arrays—to improve performance. You've also seen how to reduce OpenGL's workload by preculling large chunks of data using frustum culling. Applying these techniques should enable you to attain a higher frame rate. You're encouraged to continue to explore algorithms that enable you to arrange your code and data in a more efficient manner.

What You Have Learned

- Display lists allow you to store precompiled lists of commands on the graphics processor and are useful for representing static data.
- Vertex arrays provide an intuitive way to store large amounts of data. They allow OpenGL to operate more efficiently by caching transformed vertices that are used repeatedly. They also help avoid the overhead of repeatedly calling a large number of functions.

- Your OpenGL implementation may allow you to lock vertex arrays, which may allow it to process them more quickly because it knows you won't be changing them.
- Interleaved arrays provide an alternative to storing each vertex attribute in a separate array, but they have limited usefulness.
- Frustum culling can be used to discard large segments of non-visible geometry relatively quickly. It is used for many higher-level geometry occlusion algorithms.

Review Questions

1. Given a handle to a display list, how can you determine that it is valid?
2. What happens when you include a call that is not supported by display lists between calls to glNewList() and glEndList()?
3. How do you enable vertex arrays?
4. How do you specify more than one set of texture coordinates when using vertex arrays?
5. Why is it generally a bad idea to perform frustum culling on a per-triangle basis?

On Your Own

1. Modify the SphereInFrustum() function to return one of three values: whether the sphere is completely inside, completely outside, or partially inside the view frustum.

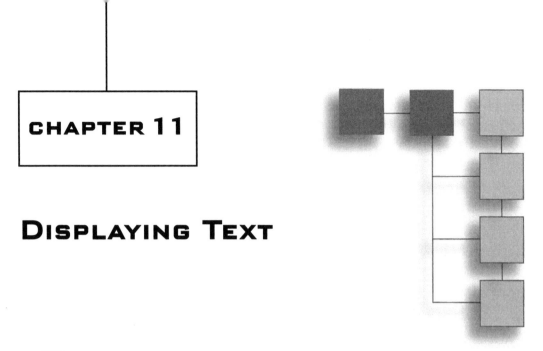

CHAPTER 11

DISPLAYING TEXT

Chances are, at some point you'll want to render text. You might use text for menus, screensavers, character dialogue, or simply for some special effects. In this chapter you'll look at some of the more common techniques for displaying text through OpenGL. The techniques you'll be looking at include bitmap fonts, outline fonts, and textured fonts. Granted, most of these techniques are operating system specific with Microsoft Windows, but we are also going to introduce a free OpenGL font library called glFont.

In this chapter we'll cover:

- Bitmap fonts
- Outline fonts
- How to use the glFont OpenGL font library

Bitmap Fonts

Bitmap fonts offer a simple way to display 2D text on the screen. Information about the characters in a bitmap font is stored as bitmap images. A drawback to bitmap fonts is that they can become jagged and primitive as they get larger (without antialiasing); however, an advantage to bitmap fonts is that they provide a high performance method for rendering text to the screen. You create them through the use of the "wiggle" function wglUse-FontBitmaps(), which generates bitmaps from font files loaded on your system.

```
BOOL wglUseFontBitmaps(HDC hdc, DWORD first, DWORD count, DWORD listBase);
```

To use bitmap fonts, the first thing you need to do is to create a display list of size 96 that will hold the character bitmaps. You accomplish this by using the glGenLists() function:

```
unsigned int base;
base = glGenLists(96);
```

After you've created the display list, you can create your font by using the Windows function CreateFont(), which is defined as:

```
HFONT CreateFont(
     int nHeight,                  // logical height of font
     int nWidth,                   // logical average character width
     int nEscapement,              // angle of escapement
     int nOrientation,             // base-line orientation angle
     int fnWeight,                 // font weight
     DWORD fdwItalic,              // italic attribute flag
     DWORD fdwUnderline,           // underline attribute flag
     DWORD fdwStrikeOut,           // strikeout attribute flag
     DWORD fdwCharSet,             // character set identifier
     DWORD fdwOutputPrecision,     // output precision
     DWORD fdwClipPrecision,       // clipping precision
     DWORD fdwQuality,             // output quality
     DWORD fdwPitchAndFamily,      // pitch and family
     LPCTSTR lpszFace              // pointer to typeface name string
);
```

This function returns a handle to the created Windows font object. You can then select a device context for this font object and use the device context as a parameter for the wglUseFontBitmaps() function, as seen here:

```
HFONT hFont;         // windows font

// create a 14pt Courier font
hFont = CreateFont(14, 0, 0, 0, FW_BOLD, FALSE, FALSE, FALSE, ANSI_CHARSET,
                   OUT_TT_PRECIS, CLIP_DEFAULT_PRECIS, ANTIALIASED_QUALITY,
                   FF_DONTCARE | DEFAULT_PITCH, "Courier");

// verify font creation
if (!hFont)
     return 0;

// select a device context for the font
SelectObject(g_HDC, hFont);
```

```
// prepare the bitmap font
wglUseFontBitmaps(g_HDC, 32, 96, base);
```

The preceding block of code builds your bitmap font display list with a 14-point Courier bold font.

Now you know how to create fonts, but how do you display them? Displaying text with bitmap fonts is actually easier than setting them up. You simply call the glListBase() and glCallLists() functions like this:

```
char *str;

glPushAttrib(GL_LIST_BIT);
    glListBase(base - 32);
    glCallLists(strlen(str), GL_UNSIGNED_BYTE, str);
glPopAttrib();
```

After the glListBase() function defines the base display list ID, the glCallLists() function calls the display list needed based on the array of characters (the text string) passed to it.

With all of this base code for using bitmap fonts, you can now develop a set of functions to use these fonts more easily. Let's look at a simple example that displays a text string in the center of the window, as shown in Figure 11.1.

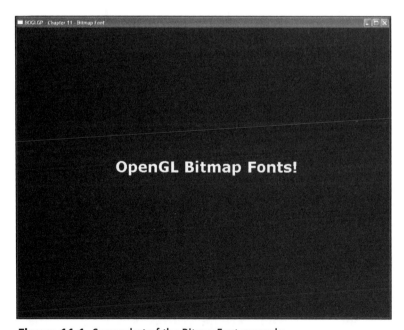

Figure 11.1 Screenshot of the BitmapFont example.

On the CD you will find the code for this example in Chapter 11, in the BitmapFont folder. In the example code, we created the private member variable m_fontListBase to store the display list base, along with three methods: CreateBitmapFont(), RenderFont(), and ReleaseFont().

The following code is for the CreateBitmapFont() method in the CGfxOpenGL class:

```
unsigned int CGfxOpenGL::CreateBitmapFont(char *fontName, int fontSize)
{
    HFONT hFont;                    // windows font
    unsigned int base;

    base = glGenLists(96);         // create storage for 96 characters

    if (stricmp(fontName, "symbol") == 0)
    {
        hFont = CreateFont(fontSize, 0, 0, 0, FW_BOLD, FALSE, FALSE, FALSE,
                            SYMBOL_CHARSET, OUT_TT_PRECIS, CLIP_DEFAULT_PRECIS,
                            ANTIALIASED_QUALITY, FF_DONTCARE | DEFAULT_PITCH,
                            fontName);
    }
    else
    {
        hFont = CreateFont(fontSize, 0, 0, 0, FW_BOLD, FALSE, FALSE, FALSE,
                            ANSI_CHARSET, OUT_TT_PRECIS, CLIP_DEFAULT_PRECIS,
                            ANTIALIASED_QUALITY, FF_DONTCARE | DEFAULT_PITCH,
                            fontName);
    }

    if (!hFont)
        return 0;

    SelectObject(hDC, hFont);
    wglUseFontBitmaps(hDC, 32, 96, base);

    return base;
}
```

The CreateBitmapFont() method first generates the display list for 96 characters. It then checks whether the desired fontName is a symbol font. If it is, then the CreateBitmapFont() function calls the CreateFont() function with the SYMBOL_CHARSET value for the fdwCharSet parameter. If the function is not a symbol font, then the ANSI_CHARSET value is set. After setting up the bitmap font for use with Windows through the `wglUseFontBitmaps()` function, the `CreateBitmapFont()` method returns the base ID for the character display list.

Next is the `RenderFont()` method, which displays a string of text using the selected bitmap font at a specified raster position:

```
void CGfxOpenGL::RenderFont(int xPos, int yPos, unsigned int base, char *str)
{
    if ((base == 0) || (!str))
        return;

    glRasterPos2i(xPos, yPos);

    glPushAttrib(GL_LIST_BIT);
        glListBase(base - 32);
        glCallLists((int)strlen(str), GL_UNSIGNED_BYTE, str);
    glPopAttrib();
}
```

The `RenderFont()` method is very simple in that it verifies the base ID and string it receives before setting the raster position and rendering the text display list. Finally, we have the `ReleaseFont()` method, which simply cleans up the font display list:

```
void CGfxOpenGL::ReleaseFont(unsigned int base)
{
    if (base != 0)
        glDeleteLists(base, 96);
}
```

The rest of the code uses these functions to display the screenshot shown in Figure 11.1. The example is set up in orthographic projection. We recommend orthographic projection when rendering with bitmap fonts because it enables you to specify the raster position coordinates in window coordinates, and you don't need to worry about the perspective projection affecting the raster position.

That's all for bitmap fonts! Let's look at another technique for putting text on the screen: outline fonts.

Outline Fonts

Outline fonts are very similar to the bitmap fonts we just discussed, but they are much more fun to play around with! Outline fonts define characters in a font as a series of lines and curves, which means they can be scaled up and down without a loss in quality. With

OpenGL, you can move outline font text around the screen in 3D, give the font text some thickness, and essentially turn any font on the current system into a 3D font with all the functionality of other 3D objects.

To use outline fonts, you first need to declare an array of 256 GLYPHMETRICSFLOAT variables, which hold information about the placement and orientation of a glyph in a character cell. The GLYPHMETRICSFLOAT structure is a special structure created specifically for using text with OpenGL. It is defined as:

```
typedef struct _GLYPHMETRICSFLOAT { // gmf
    FLOAT      gmfBlackBoxX;
    FLOAT      gmfBlackBoxY;
    POINTFLOAT gmfptGlyphOrigin;
    FLOAT      gmfCellIncX;
    FLOAT      gmfCellIncY;
} GLYPHMETRICSFLOAT;
```

You'll pass the GLYPHMETRICSFLOAT variable you create to the wglUseFontOutlines() function. This function creates a set of display lists, one for each glyph of the current outline font, which you can use to render text to the screen. This function is defined as:

```
BOOL wglUseFontOutlines(
    HDC hdc,                    // device context of the outline font
    DWORD first,                // first glyph to be turned into a display list
    DWORD count,                // number of glyphs to be turned into display lists
    DWORD listBase,             // specifies the starting display list
    FLOAT deviation,            // specifies the maximum chordal deviation from the
                                // true outlines
    FLOAT extrusion,            // extrusion value in the negative-z direction
    int format,                 // specifies line segments or polygons in display lists
    LPGLYPHMETRICSFLOAT lpgmf   // address of buffer to receive glyph metric data
);
```

Creation of the outline font is essentially the same as the bitmap font with the addition of these two items. For instance, compare the CreateBitmapFont() function we showed earlier with this CreateOutlineFont() function:

```
unsigned int CreateOutlineFont(char *fontName, int fontSize, float depth)
{
    HFONT hFont;              // windows font
    unsigned int base;

    base = glGenLists(256);      // create storage for 256 characters

    if (stricmp(fontName, "symbol") == 0)
```

```
        {
            hFont = CreateFont(fontSize, 0, 0, 0, FW_BOLD, FALSE, FALSE, FALSE,
                                SYMBOL_CHARSET, OUT_TT_PRECIS, CLIP_DEFAULT_PRECIS,
                                ANTIALIASED_QUALITY, FF_DONTCARE | DEFAULT_PITCH,
                                fontName);
        }
        else
        {
            hFont = CreateFont(fontSize, 0, 0, 0, FW_BOLD, FALSE, FALSE, FALSE,
                                ANSI_CHARSET, OUT_TT_PRECIS, CLIP_DEFAULT_PRECIS,
                                ANTIALIASED_QUALITY, FF_DONTCARE | DEFAULT_PITCH,
                                fontName);
        }

        if (!hFont)
            return 0;

        SelectObject(g_HDC, hFont);
        wglUseFontOutlines(g_HDC, 0, 255, base, 0.0f, depth, WGL_FONT_POLYGONS, gmf);

        return base;
}
```

As you can see, this function is very similar to the CreateBitmapFont() method we showed earlier, but there are a few differences. The first difference you might notice is the addition of the depth parameter, which is used by the wglUseFontOutlines() function to define the length of the outline font text along the z-axis (or essentially the depth of the font). The next difference is that you create 256 display lists instead of 96. This is because you want to provide support for all the 256 available ASCII codes. And lastly, you use the wglUseFontOutlines() function to finalize the setup of the outline fonts for OpenGL.

Displaying outline font text is exactly the same as displaying bitmap font text. Because you used all 256 ASCII codes when initializing the outline font, here is how the display code would look:

```
glPushAttrib(GL_LIST_BIT);
    glListBase(base);
    glCallLists(strlen(str), GL_UNSIGNED_BYTE, str);
glPopAttrib();
```

On the CD included with this book you will find the OutlineFont example for Chapter 11. This example renders text as an outline font to the window and rotates it. A screenshot is shown in Figure 11.2.

Figure 11.2 Screenshot of the OutlineFont example.

The majority of the code for this example is the same as the BitmapFont example, so we will focus only on the RenderFont() method because it is the most different:

```
void CGfxOpenGL::RenderFont(float xPos, float yPos, float zPos, unsigned int base,
char *str)
{
    float length = 0.0;

    if ((base == 0) || (!str))
        return;

    // center the text
    for (int idx = 0; idx < (int)strlen(str); idx++)      // find length of text
    {
        length += gmf[str[idx]].gmfCellIncX; // increase length by character's width
    }

    glTranslatef(-length/2.0f, yPos, zPos);
    glRotatef(m_angle, 1.0, 0.0, 0.0);
    glRotatef(m_angle, 0.0, 1.0, 0.0);
    glRotatef(m_angle, 0.0, 0.0, 1.0);
```

```
glPushAttrib(GL_LIST_BIT);
    glListBase(base);
    glCallLists((int)strlen(str), GL_UNSIGNED_BYTE, str);
glPopAttrib();
}
```

The RenderFont() method includes some code that centers the text on the point in space to which the text is being drawn. This is accomplished through a loop that goes through each character in the text string that you are displaying. During each iteration of the loop, you add the character's width, which you obtain from the GLYPHMETRICSFLOAT variable, to a variable that stores the sum of all the characters' widths. You then translate your coordinate system along the negative x-axis by half the total length of the text string, resulting in the text being centered on the (xPos, yPos, zPos) point in 3D space.

Also, the glRotatef() calls you see in the method are there only for demonstration purposes and should not be in the RenderFont() method during normal use.

You can also texture map outline fonts since they are constructed of polygons. Instead of trying to figure out the texture coordinates on your own, you can use OpenGL's automatic texture-coordinate generation functionality to texture map the text. You can find more information on texture-coordinate generation in Chapter 9, "More on Texture Mapping."

Using glFont

glFont is both a program executable and an API with source code that takes any Windows TrueType font and turns it into an OpenGL texture. glFont determines the appropriate texture coordinates and displays text with correct spacing and size on an OpenGL quadrilateral. Its design is not for 3D text, but rather for 2D text for use in games and other graphics applications where 3D text is overkill.

You can find glFont on the CD included with this book, or you can get it from the glFont Web site at http://students.cs.byu.edu/~bfish/glfont.php.

The Executable

The program included with glFont is glFont.exe, which is a simple-to-use program for creating font textures that the glFont API code can read and display. The process for using glFont.exe is simple:

1. Choose a font, using the standard Windows font dialog. Choose the size, style, and so on.
2. Specify the size of the texture to be used. Remember, the bigger the texture, the higher the font quality.
3. Specify the range of ASCII characters to draw onto the texture.

4. Generate the texture.

5. Save the texture to a GLF file.

The Code

Using glFont in code is almost as easy as using the glFont executable. First you need to create a GLFONT object:

```
GLFONT font;
```

Next, you need to generate an OpenGL texture object with the glGenTextures() function and then use that texture object when calling the GLFONT::Create() method:

```
unsigned int tex;
glEnable(GL_TEXTURE_2D);
glGenTextures(1, &tex);
font.Create("timesnewroman.glf", tex);
```

At this point, using glFont is just a matter of calling the GLFONT::Begin() method, displaying your text with GLFONT::DrawString(), and then finishing off the text display with GLFONT::End():

```
font.Begin();
font.DrawString("Hello world!", 5, 5, 0);
font.End();
```

A nice addition to glFont is that you can modify the source code for displaying text as you need it. For instance, you might want to display the text as a billboard for character dialogue. With glFont, you just need to create another DrawString() method for GLFONT that calculates the billboard coordinates. Remember, glFont simply uses OpenGL quads for rendering, so you can rotate fonts, scale fonts, and translate fonts however you want. Explore and experiment!

Summary

In this chapter you learned how to display and position 2D text with bitmap fonts using the wglUseFontBitmaps() function and display lists. You also learned how to display and position 3D text with outline fonts using the wglUseFontOutlines() function. Finally, we introduced the glFont OpenGL font library, which you can use and modify to suit your text rendering purposes.

What You Have Learned

- The wglUseFontBitmaps() function generates bitmap fonts from the font files loaded on the execution system.

- Display lists can be used to render each character of a font.
- When rendering bitmap fonts, you should use an orthographic perspective projection to simplify positioning the text.
- The `wglUseFontOutlines()` function creates a set of display lists, one for each glyph of the current outline font.
- The `GLYPHMETRICSFLOAT` struct is used when creating outline fonts. This struct is included particularly for rendering text with OpenGL.
- You can texture map outline fonts and specify texture coordinates with the automatic texture coordinate generation functionality provided with OpenGL.
- `glFont` is both a program executable and an API with source code that takes any Windows TrueType font and turns it into an OpenGL texture.

Review Questions

1. What "wiggle" function is used to create bitmap fonts?
2. What "wiggle" function is used to create outline fonts?
3. How do you texture map outline fonts?

On Your Own

1. Create a program that uses bitmap fonts, outline fonts, and the `glFont` library to render text.
2. Modify the `glFont` API source code to display text on a billboard polygon.

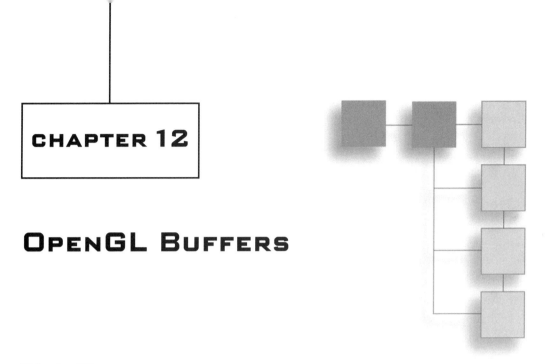

CHAPTER 12

OpenGL Buffers

W e've been discussing buffers is some form for quite some time now but haven't really taken the time to discuss them in detail. For instance, we've used the color and depth buffers in nearly every example thus far for functions such as double-buffering and hidden surface removal. In this chapter, we'll extend beyond these basic functionalities while also looking at two more buffers, called the stencil buffer and the accumulation buffer.

In this chapter, you'll learn:

- What the framebuffer is
- What general operations can be performed on buffers
- How to use the alpha test, color masking, and logic ops
- How to use the depth buffer
- How to use the stencil buffer
- How to use the accumulation buffer

What Is an OpenGL Buffer?

There are several buffers in OpenGL that you can use and manipulate, but just what exactly is a buffer? Simply put, a buffer is a set of sequential locations in memory. In OpenGL, a buffer is section of memory that is used to represent some aspect of the display. For example, the color buffer stores RGBA data for each pixel on the screen or window.

All the buffers in a system are collectively referred to as the framebuffer. So with OpenGL, the color buffer, depth buffer, stencil buffer, and accumulation buffer combine to give you a single framebuffer. When you operate on any OpenGL buffer, you are operating on the framebuffer.

Before discussing individual buffer types, we'll first look at a couple of operations that apply to all of the buffers: clearing and scissoring.

Clearing the Buffers

The most basic operation you can perform on a buffer is to clear out the previous contents. This is done using glClear():

```
void glClear(GLbitfield mask);
```

You've already seen this in action in all of the demos presented so far, so it should look familiar. The mask parameter is the bitwise logical OR of a combination of the values listed in Table 12.1.

Each buffer has a default value, and when you clear it, each element in the buffer is set to that value. As with most areas of OpenGL, you can set the default clear values to your own custom values. You do so with the following APIs:

Table 12.1 Clear Mask Values

Flag	Buffer
GL_COLOR_BUFFER_BIT	RGBA color buffer
GL_DEPTH_BUFFER_BIT	Depth buffer
GL_STENCIL_BUFFER_BIT	Stencil buffer
GL_ACCUM_BUFFER_BIT	Accumulation buffer

```
void glClearColor(GLclampf red, GLclampf green, GLclampf green, GLclampf alpha);
void glClearDepth(GLclampd depth);
void glClearStencil(GLint i);
void glClearAccum(GLclampf red, GLclampf green, GLclampf green, GLclampf alpha);
```

The GLclamp types are used for parameters that are internally clamped to fall within 0.0 and 1.0. The default values for all buffers are 0, except for the depth buffer, which is 1.0, corresponding to the value that represents elements that are farthest away from the camera.

Scissor Boxes

OpenGL allows you to define a *scissor box* that limits rendering to a sub-region of the screen. When scissoring is enabled, any pixel writes outside of the box are ignored. This applies to not only color values, but depth, stencil, and accumulation buffer values as well. Scissoring is one of the few operations that also affect the operation of glClear(); when it is enabled, only pixels inside of the scissor box will be cleared.

You can enable scissoring by passing GL_SCISSOR_TEST to glEnable(). The size of the scissor box is defined using:

```
void glScissor(GLint x, GLint y, GLsizei width, GLsizei height);
```

The x and y values correspond to the screen coordinates of the lower left corner of the box (the lower left corner of the screen is at $(0, 0)$). width and height are the dimensions of the box in pixels. The scissor box is set to the size of the window when a rendering context is first attached to it.

The following code shows an example of setting up a scissor box such as that shown in Figure 12.1.

```
glEnable(GL_SCISSOR_TEST);
glScissor(200, 250, 240, 180);
```

The Color Buffer

The color buffer stores RGBA data for each pixel on the screen. Almost everything discussed in this book relates to the color buffer in some way. There are a few operations in addition to those that we've already discussed that affect the color buffer on a per-fragment basis, and those will be described in this section.

Alpha Test

Every incoming fragment has an alpha value associated with it. Even if you don't specify it yourself, it gets set to the default value of 1. The *alpha test* can be used to discard fragments based on their alpha value. Practical applications for this include being able to discard transparent components of images.

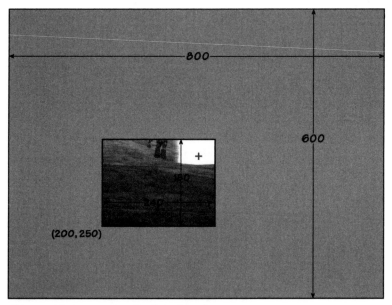

Figure 12.1 An example of a scissor box.

For example, say you are using the image in Figure 12.2 for billboarding, in which you apply the image as a texture to a screen-oriented quad to cheaply fake a 3D cactus. When applying the texture map, you would want to draw only the pixels that make up the cactus. Drawing the black area around it would ruin the effect. Alpha testing is the best way to do this.

The first step is to initialize the texture with appropriate values, such as an alpha of 0 in the black areas and 1 everywhere else. The next step is to enable the alpha test, which you would do with:

Figure 12.2 An image used as a billboard texture.

```
glEnable(GL_ALPHA_TEST);
```

Then you need to set up the alpha function. The alpha function controls exactly how the comparison is done. It is specified by using:

```
void glAlphaFunc(GLenum func, GLclampf reference);
```

func is an enumeration specifying the comparison function. Valid values are listed in Table 12.2. The incoming fragment alpha is compared against the reference value. Continuing with the cactus example, setting up the alpha function as follows would reject the black pixels (with an alpha of 0) and accept everything else.

```
glAlphaFunc(GL_GREATER, 0.0);
```

The alpha test is an easy to use tool that has many practical applications in games.

Table 12.2 Alpha Test Functions

Function	Description
GL_NEVER	Never pass, regardless of the fragment or reference alpha values.
GL_ALWAYS	Always pass, regardless of the fragment or reference alpha values. This is the default.
GL_LESS	Pass if the fragment alpha is less than the reference value.
GL_LEQUAL	Pass if the fragment alpha is less than or equal to the reference value.
GL_EQUAL	Pass if the fragment alpha is equal to the reference value.
GL_GEQUAL	Pass if the fragment alpha is greater than or equal to the reference value.
GL_GREATER	Pass if the fragment alpha is greater than the reference value.
GL_NOTEQUAL	Pass if the fragment alpha not equal to the reference value.

Color Masking

OpenGL allows you to disable writing to specific color channels. This can be used to create some interesting effects. For example, some multipass rendering algorithms require you to modify the depth buffer without actually writing color values. Another use might be to disable writing to everything but the green channel to create a cheap night vision effect.

This is known as *color masking*, and it is controlled through the following API:

```
void glColorMask(GLboolean red, GLboolean green, GLboolean blue, GLboolean alpha);
```

Passing GL_FALSE as the red, green, blue, or alpha parameter will disable writes for that channel. GL_TRUE is used to enable writes. By default, all of the channels are enabled, as you'd expect.

The color mask affects all operations that may potentially modify the color buffer, including clears.

Logical Operations

OpenGL allows you to create some interesting effects by performing logical operations between the incoming fragment and the value in the color buffer. These are executed as bitwise logical operations between each of the individual red, green, blue, and alpha components of the two colors. The resulting value is then stored in the color buffer.

Logic ops are enabled by passing GL_COLOR_LOGIC_OP to glEnable(). You can specify which specific operation to perform by using:

```
void glLogicOp(GLenum op);
```

op can be any of the enumerants listed in Table 12.3, where the fragment color is represented as *s*, the value in the color buffer is *d*, and the resulting color is *c*. The notation used corresponds to the C/C++ notation for bitwise operations.

Table 12.3 Logical Operations

Function	Description
GL_ZERO	c = 0
GL_AND	c = s & d
GL_AND_REVERSE	c = s & (~d)
GL_COPY	c = s
GL_AND_INVERTED	c = (~s) & d
GL_NOOP	c = d
GL_XOR	c = s ^ d
GL_OR	c = s | d
GL_NOR	c = ~(s | d)
GL_EQUIV	c = ~(s ^ d)
GL_INVERT	c = ~d
GL_OR_REVERSE	c = s | (~d)
GL_COPY_INVERTED	c = ~s
GL_OR_INVERTED	c = (~s) | d
GL_NAND	c = ~(s & d)
GL_SET	c = 1 (all bits set to 1)

Note

When logic ops are enabled, blending isn't performed, whether or not it is actually enabled. This is because the two operations have very similar functionality, so using them together would be ambiguous.

The Depth Buffer

You typically use the *depth buffer* (also known as the *z-buffer*) to perform hidden-surface removal on the objects in the scene. The values stored by the depth buffer for each pixel represent the distance between the object and the viewpoint. As you draw primitives, the depth buffer is checked and updated based on the distance of each object and the current depth-comparison function.

To take advantage of depth buffering, you must first be sure to request one when creating your window. You can then enable or disable depth testing by passing GL_DEPTH_TEST to glEnable()/glDisable(). It's disabled by default.

Depth-Comparison Functions

As mentioned, when you draw your scene with OpenGL, the z coordinate of each pixel on the screen is compared with the previous z coordinate already stored in the depth value as a distance. The function to determine what type of comparison you're going to use is set with the glDepthFunc() function:

```
void glDepthFunc(GLenum func);
```

You can use any of the values listed in Table 12.4 for the func parameter.

Table 12.4 Depth-Comparison Functions

Mode	Description
GL_NEVER	Never passes.
GL_LESS	Passes if the incoming z value is less than the stored z value. This is the default.
GL_EQUAL	Passes if the incoming z value is equal to the stored z value.
GL_LEQUAL	Passes if the incoming z value is equal to the stored z value.
GL_GREATER	Passes if the incoming z value is greater than the stored z value.
GL_NOTEQUAL	Passes if the incoming z value is not equal to the stored z value.
GL_GEQUAL	Passes if the incoming z value is greater than or equal to the stored z value.
GL_ALWAYS	Always passes.

OpenGL compares the current pixel's z value with the z value stored in the depth buffer at that location. If the depth-comparison function passes, then the pixel is stored in the color buffer, and the depth buffer is updated with the new pixel's depth. The default depth-comparison function is GL_LESS, which draws a pixel on if its z value is less than the z value in the depth buffer.

Tip

There's a subtle difference between using a depth function of GL_ALWAYS and simply disabling the depth test. Both methods will cause all objects to be updated in the color buffer, regardless of their depth. The difference is that when using GL_ALWAYS, each object will also update the depth buffer. The depth buffer isn't updated when the depth test is disabled.

Read-Only Depth Buffer

Being able to have objects tested against the depth buffer without updating it can enable some useful effects. For example, imagine rendering an explosion as a particle system. Each particle is transparent, and they are being additively blended, so that multiple particles in a single location will result in a brighter spot. The particles should be occluded by solid objects in the scene but not occlude each other. One way to achieve this would be to depth sort the particles and draw them in order from farthest to nearest. However, with thousands of particles, the cost of sorting could be high.

By making the depth buffer read-only and rendering the particles last, you can achieve the same effect much more easily. Read/write access to the depth buffer is controlled with glDepthMask():

```
void glDepthMask(GLboolean enable);
```

A value of GL_TRUE enables writes to the depth buffer, and GL_FALSE makes it read-only. Pseudocode for the explosion effect would look like this:

```
// depth testing is on all of the time
glEnable(GL_DEPTH_TEST);

Draw all normal objects in the scene

glDepthMask(GL_FALSE); // disable depth writes
Draw the explosion
glDepthMask(GL_TRUE); // reenable depth writes
```

> ### Z-Fighting
>
> When drawing overlapping triangles with similar depth values, a visual artifact known as *z-fighting* can manifest itself, causing the triangles to flicker as the camera moves. This is an imprecision issue; because depth values are stored in a finite (and relatively small) range, small errors introduced during their calculation can cause triangles that should be behind other triangles to show through them instead.
>
> Z-fighting usually happens when using a 16-bit depth buffer, so switching to a 24-bit depth buffer usually fixes the problem. However, to get a hardware-accelerated 24-bit depth buffer, you usually have to also request a 32-bit color buffer, which may not be possible on older systems. In addition, even with a 24-bit depth buffer, you may still experience z-fighting.
>
> The best solution is often to modify the values used for the far and near clip planes. Making the view frustum shorter allows for greater precision. Furthermore, z values are mapped to the depth buffer in a nonlinear fashion, so that objects closer to the screen have greater precision than objects farther away. Therefore, increasing the distance to the near clip plane has a more dramatic effect than decreasing the distance to the far clip plane. For instance, doubling the near plane distance from 1 to 2 doubles the precision of the depth buffer.

The Stencil Buffer

Like the depth buffer, you can use the *stencil buffer* to block out portions of the screen from view. However, the stencil buffer is a general purpose buffer that allows you to do things that aren't possible with the color buffer and depth buffer alone. One popular application is in creating reflective surfaces, where you restrict rendering to an irregular section of the screen where the reflected geometry will appear. You'll see an example of this at the end of this section. It is essential for many shadow rendering techniques, such as shadow volumes.

To use the stencil buffer, you must first make sure that your rendering window supports it. Under Windows, this means setting the `cStencilBits` field of the `PIXELFORMATDESCRIPTOR` when setting the pixel format, like this:

```
pfd.cStencilBits = 8;
```

This will create an 8-bit stencil buffer. Then you need to enable stenciling by passing `GL_STENCIL_TEST` to `glEnable()`. The next step is to set up stencil function and operation. These define how stenciling actually works, and understanding them will allow you to understand what stenciling really is.

The stencil function allows you to specify a function (which can be any of the values in Table 12.5), a reference value, and a mask. When a fragment is processed, the reference value and the value in the stencil buffer at the current pixel are logically ANDed with the mask, and the resulting values are tested using the stencil function. What happens next depends on the stencil operation. The stencil function can be set with the following API:

```
void glStencilFunc(GLenum func, GLint reference, GLuint mask);
```

The stencil operation defines three different actions:

1. What to do if the stencil test fails.
2. What to do if the stencil test passes but the depth test fails.
3. What to do if both the stencil and depth tests pass, or if the stencil tests pass and depth testing is disabled.

Each of these actions can be any of the values listed in Table 12.6. The stencil operation can be set using the following:

```
void glStencilOp(GLenum fail, GLenum zfail, GLenum zpass)
```

fail, zfail, and zpass correspond to actions 1, 2, and 3 in the list above.

Table 12.5 Stencil Functions

Function	Description
GL_NEVER	Always fails.
GL_LESS	Passes if the reference value is less than the value in the stencil buffer.
GL_LEQUAL	Passes if the reference value is less than or equal to the value in the stencil buffer.
GL_GREATER	Passes if the reference value is greater than the value in the stencil buffer.
GL_GEQUAL	Passes if the reference value is greater than or equal to the value in the stencil buffer.
GL_EQUAL	Passes if the reference value is equal to the value in the stencil buffer.
GL_NOTEQUAL	Passes if the reference value is not equal to the value in the stencil buffer.
GL_ALWAYS	Always passes. This is the default.

Table 12.6 Stencil Operations

Function	Description
GL_KEEP	The value in the stencil buffer is not changed.
GL_ZERO	The value in the stencil buffer is set to 0.
GL_REPLACE	The value in the stencil buffer is set to the reference value.
GL_INCR	The value in the stencil buffer is increased by 1.
GL_DECR	The value in the stencil buffer is decreased by 1.
GL_INVERT	Inverts the bits in the stencil buffer value.

An Example of Stencil Testing

You now know how the stencil test works on a low level, but let's look at an example to better understand it. The Marbles demo from Chapter 10, "Up Your Performance," used the stencil test to create a reflection of the marbles on the floor of the box. This was done in the following function:

```
void CGfxOpenGL::DrawReflection()
{
  glLightfv(GL_LIGHT0, GL_POSITION, NEG_LIGHT_POSITION);
  glDepthMask(GL_FALSE);
  glEnable(GL_STENCIL_TEST);
  glStencilFunc(GL_ALWAYS, 1, 0xFFFFFFFF);
  glStencilOp(GL_REPLACE, GL_REPLACE, GL_REPLACE);

  DrawBoxBottom();

  glDepthMask(GL_TRUE);
  glStencilFunc(GL_EQUAL, 1, 0xFFFFFFFF);
  glStencilOp(GL_KEEP, GL_KEEP, GL_KEEP);

  DrawMarbles(GL_TRUE);
  glDisable(GL_STENCIL_TEST);

  glLightfv(GL_LIGHT0, GL_POSITION, LIGHT_POSITION);
}
```

To set up the stencil test, this code first enables it and sets the stencil function to always pass with a reference value of 1. The mask used will not modify the reference or stencil buffer values at all. The stencil operation is set to GL_REPLACE for all possibilities, so anything that gets rendered will set the stencil buffer to the reference value.

After setting up the stencil test, the bottom of the box is rendered. When the stencil buffer was cleared (outside of this code), the entire stencil buffer was set to 0. After the call to DrawBoxBottom(), the stencil buffer will be set to 1 (the reference value) at the pixels where the box bottom was drawn and 0 everywhere else.

Then the stencil function is changed to GL_EQUAL, but the reference value is left at 1. Now fragments will pass the stencil test only when the stencil buffer is 1 at the current pixel location. So when the call to DrawMarbles() is made, it will only be drawn in the region where the box bottom is located. By setting all stencil operations to GL_KEEP, we're ensuring that the contents of the stencil buffer won't get modified by anything currently being drawn.

That's all there is to using the stencil buffer. The stencil test is useful in games for reflections, decals, and shadow volumes, among other things, so you'll definitely be using it.

Tip

To ensure that you get a hardware-accelerated stencil buffer, it's recommended that you use a 32-bit color buffer along with a 24-bit depth buffer and 8-bit stencil buffer. Color depths other than 32 may cause the stencil buffer to operate in software mode, which is extremely slow. Similarly, the depth buffer and stencil buffer are typically interleaved in memory, so using 24 bits for the depth buffer and 8 bits for the stencil buffer allows for optimal performance.

The Accumulation Buffer

The idea of the accumulation buffer is that you draw multiple images into the color buffer, one at a time, and then *accumulate* each image into the accumulation buffer. After you've accumulated all the images, you put them back onto the color buffer to be displayed on the screen. You can create some cool effects with this buffer, including motion blur, depth-of-field effects, scene antialiasing, and soft shadows.

As with other buffer types, to be able to actually use the accumulation buffer, you have to request one when you set up the pixel format. This is done by setting the cAccum bits field. The accumulation buffer typically requires more storage per pixel than other buffers, with 64 bits being a common value. This is to help maintain range and precision when accumulating multiple samples.

OpenGL provides a single function to work on the accumulation buffer:

```
void glAccum(GLenum op, GLfloat value);
```

The op parameter specifies the operation to be performed, and the value parameter specifies a number that will be used for the operation. Table 12.7 shows the available operations.

Table 12.7 Accumulation Buffer Operations

Operation	Description
GL_ACCUM	Obtains RBGA values from the color buffer, multiplying them by value and then adding them to the existing contents of the accumulation buffer.
GL_LOAD	Obtains RBGA values from the color buffer, multiplying them by value and replacing the existing contents of the accumulation buffer.
GL_ADD	Adds the value parameter to each existing value in the accumulation buffer.
GL_MULT	Multiplies the value of each pixel in the accumulation buffer by value.
GL_RETURN	Multiplies the value of each pixel in the accumulation buffer by value and sends the result to the color buffer.

To use the accumulation buffer for motion blur, you accumulate several images representing the trail of the blur by using the glAccum() function like this:

glAccum(GL_ACCUM, 1.0f/N);

where N is the number of images being accumulated. This acts as a decay factor between the images. Each time this line is called, the object's image will be fainter than the previous image. After you're finished accumulating your images into the accumulation buffer, you call the glAccum() function again to copy the contents back into the color buffer:

glAccum(GL_RETURN, 1.0);

Until recently, the accumulation buffer was not well supported in consumer-level graphics hardware, so if you use it in a game, it may not run well on older computers. Fortunately, there are alternatives for many specific effects that can be more efficient than using the accumulation buffer.

Example: Using the Accumulation Buffer

A simple demo showing two uses of the accumulation buffer can be found on the CD in the folder for this chapter in the Accum directory. This demo, shown in Figures 12.3 and 12.4, actually contains two demos, one showing motion blur and the other showing soft shadows. The demo starts off with the motion blur. You can change to the soft shadows demo by pressing the S key and then change back to motion blur with the M key. Let's look at the relevant portions of this demo.

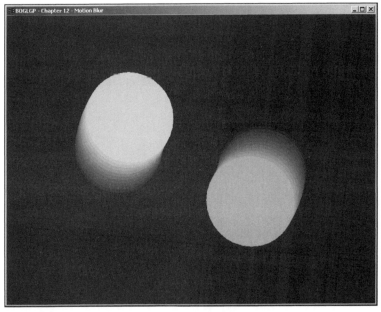

Figure 12.3 Two spheres rendered with motion blur.

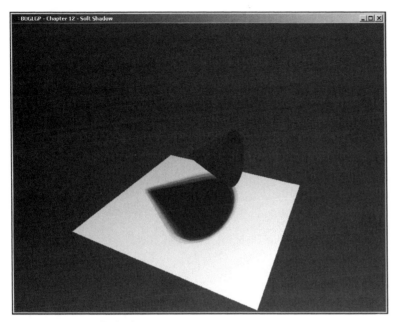

Figure 12.4 Soft shadows.

The bulk of the work for motion blur is done in the following function:

```
void CGfxOpenGL::RenderMotionBlur()
{
  glClear(GL_COLOR_BUFFER_BIT | GL_DEPTH_BUFFER_BIT);
  glLoadIdentity();
  gluLookAt(0.0, 0.0, 10.0, 0.0, 0.0, 0.0, 0.0, 1.0, 0.0);

  GLfloat angle = m_angle;
  for (int i = 0; i < SPHERE_NUM_SAMPLES; ++i)
  {
    DrawSpheres(angle);
    angle -= SPHERE_BLUR_ARC/SPHERE_NUM_SAMPLES;

    if (i == 0)
      glAccum(GL_LOAD, 1.0f/SPHERE_NUM_SAMPLES);
    else
      glAccum(GL_ACCUM, 1.0f/SPHERE_NUM_SAMPLES);
  }
  glAccum(GL_RETURN, 1.0);
}
```

During each iteration through this loop, the spheres are rotated back a bit farther along their path. Because the color buffer isn't being cleared between each iteration, the images gradually build up. At the end, they are accumulated into the depth buffer with a factor based on the total number of iterations. Spheres drawn during the first several iterations will be accumulated multiple times, so they will be brighter than the ones accumulated near the end. Finally, the results are copied back into the frame buffer.

You'll notice that on the first iteration, the color buffer is accumulated via GL_LOAD, which allows us to skip clearing the accumulation buffer at the beginning of the frame.

The main rendering function for the soft shadow portion of the demo looks like this:

```
void CGfxOpenGL::RenderSoftShadow()
{
  glClear(GL_COLOR_BUFFER_BIT | GL_DEPTH_BUFFER_BIT | GL_ACCUM_BUFFER_BIT);
  glLoadIdentity();
  gluLookAt(5.0, 8.0, 10.0, 0.0, 2.0, 0.0, 0.0, 1.0, 0.0);

  for (int i = 0; i < SHADOW_NUM_SAMPLES; ++i)
  {
    SetShadowMatrix(m_shadowMatrix, LIGHT_POS[i], FLOOR_PLANE);
    // draw the shadow
    glPushMatrix();
      glClear(GL_COLOR_BUFFER_BIT | GL_DEPTH_BUFFER_BIT);
      glEnable(GL_LIGHTING);
      glLightfv(GL_LIGHT0, GL_POSITION, LIGHT_POS[0]);
      DrawFloor();

      glDisable(GL_LIGHTING);
      glDisable(GL_DEPTH_TEST);

      glColor4f(0.0, 0.0, 0.0, 1.0f);

      // project the cone through the shadow matrix
      glMultMatrixf(m_shadowMatrix);
      DrawCone();

      glEnable(GL_DEPTH_TEST);
    glPopMatrix();
    glAccum(GL_ACCUM, 1.0f/SHADOW_NUM_SAMPLES);
  }

  glAccum(GL_RETURN, 1.0);
```

```
glLightfv(GL_LIGHT0, GL_POSITION, LIGHT_POS[0]);

// draw the cone normally
glEnable(GL_LIGHTING);
glColor3f(0.1f, 0.2f, 0.8f);
DrawCone();
glDisable(GL_LIGHTING);
}
```

This is slightly more complex due to the projective shadow code, but again we'll focus on the for loop. Each time through the loop, a different light position is used. These positions vary slightly from each other, allow us to *jitter* the light position. This allows us to simulate a light source that has volume (which is how lights in the real world work, as opposed to the infinitely small points supported by OpenGL's lighting model). A shadow projection matrix is calculated using the new light position, and then the cone is projected onto the floor plane and drawn as a black shadow. The results are accumulated with a factor based on the total number of samples.

Both the plane and shadow are drawn every iteration, but the plane remains stationary while the shadow moves slightly due to the jittered light source. The result of this is that the plane is drawn normally, but the shadow is dark in the center because the center pixels were rendered during every iteration, while the pixels near the edge of the shadow varied with each light position.

Summary

The framebuffer, composed of the color, depth, stencil, and accumulation buffers, plays a central role in OpenGL rendering. The color buffer is what ultimately gets seen, but the depth and stencil buffers both play a role in determining which pixels actually get drawn, and the accumulation buffer can be used in conjunction with the color buffer for a number of multipass rendering effects. Each buffer has several states associated with it that you can control to achieve exactly the results you want.

What You Have Learned

- All the buffers are collectively referred to as the framebuffer.
- Buffers can be cleared using glClear(). Each buffer has a clear value that you can control.
- You can define a scissor window using glScissor() that limits rendering to a subregion of the display.
- The alpha test can be used to cause fragments to be rejected based on their alpha values.

- glColorMask() allows you to disable writes to specific color channels.
- Source and destination pixels can be combined using bitwise logical operations defined with glLogicOp().
- glColorMask() allows you to disable writes to specific color channels.
- The depth buffer is used to remove hidden surfaces via a depth function you can change to fit your needs. glDepthMask() can be used to make the depth buffer read-only.
- The stencil buffer provides you with fine-grained control of what regions of the screen can be rendered to.
- The accumulation buffer is useful for several multipass rendering techniques.

Review Questions

1. What are the default clear values for the four buffers described in this chapter?
2. How is alpha testing different from alpha blending?
3. What happens to blending when logic ops are enabled?
4. True or false: Setting the depth function to GL_ALWAYS has the same effect as disabling the depth test.
5. How is the mask parameter in glStencilFunc() used?
6. Which accumulation function can be used to avoid clearing the accumulation buffer every frame?

On Your Own

1. To better understand the alpha test, create a simple program that uses it. Specify a smooth shaded quad with an alpha value of 0 in the lower left corner, 0.5 in the top left and bottom right corners, and 1 in the top right corner. Have your program cycle through several alpha reference values. Alternatively, create an image like that shown in Figure 12.2. Set the alpha value for the black regions to 0 with a value of 1 everywhere else. Set the alpha test to reject the black pixels, and apply the texture using GL_REPLACE.

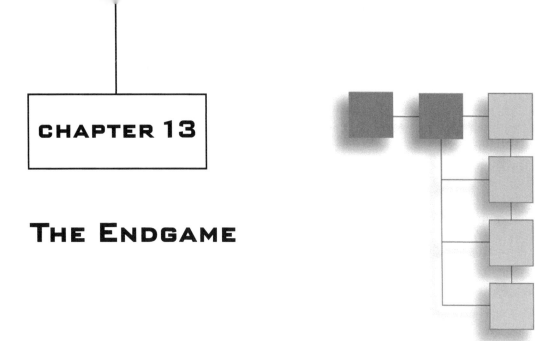

CHAPTER 13

THE ENDGAME

The endgame. This is the end, and we have a game for you. We've covered quite a bit of OpenGL in this book, and now it's time to put OpenGL to work. On the CD in Chapter 13, you will find a chess game that we have affectionately called *Chess*, which follows in the spirit of the computer chess game hit *BattleChess*. In this chapter we are going to talk a little bit about the technical design as well as cover how we used OpenGL in the game. We invite you to modify the game code and make additions if you would like. Use your imagination!

In this chapter we will cover:

- *Chess* game technical design
- How OpenGL is used in *Chess*

The Design

We had one rule when designing the chess game: keep things simple. We wanted to separate data processing from rendering as much as possible, and we wanted to keep the code portable in case you decide to copy it to another operating system. The result is a pretty solid design that we hope is expandable enough for you to modify and make changes as you see fit.

If you do a search on the Internet for "programming chess games," you will likely find Web pages that describe popular chess data structures and algorithms like "bitboards," move generations, and evaluation functions. In the spirit of keeping things simple, we didn't want to spend pages upon pages describing popular chess programming practices, so we did things our own way. In addition, we decided to keep the chess game two player, leaving the addition of chess artificial intelligence as an exercise for you.

Figure 13.1 is a diagram showing all of the classes we use in the game, along with their dependencies, similar to a minimized version of a class diagram in the Unified Modeling Language (UML). The WinMain class we have defined in the figure refers to the WinMain() function and supporting functions for main loop execution. Table 13.1 includes the rest of the classes.

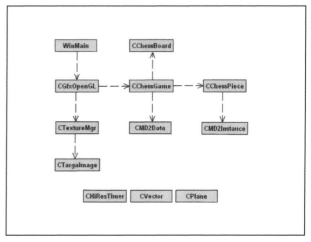

Figure 13.1 Classes and their dependencies in the game.

Now let's look at how these classes talk to each other with sequence diagram by starting from the top with initialization in WinMain(). A sequence diagram is shown in Figure 13.2 for the initialization sequence. First we initialize the high-resolution timer, CHiResTimer, which will be used during the main loop for determining the delta time between frames. Next the

Table 13.1 Chess Game Classes

Class	Description
CGfxOpenGL	The OpenGL rendering class. The majority of OpenGL rendering functionality is here.
CChessGame	The core chess game functionality. Stores the chessboard, all chess pieces, piece model loading, piece movement, capturing, and the chess game state machine.
CTextureMgr	A texture management class. Loads textures and provides access to them through a simple interface for binding OpenGL textures.
CChessBoard	A class representing the chessboard and its current state.
CChessPiece	A struct representing a chess piece, storing color, position on the board, an "in play" flag, and the piece model.
CMD2Data	A factory class for MD2 models. Loads the MD2 model data and spawns CMD2Instances.
CMD2Instance	An instance of an MD2 model.
CTargaImage	The Targa image class used for textures.
CHiResTimer	Encapsulates high-resolution timer functionality that allows us to render with frame-rate independence.
CVector	A 3D vector math class.
CPlane	A plane math class.

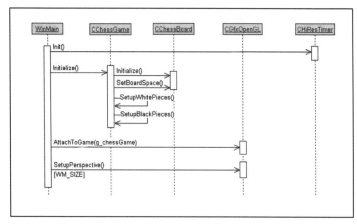

Figure 13.2 Initialize sequence diagram.

CChessBoard class is initialized, allowing the chessboard to be set up and all of the pieces to be positioned correctly and their models loaded.

Finally, we "attach" the CChessGame class pointer to the CGfxOpenGL class, which needs to know about the data stored in CChessGame in order to render the chessboard and pieces correctly.

Next we have the main game loop, whose sequence diagram is shown in Figure 13.3. The CGfxOpenGL class is used as the entry point into the rest of the game software. It is here that we call the Update() method of the CChessGame class, where we then proceed to update chess piece model animations, piece movements, captures, the game board, and the overall game state.

After performing the data update for the current frame, we then render it with the Render() method of CGfxOpenGL. Let's take a look at this method.

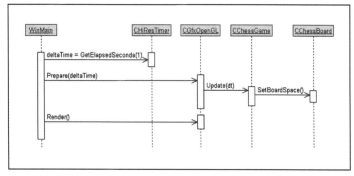

Figure 13.3 Update sequence diagram.

Using OpenGL in the Game

The Render() method in the CGfxOpenGL class is the entry point for all rendering functionality in the game.

```
void CGfxOpenGL::Render()
{
    glClearColor(0.0f, 0.0, 0.0, 0.0);
    glClear(GL_COLOR_BUFFER_BIT | GL_DEPTH_BUFFER_BIT |
            GL_STENCIL_BUFFER_BIT);

    glLoadIdentity();

    if (m_currentView == WHITE)
        gluLookAt(m_whiteViewPos.x, m_whiteViewPos.y,
                  m_whiteViewPos.z, 4.0, 0.0, 4.0, 0.0, 1.0, 0.0);
    else
        gluLookAt(m_blackViewPos.x, m_blackViewPos.y,
                  m_blackViewPos.z, 4.0, 0.0, 4.0, 0.0, 1.0, 0.0);
```

In this first block of code, you can see that we clear the color, depth, and stencil buffer bits, load the identity matrix, and set the camera position based on the current player. We clear the stencil buffer bit because we use the stencil buffer to properly render piece reflections on the chessboard.

```
    // render the wood table
    glDisable(GL_DEPTH_TEST);
    RenderTable();
    glEnable(GL_DEPTH_TEST);
```

In this section we draw the background wood table with the RenderTable() method. The background table is drawn primarily for aesthetic purposes, but since we are drawing piece reflections on the chessboard, we need to disable depth testing while drawing it; otherwise, the piece reflections will not look correct as the background table will mix into the reflected piece rendering.

```
    // prepare to write to the stencil buffer by turning off
    // writes to the color and depth buffer
    glColorMask(GL_FALSE, GL_FALSE, GL_FALSE, GL_FALSE);
    glDepthMask(GL_FALSE);

    // setup the stencil func and op to place a 1 in the stencil buffer
    // everywhere we're about to draw
    glEnable(GL_STENCIL_TEST);
    glStencilFunc(GL_ALWAYS, 1, 0xFFFFFFFF);
    glStencilOp(GL_REPLACE, GL_REPLACE, GL_REPLACE);
```

```
// render the chess board surface. Since the depth and
// color buffers are disabled,
// only the stencil buffer will be modified
RenderChessBoard();

// turn color and depth buffers back on
glColorMask(GL_TRUE, GL_TRUE, GL_TRUE, GL_TRUE);
glDepthMask(GL_TRUE);

// from this point on, only draw where stencil buffer is set to 1
glStencilFunc(GL_EQUAL, 1, 0xFFFFFFFF);

// don't modify the contents of the stencil buffer
glStencilOp(GL_KEEP, GL_KEEP, GL_KEEP);
```

The preceding section of code is responsible for setting up and rendering the chessboard to the stencil buffer. The stencil buffer is used as a cutout for determining what is actually rendered to the screen.

```
// draw reflected chess pieces first
glPushMatrix();
    glScalef(1.0, -1.0, 1.0);
    RenderPieces();
glPopMatrix();

// draw chessboard and selection square with blending
glEnable(GL_BLEND);
    RenderSelections();
    glBlendFunc(GL_SRC_ALPHA, GL_ONE_MINUS_DST_ALPHA);
    RenderChessBoard();
glDisable(GL_BLEND);

// turn off stencil testing
glDisable(GL_STENCIL_TEST);
```

With stencil testing enabled, we draw the reflected pieces and the chessboard. The stencil testing prevents anything rendered at this step from being drawn outside the bounds of the chessboard that we rendered onto the stencil buffer.

```
// draw pieces normally
glPushMatrix();
    glColor4f(1.0, 1.0, 1.0, 1.0);
    RenderPieces();
glPopMatrix();
}
```

And finally, with stencil testing disabled, we render the chess pieces normally. The result is a set of chess pieces reflecting off a marble-looking chessboard sitting on a table, as shown in Figure 13.4.

Summary

The rest of the code for the chess game deals with piece movement algorithms, model rendering and loading, and the various state machines involved. We invite you to browse the source code in detail, experiment with it, learn from it, and even make your own derivative!

Figure 13.4 A screenshot of the chess game.

More than anything, we hope you've learned a lot about OpenGL from this book and you enjoy using OpenGL as much as we have. Just remember, in today's world of 3D graphics, anything is possible!

What You Have Learned

- The chess game is designed to be easily portable.
- The chessboard is rendered to the stencil buffer to aid in rendering the chess piece reflections properly.

Review Questions

No review questions for this chapter.

On Your Own

1. Right now the chess game does not verify *check* or *checkmate*. Add this functionality to the chess game.
2. The chess game does not have a menu, nor does it display any statistics during the game. Write code to display the current player, "White" or "Black," on the screen, and add functionality for a basic menu.
3. In its current form, the game switches between only two views. Add code to view closeups of piece capture moves, rotate views of the chessboard, and zoom the view.

PART III

APPENDICES

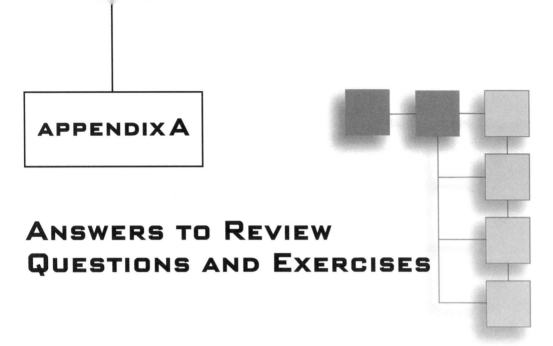

ANSWERS TO REVIEW QUESTIONS AND EXERCISES

Chapter 1

Review Questions

1. 1992

2. At the time of writing (early 2004), OpenGL's latest release is 1.5.

3. The OpenGL Architectural Review Board.

On Your Own

1. glColor3f(1.0, 0.0, 0.0) should be used for all triangle vertices, and glColor3f(0.0, 0.0, 1.0) should be used for all polygon vertices.

Chapter 2

Review Questions

1. A rendering context connects OpenGL to a window.

2. wglGetCurrentContext()

3. A PIXELFORMATDESCRIPTOR is a struct that defines the characteristics and behavior of the OpenGL rendering context.

4. glClearColor() clears the background color of the OpenGL window.

5. The DEVMODE struct is required to set up fullscreen mode.

On Your Own

1. The following should be changed: glClearColor(1.0, 1.0, 1.0, 1.0); and glColor3f(1.0, 0.0, 0.0);.

Chapter 3

Review Questions

1. Pass GL_LINE_SMOOTH to glIsEnabled(); glIsEnabled(GL_LINE_SMOOTH).

2. glEnable(GL_CULL_FACE);

3. OpenGL draws the first three vertices as a single triangle; after that, it takes every vertex specified and combines it with the previous two vertices to create another triangle. In general, every set of n triangles you can reduce to a triangle strip reduces the number of vertices from $3n$ to $n + 2$.

4. The first three vertices define a triangle, and each subsequent vertex defines a new triangle with the previous vertex and the first vertex. Fans allow you to draw n triangles while specifying only $n + 2$ vertices.

5. a. Three coordinate vertex with float data type

   b. Two coordinate vertex with integer data type, passed as an array

   c. Four coordinate vertex with double data type

   d. Three coordinate vertex with float data type, passed as an array

   e. Two coordinate vertex with short data type

On Your Own

1. Answers may vary.

```
void DrawCircleApproximation(double radius, int numberOfSides)
{
    // if edge only, use line strips; otherwise, use polygons
    if (edgeOnly)
        glBegin(GL_LINE_STRIP);
    else
        glBegin(GL_POLYGON);

    // calculate each vertex on the circle
    for (int vertex = 0; vertex < numberOfSides; vertex++)
    {
        // calculate the angle of the current vertex
                            // (vertex # * 2 * PI) / # of sides
        float angle = (float)vertex * 2.0 * 3.14159 / numberOfSides;

        // draw the current vertex at the correct radius
        glVertex3f(cosf(angle)*radius, 0.0, sinf(angle)*radius);
    }
```

```
        // if drawing edge only, then need to complete the loop with first vertex
        if (edgeOnly)
            glVertex3f(radius, 0.0, 0.0);

        glEnd();
    }
```

Chapter 4

Review Questions

1. `glTranslatef(29.0, 3.0, 15.0);`

2. `glRotatef(45.0, 1.0, 0.0, 0.0);`

3a. `glScalef(3.0, 3.0, 3.0);`

3b. `glScalef(0.5, 0.5, 0.5);`

4. Modelview matrix stack, projection matrix stack, texture matrix stack, color matrix stack

5. `glLoadIdentity()`

6. Save and restore the current matrix on the matrix stack.

On Your Own

1. Answers may vary.

```
void PositionAndRotate(float xPos, float yPos, float zPos, float xAngle,
float yAngle, float zAngle)
{
    glPushMatrix();
        // position the cube
        glTranslatef(xPos, yPos, zPos);
        // perform the rotations
        glRotatef(xAngle, 1.0, 0.0, 0.0);
        glRotatef(yAngle, 0.0, 1.0, 0.0);
        glRotatef(zAngle, 0.0, 0.0, 1.0);

        // draw the cube
        DrawCube();
    glPopMatrix();
}
```

Chapter 5

Review Questions

1. All OpenGL implementations are required to provide at least eight lights. You can find out how many are available by passing GL_MAX_LIGHTS to glGet().

2. By passing an array holding the colors to glFog() with GL_FOG_COLOR.

3. glEnable(GL_COLOR_MATERIAL);
   glColorMaterial(GL_FRONT_AND_BACK, GL_SPECULAR);

4. False. It can be taken advantage of by using the secondary color.

5. b. GL_ALPHA_SATURATE

On Your Own

1. Answers may vary.

   • Add an emissive property to the cube's material.

   ```
   // set up the cube's material
   ...
   GLfloat emmisive[] = { 0.2f, 0.2f, 0.2f, 1.0};
   glMaterialfv(GL_FRONT_AND_BACK, GL_EMISSION, emmisive);
   ```

   • Add attenuation to the red light.

   ```
   // set up static red light
   ...
   glLightf(GL_LIGHT1, GL_CONSTANT_ATTENUATION, 0.5f);
   glLightf(GL_LIGHT1, GL_LINEAR_ATTENUATION, 0.1f);
   ```

   • Make the beam of the flashlight more focused.

   ```
   // set up the flashlight
   ...
   glLightf(GL_LIGHT0, GL_SPOT_EXPONENT, 128.0);
   ```

   • Add a transparent sphere surrounding the cube, and set the material for it using color tracking.

   ```
   // after the cube has been drawn
   glEnable(GL_COLOR_MATERIAL);
   glColor4f(0.8f, 0.6f, 0.0f, 0.7f);
   glEnable(GL_BLEND);
   glBlendFunc(GL_SRC_ALPHA, GL_ONE_MINUS_SRC_ALPHA);
   gluSphere(m_pSphere, CUBE_SIZE, 64, 32);
   glDisable(GL_BLEND);
   glDisable(GL_COLOR_MATERIAL);
   ```

Chapter 6

Review Questions

1. glRasterPosi(150, 75);

   glBitmap(16, 16, 0.0, 0.0, 0.0, 0.0, m_bitmapData);

2. glDrawPixels

3. glCopyPixels

4. glPixelZoom(2.0f, 2.0f);

On Your Own

1. Answers may vary.

```
#include <stdlib.h>
void DrawRandomBitmaps(unsigned char *bitmapData)
{
    for (int idx = 0; idx < 100; idx++)
    {
        glRasterPos2i(rand() % WINDOW_WIDTH, rand() % WINDOW_HEIGHT);
        glBitmap(8, 8, 0.0, 0.0, 0.0, 0.0, bitmapData);
    }
}
```

Chapter 7

Review Questions

1. Using glEnable(GL_TEXTURE_2D);

2. Texture objects used to represent texture data and parameters. Each texture object has a state associated with it. They are accessed through an ID or handle.

3. glTexImage2D(GL_TEXTURE_2D, 0, GL_RGBA, 64, 64, 0, GL_RGBA, GL_UNSIGNED_BYTE, data);

4. Base Level: 128×128. Other Levels: $64 \times 64, 32 \times 32, 16 \times 16, 8 \times 8, 4 \times 4, 2 \times 2, 1 \times 1$

5. GL_REPEAT

6. True.

On Your Own

1. Answers may vary.

```
glEnable(GL_TEXTURE_2D);
glGenTextures(1, &myTexture);
glBindTexture(GL_TEXTURE_2D, myTexture);
gluBuild2DMipmaps(GL_TEXTURE_2D, GL_RGBA, 256, 256, GL_RGBA, GL_UNSIGNED_BYTE,
data);
...
glBindTexture(GL_TEXTURE_2D, myTexture);
glBegin(GL_POLYGON);
    glTexCoord2f(0.0f, 0.0f); glVertex3f(-0.5f, 0.5f, 0.5f);
    glTexCoord2f(1.0f, 0.0f); glVertex3f(0.5f, 0.5f, 0.5f);
    glTexCoord2f(1.0f, 1.0f); glVertex3f(0.5f, 0.5f, -0.5f);
    glTexCoord2f(0.0f, 1.0f); glVertex3f(-0.5f, 0.5f, -0.5f);
glEnd();
```

2. Answers will vary.

Chapter 8

Review Questions

1. An extension that has been officially endorsed by the OpenGL Architectural Review Board. These extensions tend to be very widely supported.

2. Presently, Windows headers and libraries for OpenGL only support OpenGL 1.1, so OpenGL 1.2, 1.3, 1.4, and 1.5 features have to be accessed via extensions.

3. By checking the extensions string for the name of the extension. Alternatively, you can try obtaining a pointer from `wglGetProcAddress()`, with a null pointer indicating failure.

4. Any time you are accessing core functions using function names that do not include the extension suffix.

On Your Own

1. Answers will vary. The program should make use of `glGetString(GL_EXTENSIONS)` and `wglGetExtensionsString()`.

Chapter 9

Review Questions

1. Creating a new texture requires memory to be allocated, which can be slow.
2. There is one for every supported texture unit.
3. GL_OBJECT_LINEAR and GL_EYE_LINEAR both make use of planes defined through GL_OBJECT_PLANE and GL_EYE_PLANE, respectively.
4. You enable a texture unit by assigning a complete, valid texture image to it and enabling the corresponding texture target. You disable the unit by disabling all texture targets for it.
5. GL_COMBINE

On Your Own

1. Answers may vary. GL_ADD adds the incoming fragment RGB with the texture RGB and multiplies the incoming fragment alpha by the texture alpha. This can be done via combiners as follows:

```
glTexEnvf(GL_TEXTURE_ENV, GL_TEXTURE_ENV_MODE, GL_COMBINE);
glTexEnvf(GL_TEXTURE_ENV, GL_COMBINE_RGB, GL_ADD);
glTexEnvf(GL_TEXTURE_ENV, GL_COMBINE_ALPHA, GL_MODULATE);
glTexEnvf(GL_TEXTURE_ENV, GL_SOURCE0_RGB, GL_PREVIOUS);
glTexEnvf(GL_TEXTURE_ENV, GL_SOURCE0_ALPHA, GL_PREVIOUS);
glTexEnvf(GL_TEXTURE_ENV, GL_SOURCE1_RGB, GL_TEXTURE);
glTexEnvf(GL_TEXTURE_ENV, GL_SOURCE1_ALPHA, GL_TEXTURE);
glTexEnvf(GL_TEXTURE_ENV, GL_OPERAND0_RGB, GL_SRC_COLOR);
glTexEnvf(GL_TEXTURE_ENV, GL_OPERAND0_ALPHA, GL_SRC_ALPHA);
glTexEnvf(GL_TEXTURE_ENV, GL_OPERAND1_RGB, GL_SRC_COLOR);
glTexEnvf(GL_TEXTURE_ENV, GL_OPERAND1_ALPHA, GL_SRC_ALPHA);
```

Chapter 10

Review Questions

1. By passing it to glIsList().
2. It is executed immediately and is not stored as part of the list.
3. By passing the appropriate flags to glEnableClientState().
4. You must first change the currently active texture unit by calling glClientActive-Texture(). You can then use glTexCoordPointer() normally to assign an array of texture coordinates.

5. The cost of doing per-triangle frustum culling on the CPU generally exceeds the cost of letting the graphics hardware do it for you.

On Your Own

1. Answers will vary.

```
// returns 1 if the sphere is in the frustum, -1 if it's partially within the
frustum, of 0 if it's completely outside
int SphereInFrustum(sphere_t sphere, frustum_t frustum)
{
  GLfloat dist;
  GLuint numOutside = 0;
  for (int i = 0; i < 6; ++i)
  {
    dist = frustum.planes[i].A * sphere.center.x +
           frustum.planes[i].B * sphere.center.y +
           frustum.planes[i].C * sphere.center.z +
           frustum.planes[i].D;

    if (dist <= -sphere.radius)
      return 0;
    if (dist > radius) // sphere is doesn't intersect this plane
      numOutside++;
  }
  if (6 == numOutside)
    return 1;
  else
    return -1;
}
```

Chapter 11

Review Questions

1. `wglUseFontBitmaps()`

2. `wglUseFontOutlines()`

3. Outline fonts may be textured by using the automatic texture coordinate generation feature of OpenGL.

On Your Own

1. Answers will vary. The program should use `wglUseFontBitmaps()`, `wglUseFontOutlines()`, and the `glFont` library to render text.
2. Answers will vary. The program should modify the `glFont` library source code by adding a new `DisplayText()` method that draws text on a billboard polygon at a given 3D position.

Chapter 12

Review Questions

1. The depth buffer is 1.0, everything else is 0.
2. Alpha testing is used to accept or reject fragments based on the alpha value. Alpha blending combines the incoming fragment with the pixel in the color buffer using the alpha value, but it does not typically reject fragments.
3. Blending is disabled internally.
4. False. See the Tip in the section titled "Depth-Comparison Functions."
5. It is logically ANDed with both the stencil reference value and the value in the stencil buffer before the two values are combined.
6. `GL_LOAD`

On Your Own

1. Answers will vary.

Chapter 13

Review Questions

1. No review questions for this chapter.

On Your Own

1. Answers will vary.
2. Answers will vary.
3. Answers will vary.

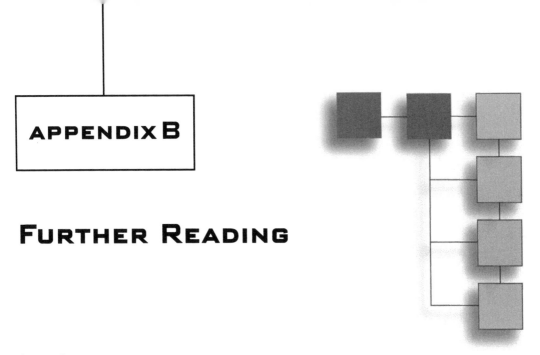

APPENDIX B

FURTHER READING

This book covered the core topics you need to understand to begin developing games and graphics applications with OpenGL, but your journey has just begun. This appendix lists Web sites and books that you may find useful in expanding your knowledge.

Online Resources

There's no better way to keep up to date on the rapidly changing world of technology than the Internet. We've collected a list of the most important Web sites covering game development and OpenGL.

Game Development

There are dozens—if not hundreds—of Web sites dedicated to game development. The ones listed here are the cream of the crop.

GameDev.net

http://www.gamedev.net

Co-founded and operated by the authors of this book, GameDev.net is the leading online resource for game developers. Features include thousands of articles, active and helpful community forums, books and software reviews, daily news, and a place to upload and showcase your games.

Garage Games

http://www.garagegames.com

Founded and operated by the developers of the *Tribes* franchise, Garage Games offers affordable tools to game developers, including the popular *Torque* game engine, based on *Tribes 2* technology.

Game Development Search Engine

http://www.gdse.com

The GDSE includes news and a handpicked selection of links to hundreds of smaller game development sites, coupled with a powerful search engine.

Game Tutorials

http://www.gametutorials.com

Game Tutorials contains dozens of short tutorial programs covering game development and OpenGL topics. The tutorials tend to be light on explanation, but if you want to see how something is done in code it's a fantastic resource.

Flipcode

http://www.flipcode.com

More graphics oriented than GameDev.net and not as frequently updated, but still contains many good articles and a community of knowledgeable developers.

Gamasutra

http://www.gamasutra.com

Produced by the people who run the Game Developers Conference and publish *Game Developer Magazine*, this site offers articles and other content taken from both the magazine and the conference.

Developer Pages

http://developer.nvidia.com
http://www.ati.com/developer

Both NVIDIA and ATI maintain sites containing a vast array of white papers, presentations, and demos covering many advanced graphics and game programming topics, many of them using OpenGL.

OpenGL

OpenGL has an active and enthusiastic online community of game and graphics programmers. A quick search of the Internet will turn up hundreds—if not thousands—of pages containing OpenGL information, but we've distilled the best of them here.

OpenGL.org

http://www.opengl.org

OpenGL.org is the official site of the OpenGL ARB. Besides regular OpenGL-related news, they maintain several FAQs full of helpful information.

NeHe Productions

http://nehe.gamedev.net

Jeff Molofee has worked hard to make NeHe one of the top OpenGL resources on the Web. In addition to more than 40 original OpenGL tutorials, he's collected an impressive suite of demo programs displaying the capabilities of OpenGL. He also routinely posts links and descriptions of new OpenGL online resources.

Delphi3D

http://www.delphi3d.net

Although all the demos are written in Delphi, this site has some of the most useful articles and demos covering advanced OpenGL topics.

Books

Whether you're looking for resources to meet the prerequisites for reading this book or ready to expand your knowledge, the books listed here should prove valuable.

C++

Accelerated C++: Practical Programming by Example
Andrew Koenig, Barbara E. Moo, Addison-Wesley, 2000

C++ Primer 3rd Ed.
Stanley Lippman, Addison-Wesley, 1998

Windows Programming

Programming Windows
Charles Petzold, Microsoft Press, 1998

3D Math

Mathematics for 3D Game Programming & Computer Graphics 2nd Ed.
Eric Lengyel, Charles River Media, 2003

3D Math Primer for Graphics and Game Development
Fletcher Dunn, Ian Parberry, Wordware, 2002

OpenGL

OpenGL Programming Guide 4th Ed.
Woo, Neider, Davis, Shreiner, Addison-Wesley, 2003

OpenGL Extensions Guide
Eric Lengyel, Charles River Media, 2003

Graphics Programming

Real-Time Rendering
Tomas Akenine-Möller, Eric Haines, A.K. Peters, 2002

Game Development

Game Programming Gems 1, 2, 3
Marc DeLoura (editor), Dante Treglia (editor), Charles River Media, 2000, 2001, 2002

Core Techniques and Algorithms in Game Programming
Daniel Sanchez-Crespo Dalmau, New Riders, 2003

Game Scripting Mastery
Alex Varanese, Premier Press, 2002

AI Techniques for Game Programming
Mat Buckland, Premier Press, 2002

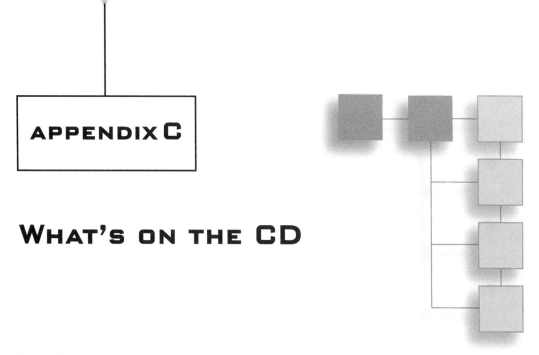

APPENDIX C

WHAT'S ON THE CD

The CD included with this book contains resources intended to be used in conjunction with the text. It includes an auto-installer, so all you have to do is insert the CD into your CD player and the installer will launch itself.

The contents of the CD are detailed in this appendix.

Source Code

Most importantly, the CD includes the full source code for all of the demos used throughout the book. These are arranged by chapter, with each project having its own directory within the chapter directory.

GLee

Many of the example programs starting in Chapter 8 use the GLee library by Ben Woodhouse for managing extensions. We've included the latest version of it on the CD.

Bonus Chapters

There were many chapters from *OpenGL Game Programming* covering topics that are not covered in this volume and that we don't intend to cover in future volumes. These chapters have been included on the CD in Adobe Acrobat format to supplement the material presented here. The chapters included are

Using Windows with OpenGL

An Overview of 3D Graphics Theory

OpenGL Quadrics

Curves and Surfaces

Using DirectX: DirectInput

Using DirectX Audio

Working with 3D Models

Making a Game: A Time to Kill

Bonus Game

In addition to the game included in Chapter 13, "The Endame," we're including the source code for the game from *OpenGL Game Programming* entitled *A Time to Kill*.

INDEX

Gamedev.net

The most comprehensive game development resource

- The latest news in game development
- The most active forums and chatrooms anywhere, with insights and tips from experienced game developers
- Links to thousands of additional game development resources
- Thorough book and product reviews
- Over 1,000 game development articles!
  - Game design
  - Graphics
  - DirectX
  - OpenGL
  - AI
  - Art
  - Music
  - Physics
  - Source Code
  - Sound
  - Assembly
  - And More!

 **Gamedev.net**

License Agreement/Notice of Limited Warranty